A-Z LA DISTRICT

CW00347521

VISITORS' ATLAS & GUIDE

CONTENTS

Grasmere View

Geographers' A-Z Map Company Ltd
Fairfield Road, Borough Green,
Sevenoaks, Kent TN15 8PP
Enquiries & Trade Sales
01732 781000
Retail Sales
01732 783422
www.a-zmaps.co.uk

Lakeland Fell

Welcome to one of Britain's most famous and popular holiday destinations. The Lake District attracts visitors from around the world to see and explore the astonishing variety of unspoiled landscape.

Besides the varied tranquil lakes, mountain peaks and fells, there are many characterful market towns and villages, also museums and houses associated with many literary and historically important people.
There are historic houses and gardens, ancient monuments, steam railways, many arts and craft outlets, a multitude of activity resources both on and off the lakes, some 60 miles of coastline with many stretches of broad sands, coastal walks and glorious views.

This is a landscape formed by the carving action of great glaciers during the ice ages. The ice, by scouring out deep valleys allowed the formation of the beautiful lakes. The vast central area of ancient volcanic rocks is a mass of great peaks and jagged crags, while to the north and south softer rocks have eroded into a smoother rounded fell landscape. To the east the surface limestone is exposed and dissolved to create the striking limestone pavements more typical of the nearby Yorkshire Dales.

The heart of the region is the Lake District National Park, at some 885 square miles the largest of the national Parks in England and Wales. Here there are over 1800 miles of public footpaths, and the National Trust is responsible for the conservation and management of approximately 1/4 of the area, including most of the central fells, 24 lakes, tarns and many individual properties and houses.

This is a landscape that has enchanted and inspired so many, not only the famous like the quintessentially English poet William Wordsworth, the Victorian writer, educationalist and artist John Ruskin or the much loved author Beatrix Potter, but also countless families and individuals who find relaxation and pleasure throughout the year.

Perhaps one of the best starting points is the National Park Centre at Brockhole in its ideally situated lakeside setting, between Ambleside and Windermere. Here a wealth of information is freely given, facilities also include gardens and games lawn, adventure playground, exhibitions, great gift shop and café. From here you can also cruise on Windermere in high season or join one of our many special events.

We hope this guide will help you to share the experience that is the incomparable Lake District.

Mountain Safety

Every year visitors to the Lake District and other mountainous regions are killed or injured either because they have gone on to the fells without adequate clothing or equipment, or that conditions had been severely underestimated. A mountain top can be icy cold on a summer's day, and weather conditions can change very quickly. Do not venture on to the fells unless you are properly equipped and have thoroughly checked weather forecasts in advance, particularly those detailing local conditions. You risk not only your own life, but also those of the voluntary Mountain Rescue Teams who have to try and find you. In the event of an emergency, dial 999 and ask either for the Police or Mountain Rescue. In the Lake District, make sure you are directed to the Cumbria Police.

Leaflets on basic mountain safety are available from most information centres. You can telephone the National Park's 24-hour Lake District Weatherline Service on 08700 550575.

Note: This atlas and guide is designed for planning lowland walking and general touring, but is not intended for use on the mountains. For these purposes, it is strongly advised that the appropriate Ordnance Survey 1:25,000 Explorer mapping be carried and used accordingly.

Tarn Hows

The Country Code

■ **Be safe - plan ahead and follow any signs.**
Even when going out locally, it's best to get the latest
information about where and when you can go; for example,
your rights to go onto some areas of open land may be
restricted while work is carried out, for safety reasons or
during breeding seasons. Follow advice and local signs, and
be prepared for the unexpected.

■ **Leave gates and property as you find them.**
Please respect the working life of the countryside, as our
actions can affect people's livelihoods, our heritage, and the
safety and welfare of animals and ourselves.

■ **Protect plants and animals, and take your litter home.**
We have a responsibility to protect our countryside now and
for future generations, so make sure you don't harm animals,
birds, plants, or trees. Fires can be as devastating to wildlife
and habitats as they are to people and property.

■ **Keep dogs under close control.**
The countryside is a great place to exercise dogs, but it's
every owner's duty to make sure their dog is not a danger or
nuisance to farm animals, wildlife or other people.

■ **Consider other people.**
Showing consideration and respect for other people makes
the countryside a pleasant environment for everyone - at
home, at work and at leisure.

■ For more information visit www.countrysideaccess.gov.uk

The Off Road Code
ADDITIONAL GUIDELINES FOR CYCLISTS

■ **Always cycle with care.** Keep your speed down and be
aware of the possibility of other off-road vehicles nearby.

■ **Keep to Public Rights of Way.** Use maps to plan your
route in advance and do not take short cuts along private
accesses or across land that you have no legal right to use.

■ **Check your bike before you set out**. Ensure that all
parts are in good working order, particular attention should
be paid to gears, brakes, lights and tyres.

■ **Take adequate supplies of essential items.** Include food
and drink, waterproofs, tools and spares. Even if you don't
need them yourself, someone in your group may.

■ **Give way to all walkers and horses.** Be considerate and
have no confrontations with riders or walkers.

■ **Ride in small groups of two to four.** Try not to create a
disturbance with large numbers of riders and always keep
your group together.

■ **Prevent erosion.** Always keep to designated bridleways,
public byways and roads used as public paths. Remember
also, that footpaths are for the sole use of walkers.

■ **Close gates behind you.** Always leave gates as you find
them, fasten them unless it is obvious that they should be
left open.

■ **Stay clear of industrial vehicles.** Do not pass forestry
workings or any similar operations until you are informed that
it is safe to do so.

Causey Pike and Derwent Water

Grasmere from Loughrigg

Bassenthwaite Lake -1C 15.
Bassenthwaite Lake is fed by the River Derwent from Derwent Water. 4 miles in length, one of the shallowest, the most northerly and the only one actually named 'Lake'. Situated beneath Skiddaw owned by the national park.

Brothers Water NT -2C 25.
Brothers Water is a small shallow rectangular lake (or large tarn) at the foot of the Kirkstone Pass. Formerly known as Broad Water, it is said to have been renamed after the drowning of two brothers on separate occasions in the early 19th century. Transferred to the National Trust in 1947.

Buttermere NT -1B 22. *See also Boating / Boats for hire*
Buttermere, 'the lake by dairy pastures', is situated in Lorton Vale at the foot of the Honister Pass from Borrowdale. Separated from its sister lake Crummock Water by a small strip of meadowland, formed of alluvial deposits. 1.25 miles long, with Fleetwith Pike (648 m or 2,126 ft) at its head, and the village of Buttermere close by its north-east shore. It is much favoured because of its beauty and accessibility for both low and high level walks.

Coniston Water -3B 30. *See also Boating / Boats for hire*
Coniston Water is, after Windermere and Ullswater, the third longest of the lakes at 5.25 miles, and about 0.5 miles wide. Coniston Water, set against the spectacular backdrop of The Old Man of Coniston, is much quieter than Windermere and is considered great for just 'messing about in boats'. Coniston Water was originally known by the Norse name Thorstein Mere and in early Victorian times was sometimes referred to as Thurston Water. Rainfall can vary the lake level by as much as 1.5 m (5 ft).
Coniston Water is famous for its connections with the world water speed record breaker Donald Campbell. A memorial stone to him, overlooking the lake, can be found at Coniston Boatlandings. The popular Bluebird café and picnic area are also located here.
Coniston Launch, operated by Coniston Ferry Services operate two main summer only cruise services on Coniston Water.
(Tel: 015394 36216, www.conistonlaunch.co.uk)
Steam Yacht Gondola, owned by the National Trust operate a Summer season only, daily, 45 minute round trip, hourly cruise.
(Tel: 015394 41288,
www.nationaltrust.org.uk/places/steamyachtgondola)

Crummock Water NT -1B 22. *See also Boating / Boats for hire*
Crummock Water, often overlooked in favour of Buttermere, at 2.5 miles long is approximately twice Buttermere's size and depth, with a circular footpath of 7 miles. Crummock Water is impressively framed by Mellbreak on the west side and the massif of Grasmoor (852 m or 2,795 ft) on the east.

Derwent Water -3D 15. *See also Boating / Boats for hire*
Derwent Water, situated south of Keswick, often referred to as the

'Queen of the English Lakes', is the widest lake in the Lake District (and England) at 1.25 miles wide, and just under 3 miles long. Ovoid in shape and shallow, with an average depth of only 4.5 m (15 ft), it is one of the first lakes to freeze in the winter. One of the most popular lakes, but still remarkably peaceful.
Keswick Launch operated by Keswick on Derwentwater Launch Company Limited operate an all year cruise service.
(Tel: 017687 72263, www.keswick-launch.co.uk)
Evening Cruise: Summer season only (7.30pm start), 60 minutes non-landing cruise with guide, weather permitting.

Elter Water -1C 31.
Elter Water, meaning the 'lake of the swans' (or swan lake), lies hidden beneath Loughrigg Fell, 2.5 miles west of Ambleside, on the road to the attractive village of Elterwater, the gateway to the beautiful and popular Great Langdale with the peaks of the famous Langdale Pikes at the end. This quiet and elusive lake is just over half a mile long with a central island almost splitting it.

Ennerdale Water -1A 22.
Ennerdale Water, or 'the lake in the valley of the River Ehen', is the most westerly of the lakes. 2.5 miles long, it is a deep (around 45 m or 148 ft) lake with crystal clear waters, fed by the River Liza and drained by the River Ehen; since 1864 it has acted as a reservoir for the coastal towns of West Cumbria.

Esthwaite Water -2D 31. *See also Boating / Boats for hire*
Esthwaite Water is a quiet unspoilt 113 hectare natural lake, 1.5 miles long and 0.25 miles wide. It is particularly picturesque at the extreme southern end (near Ridding Wood), where it is reed bordered. Regarded as one of the finest fishing waters in the Lake District, stocked with predominantly rainbow and wild brown trout with fly fishing throughout the year, in the winter it is one of the most productive pike fisheries in the country.

Grasmere NT -3A 24. *See also Boating / Boats for hire*
Grasmere, less than 1 mile long and less than 0.5 miles wide, situated in the River Rothay valley, is the 'roundest' and one of the most attractive of the main Lakeland lakes. Inextricably connected to the village of the same name which is set back from its north shore, Grasmere was home to William Wordsworth for 14 years from 1799 to 1813, who spent much of his time exploring the area.

Haweswater Reservoir -2D 25.
Haweswater Reservoir, in an isolated setting, is at just over 4 miles long, the highest and most easterly of the Lake District 'lakes'. Owned by United Utilities, it is also the North West's largest reservoir, holding 18,600 million gallons of water. At times of drought, when the water level is very low, the outline of the submerged village of Mardale Green, its roads and buildings, can still be seen at the head of the reservoir between the wooded promontory of The Rigg and the island of Wood Howe.

Loweswater NT -3A 14. *See also Boating / Boats for hire*
Loweswater is one of the quieter and more peaceful lakes. 1 mile long, with water lilies in June / July, it is framed by Darling Fell, with Holme Wood and a footpath on the west shore beneath Burnbank Fell and Carling Knott. Loweswater has the distinction of being the only lake in the Lake District whose outflow heads inland (to Crummock Water) rather than the coast.

Rydal Water (part NT) -3B 24.
Rydal Water is one of Lakeland's smaller lakes (at 0.75 miles long and 0.25 miles wide) and also one of the most popular. Extremely picturesque, set beneath the steeply rising wooded fells of Nab Scar to the north and Loughrigg Fell to the south, between Grasmere and the small hamlet of Rydal, both with many Wordsworth connections. The lake offers some of the best pike fishing in the north-west and also has perch and brown trout.

Thirlmere -1A 24.
Thirlmere, set beneath the convex slope of Helvellyn, is 3.75 mile long and the second highest (after Haweswater Reservoir). The reservoir, with a capacity of 9,000 million gallons was officially opened in October 1894, the surrounding slopes subsequently being heavily planted with spruce and larch conifers and the public excluded from much of the catchment area in an unpopular measure to protect the water quality. The 96 mile long Thirlmere Aqueduct supplies water to Manchester, the water travels at a speed of around 3 mph taking around 30 hours to reach its destination.

Ullswater -3C 17. *See also Boating / Boats for hire*
Ullswater is the second longest lake in the Lake District at 7.5 miles long, and two thirds of a mile wide. It is regarded by many as the grandest and most beautiful of the lakes, running from Pooley Bridge, where the River Eamont outflows, crossed by a narrow 16th century bridge, southwards to Glenridding, growing ever more scenic as it becomes surrounded by the mountain ring of Place Fell, St Sunday Crag, Fairfield and Helvellyn. Ullswater is home to the rare and protected schelly, a slim silver scaled fish known colloquially as a 'freshwater herring', a living relic of the last Ice Age.
Ullswater Steamers (Tel: 017684 82229, www.ullswater-steamers.co.uk) operate an all year cruise service on Ullswater.

Wast Water NT -3B 22.
Wast Water is the most impressive of the Lake District lakes, 3 miles long and comparatively remote, there is vehicular access only by a no-through road to Wasdale Head along its north-west side. The deepest lake in England at 76 m (249 ft), with its floor below sea-level. It is famous for The Screes, a massive scree slope below Illgill Head and Whin Rigg, which drops dramatically around 540 m (1,772 ft) to the lake surface below, plunging underwater and giving the lake its ominous, dark and brooding atmosphere. In the distance, at the north-east end, are the classic Lakeland silhouettes of Yewbarrow, Kirk Fell, Great Gable, Lingmell and Sca Fell whose symmetry, centred on Great Gable, was the choice for the Lake District National Park logo.

Watendlath Tarn NT -1D 23. *See also Boating / Boats for hire*
Watendlath Tarn is a small tarn set within an amphitheatre of surrounding fells, approximately 265 m (869 ft) above sea level, beside the popular hamlet of Watendlath. The whole of Watendlath is owned by the National Trust.

Windermere -3D 31. *See also Boating / Boats for hire*
Windermere, the name derived from the Norse Vinandr's Lake subsequently Vinandr's Mere, is the largest natural freshwater lake in England, and at 10.5 miles long the longest in the Lake District. It is 1.25 miles wide at its widest, with a maximum depth of 64 m (210 ft), the second deepest lake after Wast Water, and the lowest below sea-level. It is also without doubt the most famous, and consequently the busiest, of the lakes although the scenery here is nowhere near as dramatic as that at Ullswater or Wast Water. The south end of the lake is fairly low lying but the north end is framed by high mountains, Loughrigg Fell and the Fairfield Horseshoe group above Rydal. In 'The Great Frost' of February 1895 the entire Windermere lake was frozen from end to end to a depth of over a foot thick, with 2 m (6.5 ft) snow drifts, with on one day as many as 20,000 people descending on the lake.
Windermere Steamboats and Museum is an essential visit for information on Lakeland boating history.
Windermere Lake Cruises operate two main all year services. (Tel: 015395 31188 / 015394 32225)
www.windermere-lakecruises.co.uk
Windermere Ferry (foot and vehicular): A ferry has operated across Windermere for over 500 years. The current Windermere Ferry operates all year from Ferry Nab (east side) to Ferry House (west side). The ferry operates every 20 minutes, approximately between the hours of 7am & 10pm but may be suspended in very windy weather.
Lake Wardens at Ferry Nab (015394 42753), Lake Ranger (01539 724555).

Loughrigg Tarn

ACTIVITIES

ACTIVITY CENTRES

Bigland Hall Estate, Backbarrow, Newby Bridge, Ulverston, LA12 8PB. Tel: 015395 31728. -2B 36.

Calvert Trust, Keswick, The, Little Crossthwaite, Underskiddaw, Keswick, CA12 4QD. Tel: 017687 72255. -2C 15.

Cockermouth Climbing Wall, Cockermouth Leisure Centre, Castlegate Drive, Cockermouth, CA13 9JR. Tel: 01900 823596. see Cockermouth plan -2D.

Derwentwater Marina, Portinscale, Keswick, CA12 5RF. Tel: 017687 72912. -3D 15.

Eden Climbing Wall, Penrith Leisure Centre, Southend Road, Penrith, CA11 8JH. Tel: 01768 863450. see Penrith plan -4D.

Glaramara Centre, The, Borrowdale, Seatoller, Keswick, CA12 5XQ. Tel: 017687 77222. -2C 23.

Glenridding Sailing Centre, The Spit, Beach Head Area, Glenridding, Penrith, CA11 0PA. S. Tel: 017684 82541. -1B 24.

Go Ape!, Grizedale Visitor Centre, Grizedale Forest Park, Grizedale, Ambleside, LA22 0QJ. Tel: 0870 4445562. -3C 31.

Greystoke Castle, Greystoke, Penrith, CA11 0TG. Tel: 017684 83722. -1C 17.

Hinning House Outdoor Education Centre, Hinning House, Seathwaite, Broughton-in-Furness, LA20 6EG. Tel: 01229 716307. -2A 30.

Howtown Outdoor Centre, Howtown, Martindale, Pooley Bridge, Penrith, CA10 2ND. Tel: 017684 86508. -1C 25.

Kendal Artificial Ski Slope, Canal Head North, Kendal, LA9 7AL. Tel: 01539 732948. see Kendal plan -3D.

Keswick Climbing Wall & Activity Centre, Southey Hill Trading Estate, Carding Mill Lane, Main Street, Keswick, CA12 5NR. Tel: 017687 72000. see Keswick plan -2B.

Lakeland Climbing Centre (Kendal Wall), Unit 27, Lake District Business Park, Mint Bridge Road, Kendal, LA9 6NH. Tel: 01539 721766. -3C 33.

Low Bank Ground Outdoor Education Centre, Low Bank Ground, Coniston, LA21 8AA. Tel: 015394 41314. -2C 31.

Low Wood Watersports & Activity Centre, English Lakes Hotels Ltd., Low Wood, Ambleside Road, Troutbeck Bridge, Windermere, LA23 1LP. S. Tel: 015394 39441. -1D 31.

Newlands Adventure Centre, Stair, Keswick, CA12 5UF. Tel: 017687 78463. -3C 15.

Nichol End Marine, Portinscale, Keswick, CA12 5TY. Tel: 017687 73082. -3D 15.

Outward Bound Eskdale, Gate House, Eskdale Green, Holmrook, CA19 1TE. Tel: 019467 23281. -1C 29.

Outward Bound Ullswater, Watermillock, Penrith, CA11 0JL. Tel: 017684 85000. -3C 17.

Platty+, Lodore Landing Stage / Boat Landings, Lodore, Borrowdale, Keswick, CA12 5SL. Tel: 017687 77282 / 76572. -1D 23.

Rookin House Farm Equestrian & Activity Centre, Rookin House Farm, Troutbeck, Penrith, CA11 0SS. Tel: 017684 83561. -2B 16.

Summitreks Adventure Activities, Unit 2, Lake Road Workshops, Lake Road, Coniston, LA21 8EW. Tel: 015394 41212. see Coniston plan -2C.

Tower Wood Outdoor Education Centre, Tower Wood, near Bowness-on-Windermere, Windermere, LA23 3PL. Tel: 015395 31519. -3D 31.

Vivid Events, Denton House, Penrith Road, Keswick, CA12 4JW. Tel: 017687 75351. see Keswick plan -2D.

White Cross Bay Watersports Centre, White Cross Bay Leisure Park & Marina, White Cross Bay, Ambleside Road, Troutbeck Bridge, Windermere, LA23 1LF. Tel: 015394 46131. -1D 31.

Windermere Outdoor Adventure, Leigh Groves Building, Rayrigg Road, Windermere, LA23 1BP. S. Tel: 015394 47183. see Windermere plan -2B.

BOATING / BOATS FOR HIRE

Buttermere
Dalegarth Boat Hire, Dalegarth Guest House, Buttermere, Cockermouth, CA13 9XA. S. Tel: 017687 70233. -1B 22.

Coniston Water
Coniston Boating Centre, Lake Road, Coniston, LA21 8EW. S. Tel: 015394 41366. see Coniston plan -2C.

Crummock Water
Wood House Boat Hire, Wood House, Buttermere, Cockermouth, CA13 9XA. S. -1B 22.

Derwent Water
Derwentwater Marina, Portinscale, Keswick, CA12 5RF. S. Tel: 017687 72912. -3D 15.
The Keswick Launch Company, Lake Road, Keswick, CA12 5DJ. S. Tel: 017687 72263. see Keswick plan -4B.
Nichol End Marine, Portinscale, Keswick, CA12 5TY. Tel: 017687 73082. -3D 15.
Platty+, Lodore Landing Stage / Boat Landings, Lodore, Borrowdale, Keswick, CA12 5SL. Tel: 017687 77282 / 76572. -1D 23.

Esthwaite Water
Esthwaite Water Fishery, The Boathouse, Ridding Wood, Hawkshead, Ambleside, LA22 0QF. Tel: 015394 36541. -2D 31.

Grasmere
Faeryland, Red Bank Road, Grasmere, Ambleside, LA22 9PX. Tel: 015394 35060. see Grasmere plan -3A.

Loweswater
Water End Farm Boat Hire, Water End Farm, Waterend, Loweswater, Cockermouth, CA13 0SU. S. Tel: 01946 861465. -3A 14.

Ullswater
Glenridding Sailing Centre, The Spit, Beach Head Area, Glenridding, Penrith, CA11 0PA. S. Tel: 017684 82541. -1B 24.
Lakeland Boat Hire, Pooley Bridge, Penrith, CA10. S. Tel: 0777 3671399. -3D 17.
St Patrick's Boat & Bike Hire, St Patrick's Boat Landing, Glenridding, Penrith, CA11 0QQ. S. Tel: 017684 82393. -1B 24.
Ullswater Marine, Rampsbeck Cottage, Watermillock, Penrith, CA11 0LP. Tel: 017684 86415. -3D 17.

Watendlath Tarn
Watendlath Tarn Trout Fishery, Fold Head Farm, Watendlath, Keswick, CA12 5UW. S. Tel: 017687 77255. -1D 23.

Windermere
Fell Foot Park, Newby Bridge, Ulverston, LA12 8NN. S. Tel: 015395 31273. -1B 36.
Low Wood Watersports & Activity Centre, English Lakes Hotels Ltd., Low Wood, Ambleside Road, Troutbeck Bridge, Windermere, LA23 1LP. S. Tel: 015394 39441. -1D 31.
Shepherds (Windermere) Ltd., Glebe Road, Bowness Bay, Bowness-on-Windermere, Windermere, LA23 3HE. Tel: 015394 44031 / 45395. see Windermere plan -5B.
Windermere Lake Cruises Ltd., Bowness Pier, Promenade, Bowness Bay, Bowness-on-Windermere, Windermere, LA23 3HQ. S. Tel: 015394 42600. see Windermere plan -5B.
Windermere Lake Cruises Ltd., Waterhead Pier, Waterhead, Ambleside, LA22 0EY. S. Tel: 015394 32225 / 015395 31188. see Ambleside plan -5B.

CYCLE HIRE

Ainfield Cycle Centre, Ainfield, Jacktrees Road, Cleator, Whitehaven, CA23 3DW. Tel: 01946 812427. -2C 21.
Arragons Cycle Centre, Brunswick Road, Penrith, CA11 7LU. Tel: 01768 890344. see Penrith plan -3C.
(Askew Cycles), The Old Brewery, Wildman Street, Kendal, LA9 6EN. Tel: 01539 728057.

see Kendal plan -2C.
Biketreks, Compston Road, Ambleside, LA22 9DJ. Tel: 015394 31505. see Ambleside plan -3A.
Country Lanes, The Railway Station, Windermere, LA23 1AH. Tel: 015394 44544. see Windermere plan -1D.
Easyriders, Waterhead Pier, Waterhead, Ambleside, LA22 0EY. Tel: 015394 32902 see Ambleside plan -5B.
Ghyllside Cycles, The Slack, Ambleside, LA22 9DQ. Tel: 015394 33592. see Ambleside plan -3B.
Gill Cycles, 1 The Gill, Ulverston, LA12 7BJ. S. Tel: 01229 581116. see Ulverston plan -3B.
Gone Mountain Biking, Portinscale, Keswick, CA12. Tel: 017687 80812. -3C 15.
Grizedale Mountainbikes, Grizedale Visitor Centre, Grizedale Forest Park, Grizedale, Ambleside, LA22 0QJ. Tel: 01229 860369. -3C 31.
Haven Cycles, Preston Street Garage, Preston Street, Whitehaven, CA28 9DL. Tel: 01946 632630. see Whitehaven plan -4B.
(Keswick Motor Company), Lake Road, Keswick, CA12 5BX. Tel: 017687 72064. see Keswick plan -3C.
Keswick Mountain Bike Centre, Units 1-2, Southey Hill Trading Park, Main Street, Keswick, CA12 5ND. Tel: 017687 75202. see Keswick plan -2B.
Millennium Cycles, Bankside Barn, Crook Road, Staveley, Kendal, LA8 9NG. Tel: 01539 821167. -2B 32.
St Patrick's Boat & Bike Hire, St Patrick's Boat Landing, Glenridding, Penrith, CA11 0QQ. S. Tel: 017684 82393. -1B 24.
Summitreks, 14 Yewdale Road, Coniston, LA21 8DU. Tel: 015394 41822. see Coniston plan -1B.
Wheelbase UK Ltd., Staveley Mill Yard, Back Lane, Staveley, Kendal, LA8 9LR. Tel: 01539 821443. -2B 32.

HORSE RIDING

Bank House Equestrian, Bank House, Little Salkeld, Penrith, CA10 1NN. Tel: 01768 881257. -1B 18.
Bigland Hall Riding Centre, Backbarrow, Newby Bridge, Ulverston, LA12 8PB. Tel: 015395 31728. -2B 36.
Birkby Cottage Stables, Birkby Hall Cottage, Cartmel, Grange-over-Sands, LA11 7NP. Tel: 015395 36319. -3B 36.
Bradley Riding Centre, Low Cock How, Kinniside, Ennerdale Bridge, Lamplugh, Cleator, CA23 3AQ. Tel: 01946 861354. -2D 21.

Calvert Trust Riding Centre, Little Crossthwaite, Underskiddaw, Keswick, CA12 4QD. Tel: 017687 72255. see Keswick plan -1E.
Crook Barn Stables, Torver, Coniston LA21 8BP. Tel: 015394 41088. -3B 30.
Hipshow Farm Riding Stables, Hipshow Farm, Patton, Kendal, LA8 9DR. Tel: 01539 735689 / 728221 / 723341. -2C 33.

Holmescales Riding Centre, Holmescales, Old Hutton, Kendal, LA8 0NB. Tel: 01539 729388. -1B 38.
Lakeland Pony Trekking, Limefitt Park, Patterdale Road, Troutbeck, Windermere, LA23. Tel: 015394 31999. -1A 32.
Lakeland Riding Centre, Lakeland Leisure Park, Moor Lane, Flookburgh, Grange-over-Sands, LA11 7LT. S. Tel: 015395 58131. -3B 36.
Larkrigg Riding School, Larkrigg, Natland, Kendal, LA9 7QS. Tel: 015395 60245. -1A 38.
Leacett Cottage Stables, South Whinfell, Melkinthorpe, Penrith, CA10 2DS. Tel: 01768 862153. -2B 18.
Parkfoot Trekking Centre, Howtown Road, Pooley Bridge, Penrith, CA10 2NA. S. Tel: 017684 86696. -3D 17.
Rookin House Farm Equestrian & Activity Centre, Rookin House Farm, Troutbeck, Penrith, CA11 0SS. Tel: 017684 83561. -2B 16.
Sockbridge Pony Trekking Centre, The Cottage, Sockbridge, Tirril, Penrith, CA10 2JT. Tel: 01768 863468. -2D 17.
Spoon Hall Pony Trekking, Haws Bank, Coniston, LA21 8AW. S. Tel: 015394 41391. see Coniston plan -3A.
Witherslack Hall Equestrian Centre, Witherslack Hall Farm, Witherslack, Grange-over-Sands, LA11 6SD. Tel: 015395 52244. -1C 37.

REFERENCE

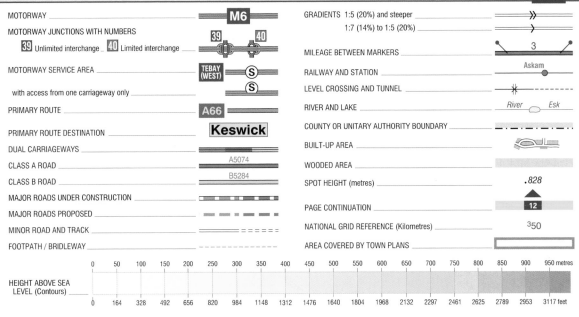

MOTORWAY	M6	GRADIENTS 1:5 (20%) and steeper	
MOTORWAY JUNCTIONS WITH NUMBERS	39 40	1:7 (14%) to 1:5 (20%)	
39 Unlimited interchange 40 Limited interchange		MILEAGE BETWEEN MARKERS	3
MOTORWAY SERVICE AREA	TEBAY (WEST) (S)	RAILWAY AND STATION	Askam
with access from one carriageway only	(S)	LEVEL CROSSING AND TUNNEL	
PRIMARY ROUTE	A66	RIVER AND LAKE	River Esk
PRIMARY ROUTE DESTINATION	Keswick	COUNTY OR UNITARY AUTHORITY BOUNDARY	
DUAL CARRIAGEWAYS		BUILT-UP AREA	
CLASS A ROAD	A5074	WOODED AREA	
CLASS B ROAD	B5284	SPOT HEIGHT (metres)	.828
MAJOR ROADS UNDER CONSTRUCTION		PAGE CONTINUATION	12
MAJOR ROADS PROPOSED		NATIONAL GRID REFERENCE (Kilometres)	350
MINOR ROAD AND TRACK		AREA COVERED BY TOWN PLANS	
FOOTPATH / BRIDLEWAY			

HEIGHT ABOVE SEA LEVEL (Contours)

0 50 100 150 200 250 300 350 400 450 500 550 600 650 700 750 800 850 900 950 metres
0 164 328 492 656 820 984 1148 1312 1476 1640 1804 1968 2132 2297 2461 2625 2789 2953 3117 feet

TOURIST INFORMATION

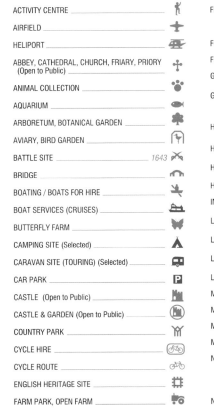

ACTIVITY CENTRE	FERRY (Vehicular)	NATURAL ATTRACTION
AIRFIELD	(Foot)	PICNIC SITE
HELIPORT	FOREST WALK, NATURE TRAIL	PLACE OF INTEREST (General)
ABBEY, CATHEDRAL, CHURCH, FRIARY, PRIORY (Open to Public)	FORTRESS, HILL FORT	POST OFFICE
ANIMAL COLLECTION	GARDEN (Open to Public)	PREHISTORIC MONUMENT
AQUARIUM	GOLF COURSE 9 HOLE	RAILWAY (Heritage, Narrow Gauge)
ARBORETUM, BOTANICAL GARDEN	18 HOLE	(Miniature Railway)
AVIARY, BIRD GARDEN	HISTORIC BUILDING (Open to Public)	ROMAN REMAINS
BATTLE SITE 1643	HISTORIC BUILDING & GARDEN (Open to Public)	SPOT HEIGHT (metres) • 241
BRIDGE	HORSE RACECOURSE	THEME PARK
BOATING / BOATS FOR HIRE	HORSE RIDING	TOILET
BOAT SERVICES (CRUISES)	INDUSTRIAL MONUMENT	(without facilities for the disabled)
BUTTERFLY FARM	LAKE DISTRICT NATIONAL PARK	(with facilities for the disabled)
CAMPING SITE (Selected)	LEISURE PARK, LEISURE POOL	(for exclusive use by the disabled)
CARAVAN SITE (TOURING) (Selected)	LIGHTHOUSE	TOURIST INFORMATION CENTRE (All year)
CAR PARK	LONG DISTANCE FOOTPATH Dales Way	(Summer Season Only)
CASTLE (Open to Public)	MINE, CAVE	VIEWPOINT 180° 360°
CASTLE & GARDEN (Open to Public)	MONUMENT, FOLLY	VINEYARD, CIDERMAKER, DISTILLERY
COUNTRY PARK	MOTOR RACING CIRCUIT	VISITOR / INFORMATION CENTRE
CYCLE HIRE	MUSEUM, ART GALLERY	National Park NP
CYCLE ROUTE	NATIONAL TRUST PROPERTY	National Trust NT
ENGLISH HERITAGE SITE	(Always Open) NT	WILDLIFE PARK
	(Restricted Opening) NT	WINDMILL
FARM PARK, OPEN FARM	NATURE RESERVE, BIRD SANCTUARY	YOUTH HOSTEL
		ZOO, SAFARI PARK

SCALE

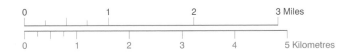

1:70,000

1.1 Miles to 1 inch

0.7 Kms (0.435 Miles) to 1 cm

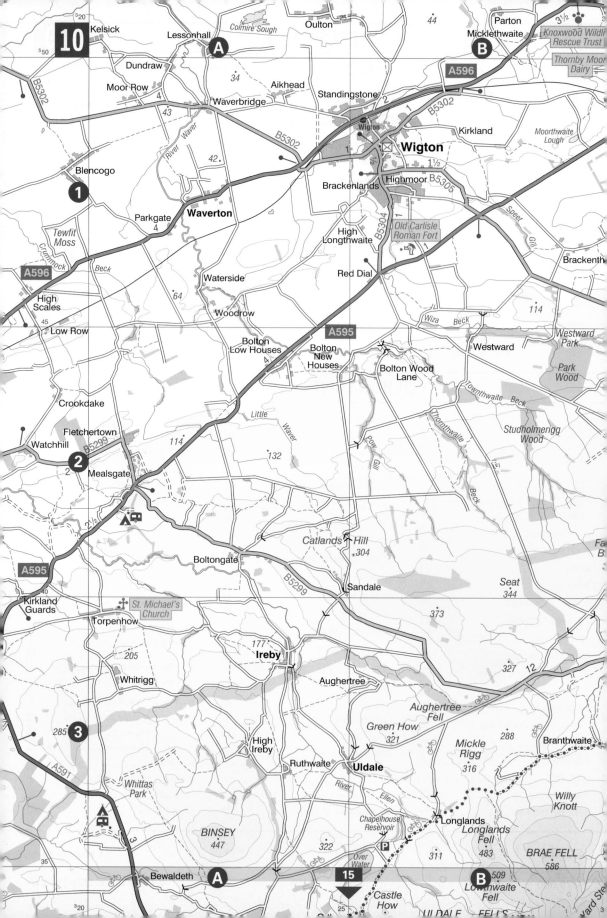

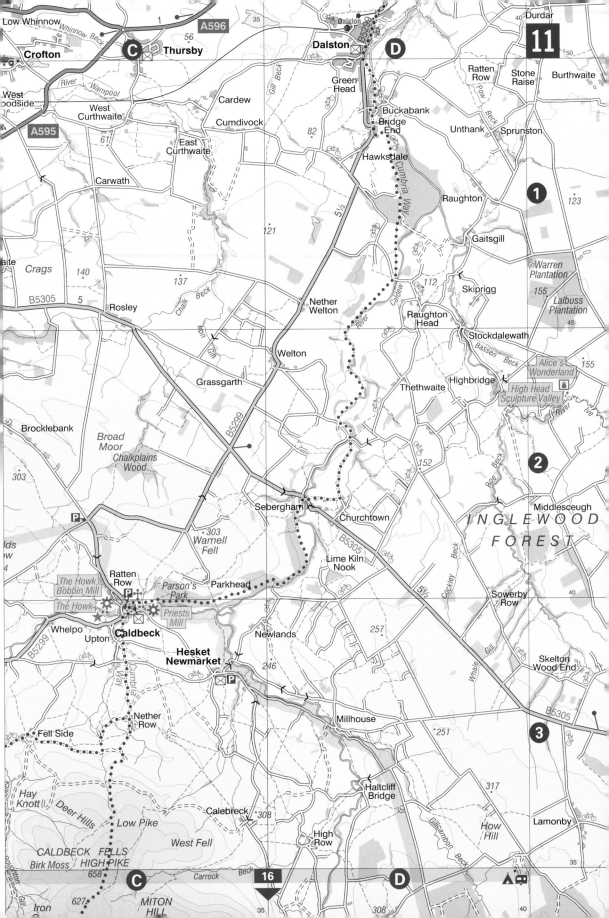

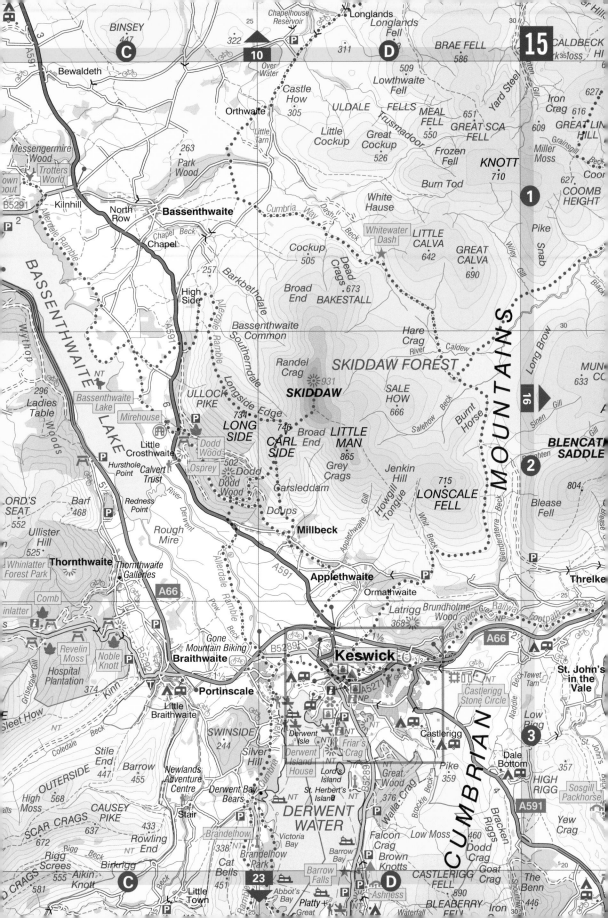

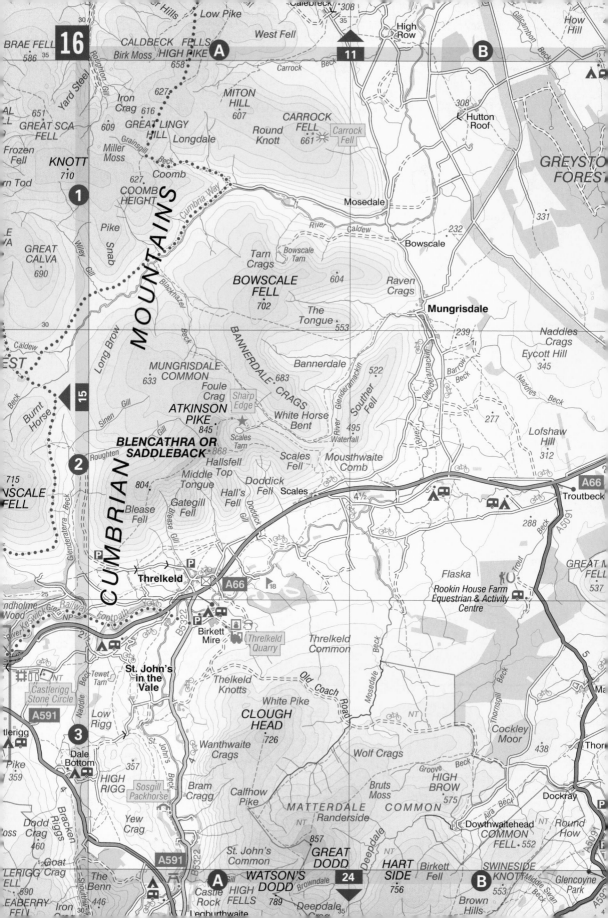

BRAE FELL 586 35

CALDBECK FELLS HIGH PIKE 658

Low Pike

West Fell

Caldbeck 308 35

High Row

How Hill

Gillamoor Beck

Birk Moss

Carrock Beck

Yard Steel

Roughton Gill

Iron Crag

627

616

MITON HILL 607

308

Hutton Roof

GREAT SCA FELL 651

Frozen Fell

GREAT LINGY HILL 609

Longdale

CARROCK FELL 661

Carrock Fell

GREYSTO FOREST

rn Tod

KNOTT 710

Miller Moss

627

Coomb

Round Knott

331

COOMB HEIGHT

Grainsgill Beck

River Caldew

Mosedale

232

Bowscale

GREAT CALVA 690

Pike Snab

Cumbria Way

Tarn Crags

Bowscale Tarn

604

Raven Crags

Naddles Crags

Wiley Gill

Blackhazel Beck

BOWSCALE FELL 702

The Tongue 553

Mungrisdale

239

Eycott Hill 345

Caldew

EST

Long Brow

MUNGRISDALE COMMON 633

BANNERDALE CRAGS

Bannerdale 683

522

Glenderamackin

Barrow Beck

277

Lofshaw Hill 312

Burnt Horse

Sinen Gill

Foule Crag

Sharp Edge

White Horse Bent

Souther Fell

Naddles Beck

Roughten Gill

ATKINSON PIKE 845

Scales Tarn

495

277

Gill

Glenderaterra Beck

868

Waterfall

715

BLENCATHRA OR SADDLEBACK

Hallsfell Top

Scales Fell

Mousthwaite Comb

River Glenderamackin

SCALE FELL

Bease Gill

Middle Tongue 804

Doddick Fell

Scales

A66

Troutbeck

Gategill Fell

Hall's Fell

4½

288

A5091

Blease Fell

Doddick Gill

GREAT M FELL 537

P

Threlkeld

A66

18

Flaska

Rookin House Farm Equestrian & Activity Centre

Trout

Keswick

Great NP

Railway

B5322

Birkett Mire

Threlkeld Quarry

Threlkeld Common

Mosedale Beck

Thornsgill Beck

Cockley Moor 438

Thor

ndholme Wood

Footpath

St. John's in the Vale

Thelkeld Knotts

White Pike

Old Coach Road

NT

HIGH BROW 575

Dockray

CASTLERIGG

Castlerigg Stone Circle

NT

Tewet Tarn

St. John's Beck

Low Rigg

CLOUGH HEAD 726

Wolf Crags

Groove Beck

Aira Beck

A591

Pike 359

Dale Bottom 357

HIGH RIGG

Wanthwaite Crags

Bram Cragg

Matterdale COMMON

Bruts Moss

Dowthwaitehead COMMON FELL 552

Round How

Dodd Crag 460

Bracken Riggs

Sosgill Packhorse

Yew Crag

Calfhow Pike

Randerside

NT

SWINESIDE KNOTT 553

Glencoyne Park

LERIGG ELL 590

Goat Crag

The Benn 446

Castle Rock

B5322

St. John's Common

WATSON'S DODD

HIGH FELLS 789

857

GREAT DODD

Browndale

Deepdale

HART SIDE 756

Birkett Fell

Brown Hills

Aira Beck

Middle Swan

EABERRY FELL

Iron Cra

35

MOUNTAINS

CUMBRIAN

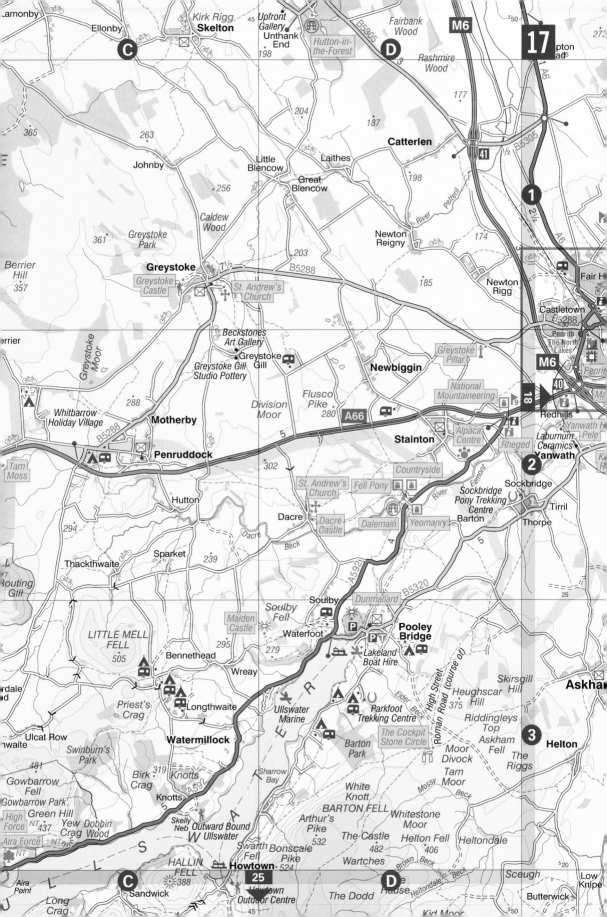

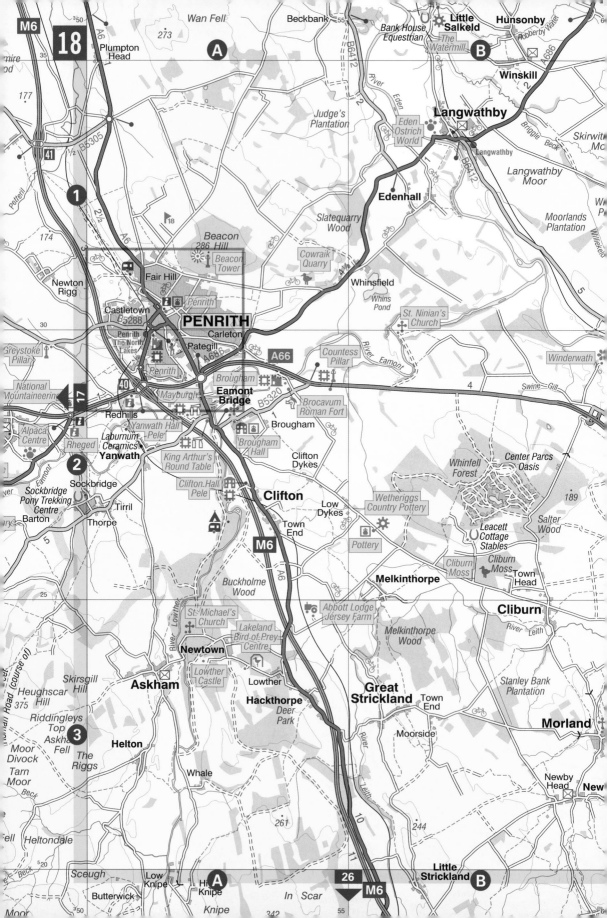

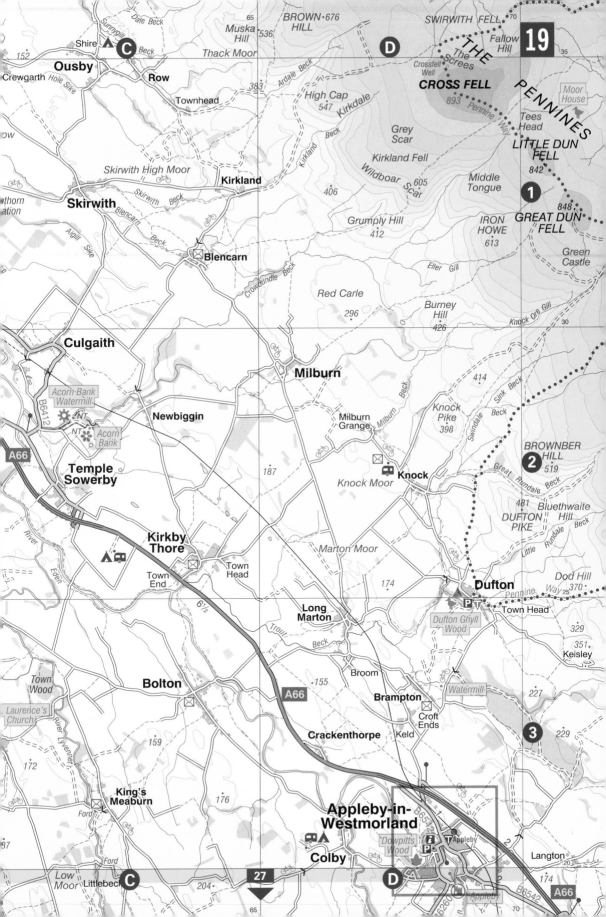

Parton Bay
Parton
Low
Moresby
Parton
A595
Quality
Corner
Tanyard
Bay
Bleachgreen
Redness
Point
Branstby
Scilly
Banks
162
WHITEHAVEN
Whitehaven
Harras
Moor
Round
Close
Park

1

The Quest
The Beacon
Harras
Park
Haig Colliery
Mining
18
Billy Bears
Corkickle
Corkickle
B5295
Saltom Pit
Kells
Hensingham

Woodhouse

SALTOM
BAY
Mirehouse

129
A595
Westlak
& Techn

St. Bees
Head
Sandwith
94

North Head
Hannah
Moor
Sandwith
Newtown
111
Linethwaite

2

ST. BEES
HEAD
Bigrig

St. Bees
Head
141
Rottington

South Head
Priory
Church
Pow Beck

Lifeboat
Station
St. Bees
St. Bees
117
9
B5345

I R I S H

Coulderton

S E A
Middleto

3

Nethertown
Nethertown

Brayston

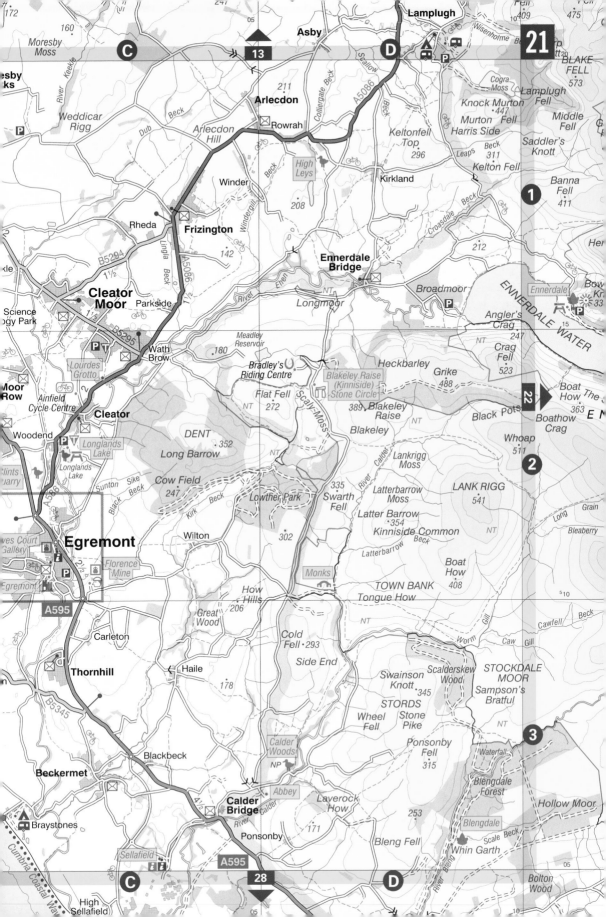

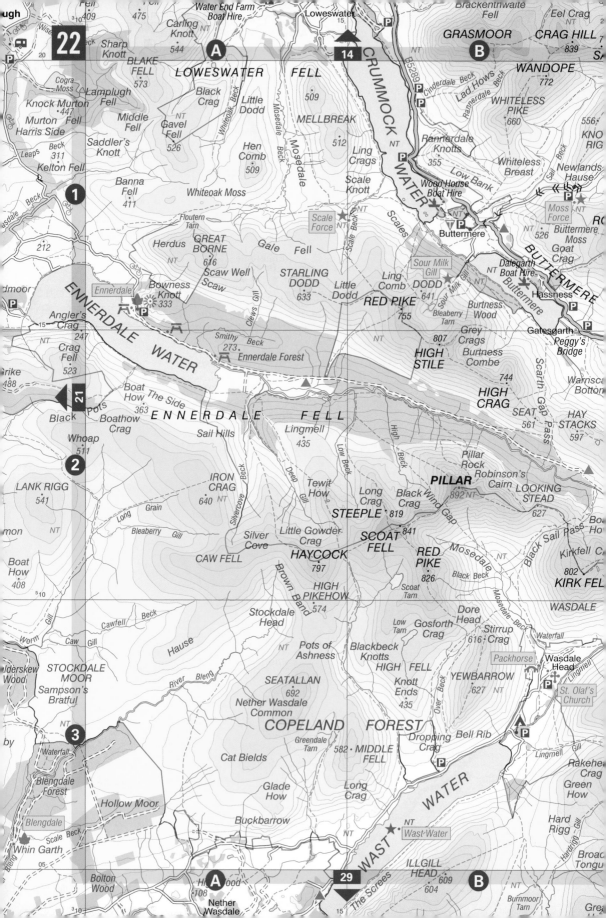

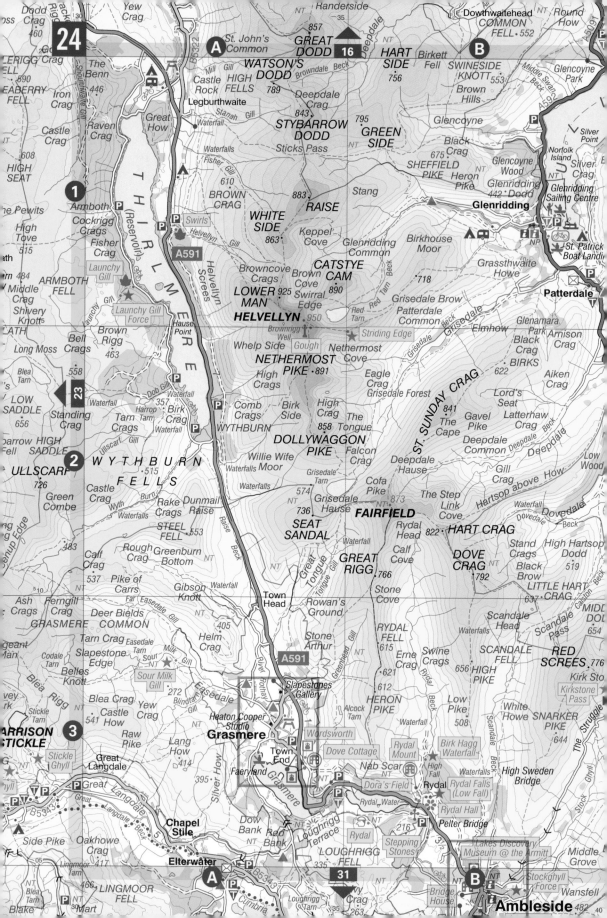

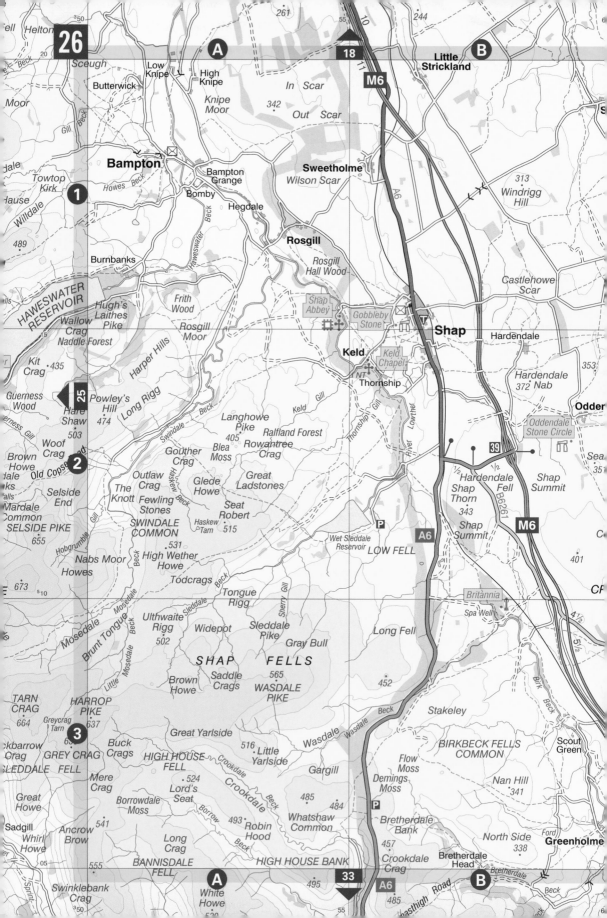

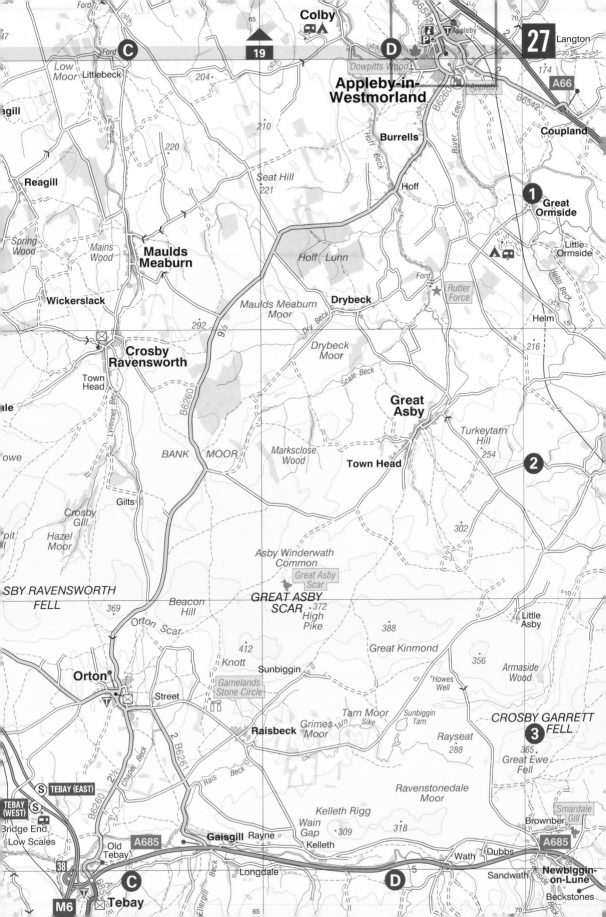

Braystones

Braystones

A ℹ️

21 A595

B Blengdale

Ponsonby

171

Bleng Fell

Whin Garth

253

Scale Beck

River Bleng

Sellafield

High Sellafield

Cumbria Coastal Way

Works

Wellington

P 🚐

Cross

Gosforth

Gosforth Pottery

Sellafield

Newmill Beck

Lacor

1

Grey Croft Stone Circle

18

B5344

2½

Seascale

Seascale

P 🚐

A595

Hallsenna Moor

Whitriggs Scar

🚴 5½

Hallsenna Moor

Irton Cross

500

Stubble Green

Holmrook

Drigg

Drigg

River Irt

B5344

P

2

Barn Scar

DANGER AREA

Kokoarrah

Dunes

Mur

127

Saltcoats

P 🚐

NP

Drigg Dunes

Railway

Ravenglass for Eskdale

Ravenglass

Munca Cast

Roman Bath House (Walls Castle)

95

I R I S H

Drigg Point

RIVER ESK

Eskmeals Dunes

DANGER AREA

Newbiggin

S E A

Dunes

Waber

3

DANGER AREA

P 🚐

90

Tarn Bay

A

B

Hycen

300

05

Selker Bay

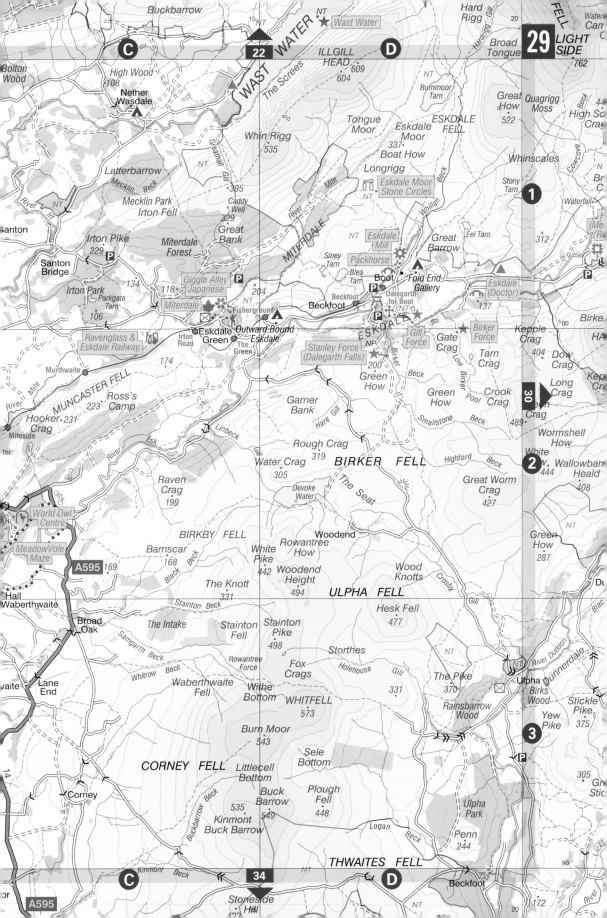

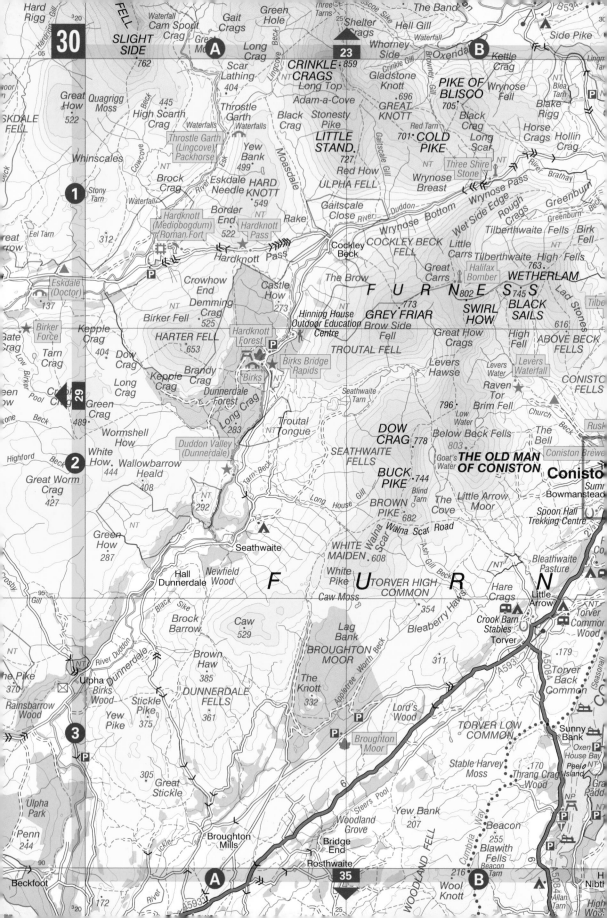

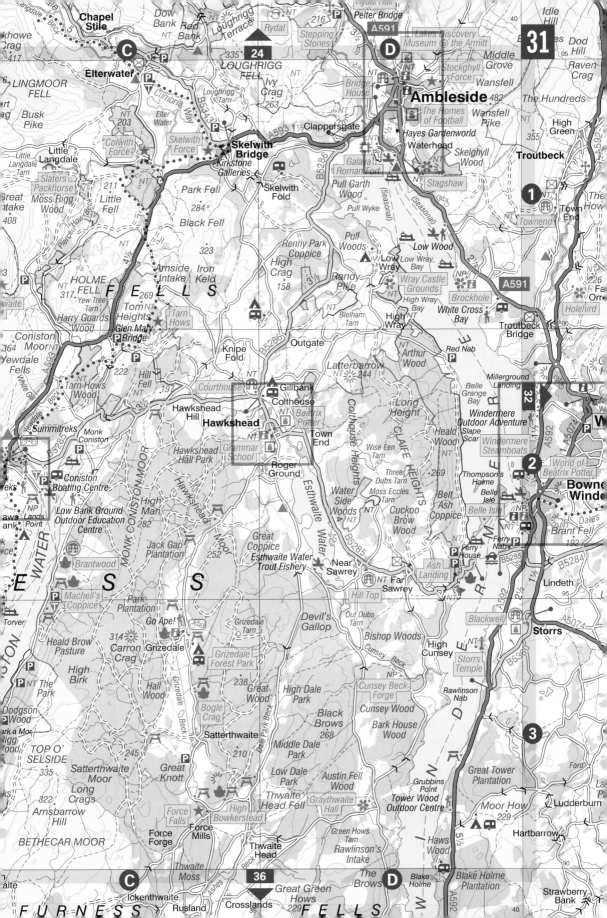

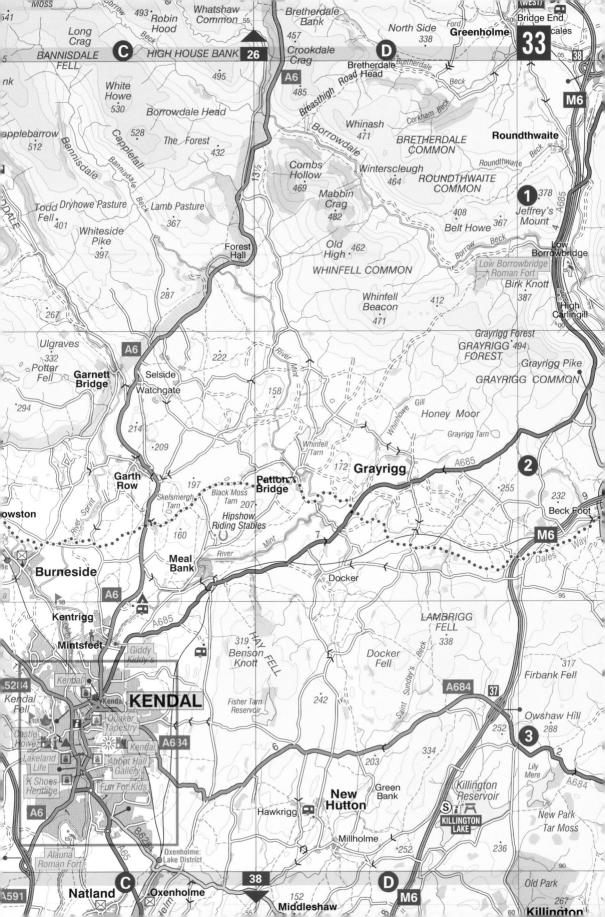

MOSS 541

493 Robin Hood

Long Crag

Whatshaw Common 55

Bretherdale Bank

North Side 338

Ford

60 Bridge End scales

BANNISDALE FELL

C

HIGH HOUSE BANK 26

A6

Greenholme

33

D

WEST

M6

nk

White Howe 530

495

Breasthigh Road Head

Crookdale Crag 457

485

Bretherdale

Beck

Borrowdale Head

528

Capplebarrow 512

Cropplefall

The Forest 432

Borrowdale

131?

Whinash 471

Corkham Beck

Roundthwaite

BRETHERDALE COMMON

Roundthwaite Beck

Bannisdale Beck

DALE

Todd Fell 401

Dryhowe Pasture

Lamb Pasture

Combs Hollow 469

Winterscleugh 464

ROUNDTHWAITE COMMON

Mabbin Crag 482

Belt Howe 408

367

1 378

Jeffrey's Mount

A685

M6

4

Whiteside Pike 397

367

Old High 462

Forest Hall

WHINFELL COMMON

Borrow Beck

Low Borrowbridge

Low Borrowbridge Roman Fort

Birk Knott

287

Whinfell Beacon 471

412

High Carlingill 387

500

267

Grayrigg Forest

GRAYRIGG 494 FOREST

Ulgraves 332

A6

222

River Mint

GRAYRIGG COMMON

Grayrigg Pike

Potter Fell

Garnett Bridge

Selside

158

Watchgate

Whinhowe Gill

Honey Moor

Grayrigg Tarn

294

214

.209

Whinfell Tarn

172

Grayrigg

A685

255

232 9

Beck Foot

Garth Row

197

Black Moss Tarn

Patton Bridge

owston

Skelsmergh Tarn

207 160

Hipshow Riding Stables

River Sprint

Mint

7

River

Mint

M6

Dales Way

95

Burneside

Meal Bank

Docker

LAMBRIGG FELL 338

A6

Kentrigg

A685

Docker Fell

Saint Sunday's Beck

317 Firbank Fell

5284

Mintsfeet

Giddy Kiddy's

319

HAY FELL

Benson Knott

242

A684

37

252

Owshaw Hill 288

Kendal Fell

Kendal

Kendal

KENDAL

Quaker Tapestry

Fisher Tarn Reservoir

334

3

Castle Howe

Lakeland Life

Abbot Hall Gallery

Kendal

A6 34

6

203

Lily Mere

A684

K Shoes Heritage

Fun For Kids

A6

B6254

Hawkrigg

New Hutton

Green Bank

Killington Reservoir

S

KILLINGTON LAKE

New Park Tar Moss

Alauna Roman Fort

Oxenholme: Lake District

B6254

Millholme

252

236

90

A591

C

Natland

38

Oxenholme

Kelm

D

M6

Old Park 267

55

Middleshaw

152

60

Killington

A

29

THWAITES B FELL

³10

90

Kinmont
Buck Barrow

549

448

Logan

Beck

Park

Penn
244

Kinmont Beck

NT

Beckfoot

Hycemoor

A595

Stoneside
Hill
422

NT

277

Bootle

BOOTLE FELL
Little
Grassoms

Swinside
Fell

Swinside (Sunkenkirk)
Stone Circle

Duddon
Ironworks

NP

Bootle

Great
Grassoms

456

218

Wrayslack

Duddon
Bridge

Hyton

1

Kiskin

River Annas

Little Fell

472

Gray
Stones

Knott
Hill
281

Soupdale
Crags
396

Annaside

Barfield
Tarn

417

White
Combe

Baystone Bank
Reservoir

A595

Lady
Hall

Millergill

Amaside Banks

85

BLACK COMBE

311

Black Beck

Hallthwaites

600

3

Gutterby Spa

Whitbeck

3

The Green

Arnaby

A5093

Strands

2

Townend
Knotts

Black
Crags

Whicham Valley

Whicham

Green Road

A595

Millom Park

**The
Hill**

Whicham

A5093

Silecroft
Silecroft

A5093

189

Lacra
Stone Circles

Millom
Castle

DUI

P

Giant's
Grave

Kirksanton

Beck
Wood

Millom
Folk

Millom
Ironworks

Borwick Rails
Harbour

9

A5093

7

⁴80

Haverigg

Pool

Millom

I R I S H

RAF Millom

Haverigg

Hodbarrow

Cumbria Coastal Way

Port Haverigg
Railway

Hodbarrow
Point

3

Haverigg
Point

Wortbrig
Scar

S E A

DUDDON SANDS

Sandscale
Haws

NT

Sandscale
Haws

A

B

Lowsy Point

75

³10

15

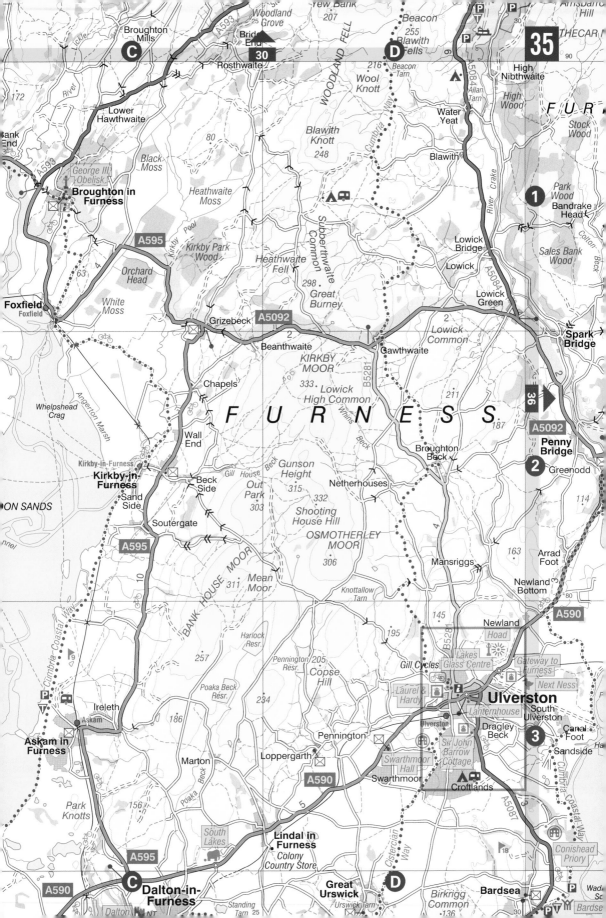

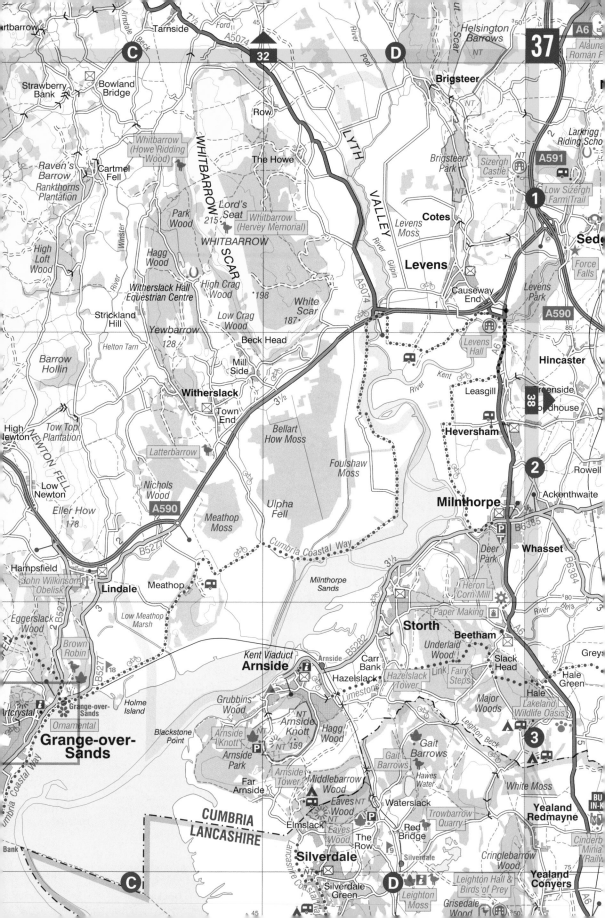

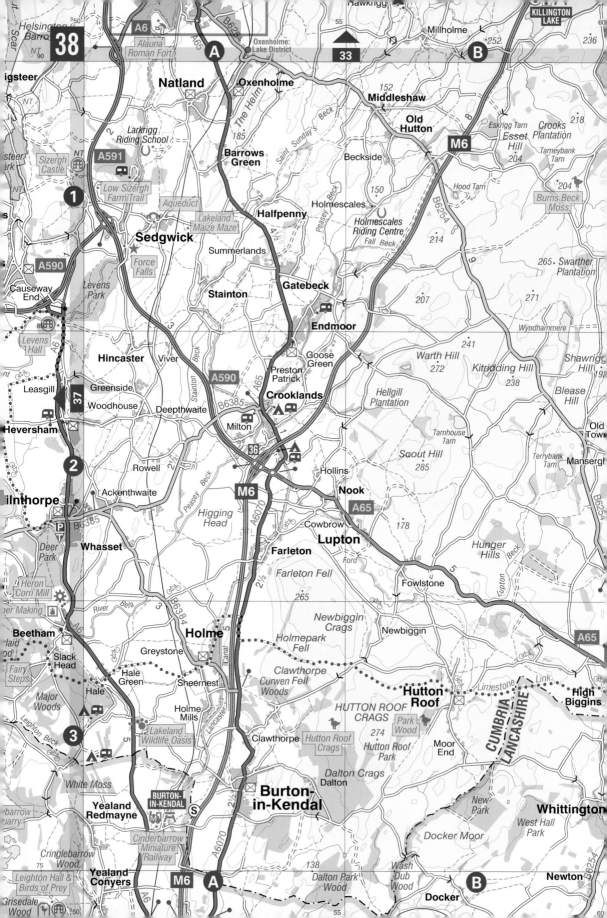

INDEX TO TOWNS, VILLAGES, HAMLETS and LOCATIONS

INDEX TO TOWNS, VILLAGES, HAMLETS and LOCATIONS

TOWN PLANS

REFERENCE

MOTORWAY — **M6**

PRIMARY ROUTE — **A65**

CLASS A ROAD — A5271

CLASS B ROAD — B5289

DUAL CARRIAGEWAYS

ONE-WAY STREET
Traffic flow on A Roads is also indicated by a heavy line on the drivers left.

RESTRICTED ACCESS

PEDESTRIANIZED ROAD

HOUSE NUMBERS
A & B Roads only — 10 / 87 / 124

LONG DISTANCE FOOTPATH

CYCLE ROUTE

TRACK

FOOTPATH

RESIDENTIAL WALKWAY

RAILWAY — Level Crossing / Station / Tunnel

BUILT-UP AREA — LAKE / ROAD

CAR PARK (Selected) — P

CHURCH OR CHAPEL — †

FIRE STATION — ■

HOSPITAL — H

NATIONAL GRID REFERENCE (Kilometres) — $^{3}30$

POLICE STATION — ▲

POST OFFICE — ⊠

TOILET
without facilities for the disabled — ▽
with facilities for the disabled — ▽
for exclusive use by the disabled — ▽

EDUCATIONAL ESTABLISHMENT

HOSPITAL OR HOSPICE

INDUSTRIAL BUILDING

LEISURE OR RECREATIONAL FACILITY

PLACE OF INTEREST

PUBLIC BUILDING

SHOPPING CENTRE OR MARKET

OTHER SELECTED BUILDINGS

SCALE

1:15,840

4 inches (10.61 cm) to 1 Mile
6.3 cm (2.49 inches) to 1 Km

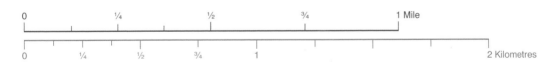

0   ¼   ½   ¾   1 Mile

0   ¼   ½   ¾   1   2 Kilometres

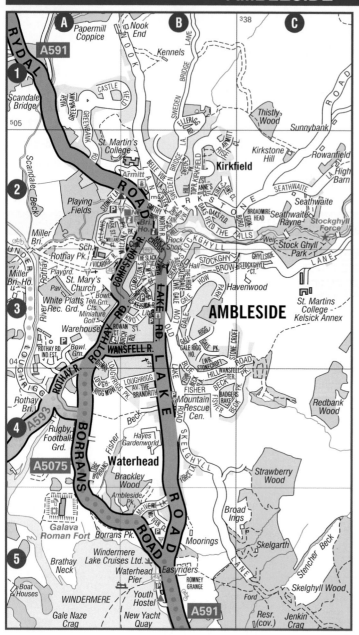

Ambleside is a compact town of distinctive grey-green slate buildings, beneath a fine scenic mountain backdrop. The town with its narrow paths, and congested roads in the summer, is extremely popular with tourists.

Although mostly Victorian in character, occupation near Ambleside dates back to the Romans (see 'Galava Roman Fort'), followed by Viking influence; the town was granted its Market Charter in 1650. The market cross, a headless sandstone cross-shaft, which once had a sundial, still survives today, moved to its present site in 1885. The oldest part of the town is the narrow North Road, Smithy Brow and Chapel Hill, the old main road until bypassed by the building of Rydal Road in 1843. The channelling of the adjacent Stock Beck in the 1890s allowed the reclamation of the low

lying marshy area now part occupied by Rothay Park. The oldest building is the 400 year old How Head on Smithy Brow, part of the demolished Ambleside Hall (seat of the Braithwaite family), remnants of which are included in parts of buildings in the area of the Golden Rule public house.

Until the 1840s Ambleside prospered from the wool trade, and its readily available water power was used in many cloth, fulling, corn, paper, bark and bobbin mills that lined Stock Beck, which flows into the River Rothay just downstream of Miller Bridge. The current environment belies the incessant noise and smell that these mills would have created. Some of these buildings, put to other uses, survive. Most noticeable of these are the waterwheel in Rydal Road, a former bark mill on North Road with a replica electrically powered waterwheel, and the converted Horrax bobbin mill on the north bank off The Falls. Remains of the weir at the entrance to the mill race can be seen from Stock Ghyll Park.

The town developed in Victorian times with visitors arriving by paddle steamer from either Bowness-on-Windermere or Newby Bridge from 1845, or by coach from the new railway terminal at Windermere from 1847. To accommodate these new visitors, the present Victorian houses and shops in Lake Road, Compston Road, Compston Street, Church Street and Rothay Road were built in the 1880s. Both these modes of transport may not have survived had The Ambleside Railway scheme succeeded, a proposal for an extension of the railway at Windermere to Ambleside, submitted to parliament in 1886-7. The scheme was not supported by the London and North Western Railway, (L.N.W.R.), who owned the Windermere line.

Bridge House - Ambleside

The most notable building in Ambleside is St Mary's parish church, on Vicarage Road. Built in 1850-4, in Early English Gothic Revival style, as a replacement for the outgrown St Anne's church in old Ambleside. Incorporating aesthetics from the Oxford Movement (a catholic revival in the Church of England), it is unique in the Lake District being the only church in Cumbria designed by Sir George Gilbert Scott (senior, 1811-78), Professor of Architecture at the Royal Academy from 1866-73. St Mary's, with its 55 m (180 ft) sandstone spire, has at its west end a long and lively mural of 1944 by G. Ransom depicting the rushbearing ceremony which is still held at this church on the first Saturday in July. Rushbearing, a parade through the village by children carrying rushes and flowers, dates back to medieval times when rushes, usually changed several times a year, were used to cover the earthen floors of churches before flagstones became common in the 19th century. There is notable stained glass, including work by Henry Holiday and William Wordsworth. Wordsworth is commemorated in a memorial chapel and by windows to himself and members of his family.

Ambleside is associated with many famous people including:

William Wordsworth, the famous 19th century romantic poet, who in 1813 obtained the lucrative job of postmaster and Distributor of Stamps for Westmorland, based in premises at the top of Church Street (no. 3, now the Old Stamp House).

The Armitt Sisters, Sophia (1847-1908), Anna Marie (1850-80) and Mary Louisa (1851-1911) who were born and brought up in Manchester studying art, botany, literature, natural history and music. The two surviving sisters moved to Hawkshead in 1886, and then to Manor Cottage, Rydal (now a guest house) in 1896, where they were popular within the community for their artistic and academic gifts.

Charlotte Mason (1842-1923) who established her House of Education in Ambleside in 1892. Initially a training institution for governesses of home-educated children of middle class backgrounds. She was closely involved with the Parents' National Education Union, developing the ideas that children are individuals, and should be taught as such with a broad syllabus, an innovation for her time. In 1894 the main base of the college moved to Scale How (where she lived the rest of her life to age 81), Charlotte Mason College continuing to this day as a part of St Martin's College.

Harriet Martineau (1802-76) who wrote books, articles and pamphlets on historical, political and philosophical topics, as well as championing many issues affecting women. She built a house called The Knoll, off Rydal Road, in 1846.

Thomas Arnold (1795-1842), a former headmaster of Rugby School (from 1828) who was influential in the development of public school education, and had the retreat at Fox How on Under Loughrigg built in 1832-3. His granddaughter Mary Augusta Ward (or Mrs Humphrey Ward, 1851-1920) was one of the prolific popular novelists of the late 19th century and wrote 'Milly and Olly' (also titled 'A Holiday among the Mountains') in 1881, an early children's novel set in the Lake District using Fox How as a setting.

Alfred Heaton Cooper (1864-1929), one of the most famous Lake District watercolour artists of his time, whose imported Norwegian log cabin studio (now 'The Log House' restaurant) can still be seen on Lake Road, roughly opposite Low Fold car park.

John Kelsick, known locally, who in 1723 set up an educational trust in his will to start a free school for boys eventually becoming known as the Kelsick Grammar School.

The town has many shops catering for the hiking and climbing fraternity as well as galleries, gift shops and tea-rooms. The Market Cross development, the Rock Shop on North Road, with its display of rocks, minerals and fossils from Cumbria and around the world, Zeffirellis cinema and retail outlet on Compston Road and Hayes Gardenworld, with its Crystal Palace style greenhouse, are all of note. Waterhead Pier is popular for lake cruises or for feeding the waterfowl. Rothay Park and White Platts Recreation Ground, with its miniature golf, should not be missed, whilst for those seeking a quieter environment there is Borrans Park with its lakeside setting.

There are many popular medium distance walks from Ambleside:
■ To the north-west a walk to the Rydal Stepping Stones via Miller Bridge and the Under Loughrigg road, which can be extended via Pelter Bridge (Rydal) to Loughrigg Fell with Rydal Cave and the Loughrigg Terrace viewpoint, a famous view over Grasmere.

Pike and Nab Scar, returning to Rydal, and then Ambleside via the footpath through Rydal Park.

Early Closing- Thursday.
Market Days- King Street car park (outdoor), Wednesdays.

PLACES OF INTEREST
Tourist Information Centre (All year) - 2B. Central Buildings, Market Cross, Ambleside. Tel: 015394 32582.
Information Centre **NT** - 2B. Bridge House, Rydal Road. Tel: 015394 32617.
● BRIDGE HOUSE- 2B. A curious tiny 2 storey early 18th century vernacular stone building bridging Stock Beck (Stock Ghyll), the subject of countless picture postcards. Built as a summerhouse, or apple store, (or both) to Ambleside Hall (which used to stand near Smithy Brow), it is said to have been built over the river to avoid land tax. It has subsequent claims to other uses, including a counting house for a woollen mill, tea-room, cobbler's shop and most famously a mid 19th century Victorian two room residence for 'Chairy'

Ambleside

■ To the north a footpath from Scandale Bridge, via Rydal Park and Rydal Hall, joining the Coffin Path via White Moss Common to Grasmere.
■ To the east, a short but steep walk up Wansfell (482 m or 1,581 ft).
■ To the south-east to Jenkin Crag viewpoint in Skelghyll Wood, with its stunning views over the north end of Windermere.
■ For the well equipped fell walker, the spectacular 'Fairfield Horseshoe' walk to the north beckons, as the name implies a horseshoe amphitheatre traced by a route almost encircling the Rydal Beck valley with Fairfield (873 m or 2,864 ft), at the north-west of the arc. This popular route is 10 miles long via Nook Lane, Ambleside to High Sweden Bridge, High Pike, Dove Crag, Hart Crag, Fairfield, Great Rigg, Heron

Rigg (a chair-repairer), his wife and 6 children, said to be the smallest house in England. Acquired by the National Trust by subscription in 1926, it is now home to the National Trust's first information centre (opened 1956) and also a small exhibition situated on the upper floor. A subject for the English landscape artist J. M. W. Turner, an engraving of the summer house in 1834 by Thomas Allom shows a fascinating scene with the building sprouting from river level in an idyllic sylvan setting without the adjacent busy main road of 1843, and the walled river course. Rydal Road. Tel: 015394 32617.

● GALAVA ROMAN FORT- 5A. Clear foundations of a typical rectangular plan Roman fort built c.120 AD by Hadrian once housing a garrison consisting of a cohort of some 500 infantrymen. Placed on a strategic site at the head of Windermere, at the confluence of the rivers Brathay and Rothay, the fort, part of a network, controlled the junction of the Roman road north-east over the fell of High Street to Penrith, south-east to Kendal and west via Hardknott (Mediobogdum) Roman Fort to the Roman port of Ravenglass. Galava was constructed on an oblong platform and once had castellated walls and corner turrets over 4 m (13 ft) high.

The remains include the main double opening gateway (leading from the road in the east), the north, south and west (river) gates, and the foundations of the main stone buildings block running across the oblong including the central Praetorium, the chief building of the fort located in the middle and used as the administration and religious centre, flanked by the granaries and commanding officers house. The rest was occupied with wooden barracks. The fort was a replacement for an abandoned timber fort of half the size built c.90 AD. Galava was acquired by the National Trust in 1913 to prevent its development, little being known about the site until it was excavated by the archaeologist Robin George Collingwood, son of William Gershom Collingwood, between 1913 and 1920. There are descriptive plaques. Borrans Field, Borrans Road, Waterhead.

● HOMES OF FOOTBALL, THE - 3B. Opened in 1997 in a new permanent home in Ambleside by photographer Stuart Clarke. The pictures capture the atmosphere of football grounds and the passion of the supporters for their clubs since the Hillsborough tragedy of 1989. Showing British grounds as they were, pre-Hillsborough, in their last incarnations of the pre and post war era before the new steel and concrete all seater stands were built to modern day requirements for safety and comfort. The collection, with its panoramic shots of the grounds and close up of the crowds, has become a unique and unrivalled 65,000 photographic archive of all levels of the English and Scottish game and of international events. 100 Lake Road. Tel: 015394 34440.

● LAKES DISCOVERY MUSEUM @ THE ARMITT, THE - 2B. Many famous Lakeland personalities are covered by this museum including John Ruskin, Beatrix Potter, the Collingwood family, the Abraham brothers (early climbing photographers) and locals such as the Armitt Sisters, Charlotte Mason, Harriet Martineau, Thomas Arnold, Herbert Bell, William Green (one of first artists to produce accurate and objective, as opposed to purely romantic, images of the Lake District), Alfred Heaton Cooper and others. The museum contains over a million objects of local, national and international importance covering subjects such as art, archaeology, geology, photography and local history. There are over 400 of Beatrix Potter's original watercolours and drawings depicting fungi, fossils and Roman archaeology, and Victorian photographs including local scenes and people, mainly by local photographers such as Herbert Bell (1856-1946, who set up a studio in 1894 and immediately captured the 'Great Frost' of February 1895) whose pictures are set in an interactive birds-eye view of the Lakeland landscape. Also included are interactive 'hands-on' exhibits, audios of John Ruskin, personal items including a lock of John Ruskin's hair and Dorothy Wordsworth's scarf and a changing programme of temporary exhibitions.

The Armitt Library, founded by Mary Louisa Armitt who in 1909 gave money for a library in Ambleside, was opened in November 1912 (after her death in 1911), incorporating the Ruskin Library which had been founded after John Ruskin's death. Today the reference library, which is open to the public, is above the museum and amounts to over 10,000 titles relating to the Lake District including Canon Hardwicke Rawnsley's book collection, early guide books, local history, Charlotte Mason's educational theories, books by Beatrix Potter and Arthur Ransome, early mountaineering subjects, archives, and photographs and glass plates produced by the Abraham Brothers. Rydal Road / Nook Lane. Tel: 015394 31212.

● STOCKGHYLL FORCE - 2C. Situated in the wooded Stock Ghyll Park, on Stock Ghyll or Beck. A half a mile uphill walk along Stockghyll Lane, signposted behind the Ambleside Salutation Hotel. With a drop of approximately 21.5 m (70 ft), the fall is viewed from railed viewpoints on either side. Footbridges up and downstream allow a circuit via the south and north banks along a footpath route, through landscaped grounds with picnic tables, clearly waymarked with red arrows. Often painted in its wooded dell, very much a Victorian romantic idyll, it was first described in the 1770s and soon became more popular than Rydal Falls nearby. Missed by most of the tourists visiting the shops at Ambleside this beautiful and easily accessible waterfall should not be missed. 'Force' is a corruption of 'Foss', the old Norse word for a waterfall, it is not a reflection of the power of the waterfall. Stock Ghyll Park, Stockghyll Lane.

ENTERTAINMENT
● Cinemas - Zeffirellis, Millans Park. Tel: 015394 33845.
● Libraries - Kelsick Road. Tel: 015394 32507.

SPORT and LEISURE
● Boating / Boats for hire - Windermere Lake Cruises Ltd., Waterhead Pier, Waterhead. Tel: 015394 32225 / 015395 31188.
● Bowling Greens - Rothay Road. White Platts Recreation Ground, Rothay Road.
● Children's Entertainment - Rothay Park Adventure Playground, Rothay Park, Vicarage Road.
● Crazy Golf Courses - White Platts Obstacle Golf, White Platts Recreation Ground, Rothay Road.
● Cricket Grounds - Ambleside Cricket Ground, Rydal Road, Rydal (NW of Ambleside).
● Cycle Hire - Biketreks, Compston Road. Tel: 015394 31505. Easyriders, Waterhead Pier, Waterhead (conventional and electric bikes). Tel: 015394 32902. Ghyllside Cycles, The Slack. Tel: 015394 33592.
● Horse Riding - Lakeland Pony Trekking, Limefitt Park, Patterdale Road, Troutbeck (E of Ambleside). Tel: 015394 31999.
● Parks and Gardens - Borrans Park, Borrans Road, Waterhead. Rothay Park, Vicarage Road. Rydal Park, Rydal Road, Rydal (NW of Ambleside). Stock Ghyll Park, Stockghyll Lane. White Platts Recreation Ground, Rothay Road.
● Pitch and Putt Courses - White Platts Recreation Ground, Rothay Road.
● Putting Greens - White Platts Recreation Ground, Rothay Road.
● Sports and Leisure Centres - St Martin's College Sports Centre, Nook Lane (term time). Tel: 015394 30210.
● Tennis Courts - White Platts Recreation Ground, Rothay Road.

APPLEBY-IN-WESTMORLAND

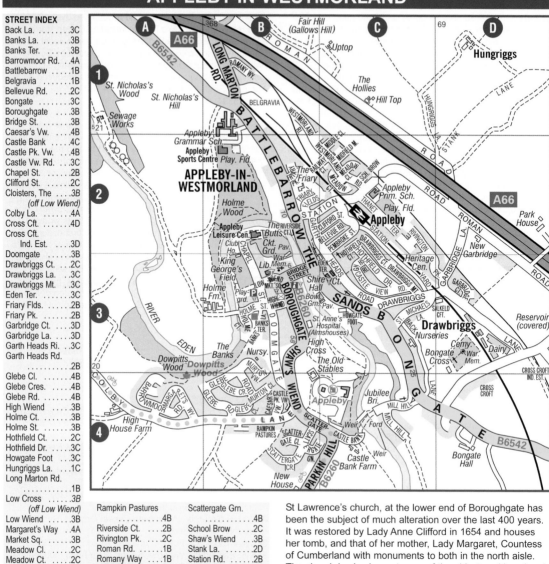

Appleby-in-Westmorland was formerly the county town of Westmorland until 1974 when that county was incorporated in the administrative county of Cumbria. Situated in a loop of the River Eden this picturesque small market town is dominated by the fine sight of the wide main thoroughfare of Boroughgate with its historic buildings, linking the cloisters and church at the lower end with the castle at the top, the ends being marked by the High and Low Crosses, which formed the original boundaries of the market.

A pleasant walk follows the river, beside the cricket ground and King George's Field between the two bridges. Running parallel behind Boroughgate are Doomgate and Chapel Street, connected to it by the narrow streets of High Wiend and Low Wiend.

St Lawrence's church, at the lower end of Boroughgate has been the subject of much alteration over the last 400 years. It was restored by Lady Anne Clifford in 1654 and houses her tomb, and that of her mother, Lady Margaret, Countess of Cumberland with monuments to both in the north aisle. The church is also home to one of the oldest working church organs in England.

The arcaded Cloisters at the bottom of Boroughgate were designed in 1811 by Sir Robert Smirke, the architect of Lowther Castle. St Anne's Hospital (at the upper end of Boroughgate), a quiet group of almshouses set around a cobbled and gardened courtyard, was established by Lady Anne Clifford in 1653 to provide accommodation for 13 poor widows of her estate. The almshouses are still maintained by a trust endowed by her and visitors may view the courtyard. The restored Moot Hall of 1596 (home to the tourist information centre) is still used as a council chamber by the town council.

The famous Appleby Horse Fair, one of the largest horse trading fairs in Europe, is held annually every June. The fair, which runs for a week (ending on the second Wednesday in the month) in a field known as Fair Hill just off the A66 junction on the road to Brampton, is attended by travelling people and gypsies from all over the country. The fair was set up by Royal Charter in 1685 and moved here from the

Appleby-in-Westmorland

town centre in 1750. Sights to see are the display of horses which are trotted along part of the Appleby-Brampton road, the open air market held in the adjacent field, occasional harness racing held on Holme Farm Field just to the west of the town centre and the daily washing of horses in the River Eden, (horses are not permitted into the town centre during fair week).

Appleby railway station is a major stopping point on the former Midland Railway's scenic Settle and Carlisle line. Steam train excursions can occasionally be seen taking water using the water tower and crane installed here.

Early Closing- Thursday.
Market Days- Market Square, Boroughgate (outdoor), Saturdays. Public Hall, Boroughgate (indoor), Fridays.

PLACES OF INTEREST
Tourist Information Centre (All year) - 3B. Moot Hall, Boroughgate. Tel: 017683 51177.
● APPLEBY CASTLE - 4C. Begun as a motte castle above the River Eden, Appleby became an enclosure castle, with sandstone rubble curtain walls built around the foot of the motte and (with the exception of the River Eden side), was surrounded by moats. Caesar's Tower, a 25 m (82 ft) high, 4 storey, square-plan great tower, or keep, was built inside c.1170. The castle became the stronghold of the Clifford family and was later restored by Lady Anne Clifford. A late 17th century Great Hall dwelling house (not open) forms the east range with portraits and furnishings. Surrounding the castle are 10 hectares of grounds providing a setting for beautiful river walks. The deer park grounds have an interesting collection of waterfowl and other birds and there is a children's animal garden with sheep, rabbits, guinea pigs and hens. Boroughgate. Tel: 017683 51402.

● DOWPITTS WOOD NATURE TRAIL - 4A. Nature trail through wood comprising typically oak, ash, beech, hazel, sycamore, rowan and alder on the south bank of the River Eden, a short walk from Appleby town centre. A leaflet detailing the 7 point trail is available from the tourist information centre. 'Dowpitts' refers to two beds of heavy clay which were once worked within the wood. Holme Wood nearby, north of the river, is also worth visiting. Banks Lane.

ENTERTAINMENT
● Libraries - Low Wiend. Tel: 017683 51170.

SPORT and LEISURE
● Bowling Greens - The Sands.
● Children's Entertainment - Barrowmoor Road. King George's Field Playground, Chapel Street.
● Cricket Grounds - The Butts, Chapel Street.
● Golf Courses - Appleby Golf Course, Brackenber Moor (18 hole) (SE of Appleby). Tel: 017683 51432.
● Parks and Gardens - The Butts, Chapel Street. Coronation Park, Garth Heads Road. King George's Field, Chapel Street.
● Sports and Leisure Centres - Appleby Leisure Centre, Chapel Street. Tel: 017683 51212.
● Squash Courts - King George's Field Club House, Chapel Street.
● Swimming Pools - Appleby Leisure Centre, Chapel Street (indoor). Tel: 017683 51212.
● Tennis Courts - Appleby Grammar School, Battlebarrow.

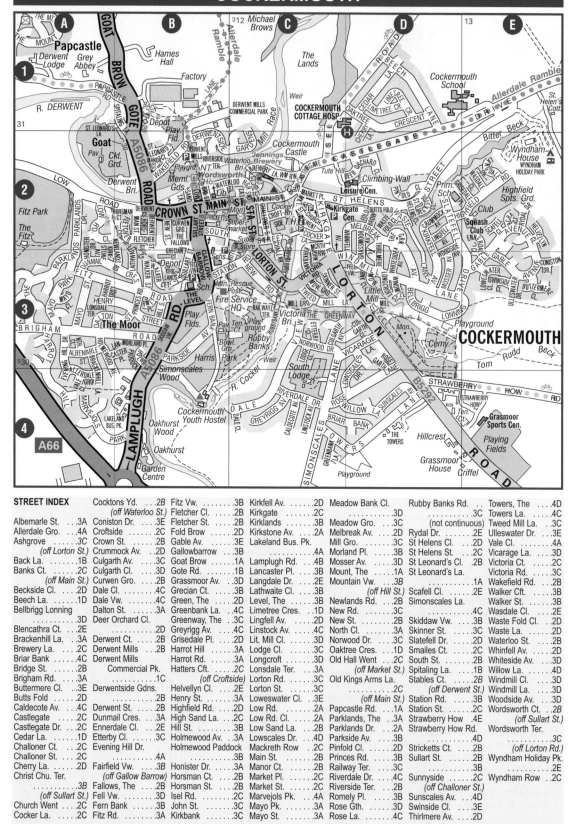

Cockermouth, an historic market town granted a Market Charter in 1221, is set at the confluence of the rivers Cocker and Derwent, on the fringe of the national park. The town is famous for being the birthplace and childhood playground of the romantic poet William Wordsworth, who was born here in Wordsworth House. With its wide tree-lined Main Street, domestic Georgian architecture and its sea of daffodils in the spring, it is a quiet town of great character sadly often by-passed by many of Lakeland's visitors.

An exploration of the town can be made by using the town trail marked by numbered cast iron plaques. The Mayo statue dominating the centre of Main Street, is a fine marble sculpture of Richard Southwell Bourke, 6th Earl of Mayo and MP for Cockermouth between 1857 and 1868. A bronze bust of William Wordsworth, opposite Wordsworth House was erected in 1970, the bicentenary of his birth.

Wordsworth House

The principal shopping areas are along the broad, attractive Main Street, Station Street and the tree-lined Market Place. Many of the shops have their original facades. More recent shopping developments include Old Kings Arms Lane and Lowther Went. The towns' major recreational area is Harris Park, containing a playground, and fountain with a graceful bronze figure of a child, a memorial to Dorothy and William Wordsworth, erected in 1896 by Canon Hardwicke Rawnsley, whilst the landscaped Greenway footpath / cycleway passes just to the north.

Early Closing - Thursday.
Market Days - Market Place (outdoor).

PLACES OF INTEREST
Tourist Information Centre (All year) - 2C. Town Hall, Market Street. Tel: 01900 822634.
● ALLERDALE RAMBLE - 1E to 1B.
● COCKERMOUTH CASTLE - 2C. An imposing ruin on a high spur of land, strategically set above the meeting of the rivers Cocker and Derwent. Best seen from the opposite bank of the Derwent, this Norman enclosure castle was originally built in the 12th century partly using stone robbed from Derventio Roman Fort at Papcastle close by. The curtain wall, towers and inner gatehouse date from the 13th century with an outer gatehouse and barbican added in the 14th. The conspicuous round tower at the apex formed by the rivers is known as the Bell Tower or Lady's Apartment. The castle may be open for guided visits, booked with the tourist information centre, during the Cockermouth Festival in July. Castlegate.

● JENNINGS BREWERY - 2C. Jennings Brewery was originally established as a true family concern back in 1828, in the village of Lorton. The company moved to its current location in 1874, in the historic market town of Cockermouth, in the shadow of Cockermouth Castle, at the point where the rivers Cocker and Derwent merge. Jennings regards itself as a traditional brewer - traditional in a number of different ways. Pure Lakeland water is still used for brewing, drawn from the brewery's own well, and only the finest natural ingredients are added. Find out how the real ales are still brewed with care and attention, by taking the friendly, guided tour of the brewery. Please allow one and a half hours for your visit. Several stairs and gridded walkways must be negotiated during the tour so it may not be suitable for everyone. Prebooking is recommended: Jennings Brewery, Castle Brewery, Cockermouth, Cumbria CA13 9NE. Tel: 0845 1297190
● PRINTING HOUSE WORKING MUSEUM OF PRINTING, THE - 2B. The history of printing from its mid 15th century origins to automated machinery, is explained in displays of printing presses and equipment from all over Britain. Dating back to 1886, is the impressively complicated 'state of the art' automatic typesetting Linotype Model 78 with hot metal casting. Described by Thomas Edison as the 'eighth wonder of the world'. 102 Main Street. Tel: 01900 824984.
● WORDSWORTH HOUSE - 2B. The birthplace of the famous romantic poet William Wordsworth in a Georgian town house built in 1745. William Wordsworth was born on 7th April 1770 and his sister Dorothy on 25th December 1771. Acquired via public subscription by the National Trust in 1938, the interior is furnished in 18th century style. Outside are the original kitchen garden and replanted Georgian garden. William's childhood enjoyment of this environment was to develop into the deep attraction he felt for the Lakeland landscape, inspiring his future writings, and passionate belief in the conservation of the countryside. Main Street. Tel: 01900 824805.

ENTERTAINMENT
● Cinemas - Kirkgate Centre, Kirkgate. Tel: 01900 826448.
● Libraries - Main Street. Tel: 01900 325990.
● Theatres - Kirkgate Centre, Kirkgate. Tel: 01900 826448.

SPORT and LEISURE
● Activity Centres - Cockermouth Climbing Wall, Cockermouth Leisure Centre, Castlegate Drive. Tel: 01900 823596.
● Bowling Greens - The Croft, Croftside. Harris Park, Fern Bank.
● Children's Entertainment - Bellbrigg Lonning Playground, Bellbrigg Lonning. Harris Park Playground, Fern Bank. Memorial Gardens Playground, Wakefield Road.
● Cricket Grounds - Sandair Cricket Ground, Gote Road, Goat.
● Golf Courses - Cockermouth Golf Course, Embleton (18 hole) (E of Cockermouth). Tel: 017687 76223.
● Parks and Gardens - Fitz Park, Low Road. Harris Park, Fern Bank. Memorial Gardens, Wakefield Road.
● Putting Greens - Harris Park, Fern Bank.
● Sports and Leisure Centres - Cockermouth Leisure Centre, Castlegate Drive. Tel: 01900 823596. Grasmoor Sports Centre, Strawberry How Road. Tel: 01900 824884.
● Squash Courts - Highfield Sports and Social Club, Highfield Road.
● Swimming Pools - Cockermouth Leisure Centre, Castlegate Drive (indoor). Tel: 01900 823596.
● Tennis Courts - Grasmoor Sports Centre, Strawberry How Road. Harris Park, Fern Bank.

CONISTON

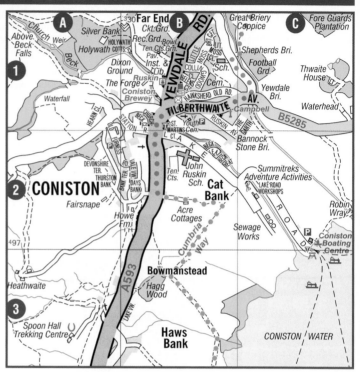

Coniston

Coniston is situated in a stunning setting at the northern end of Coniston Water, dominated by the dark massif of The Old Man of Coniston. A mixture of grey local stone, whitewashed buildings and slate roofs, the village grew from a sparse rural community to its present size because of the mineral wealth generated by the local copper and slate industries, as well as the tourism generated from the arrival of the railway. Coniston and its lake have close associations with no less than 4 famous people: John Ruskin, Arthur Ransome, Donald Campbell and William Gershom Collingwood.

The much visited grave of the heroic Donald Campbell (of world water speed record fame), with its carved Bluebird headstone and blue bird motif, is in a cemetery off Hawkshead Old Road, which runs behind the Crown Hotel opposite the church. A memorial to him is also located on the village green and there is also a memorial stone, overlooking the lake, at Coniston Boatlandings.

The oldest building to survive in the area is the Elizabethan Coniston Hall, with its massive round chimneys, situated just under a mile south-east of Coniston (near Haws Bank on the west shoreline of Coniston Water). Coniston Hall was retained as a hunting lodge for the surrounding deer park, until around 1710 when the park fell out of use, being converted to a farmhouse in 1815 and then acquired by the National Trust in the early 1970s. It is now let to a tenant and is not open to the public.

A popular walk is to Coppermines Valley to see the evocative remains of the Coniston copper mines. For well equipped walkers the summit of The Old Man of Coniston beckons, or the noted 7.75 mile Coniston 'round' or 'horseshoe' circuit. Coppermines Valley can be reached by starting from the Sun Hotel at the end of Station Road, or along 'Coppermines Road' past The Black Bull Hotel, on the north-east side of the beck. The two paths meet at Miners Bridge half a mile west of Coniston, with one of the largest waterfalls on the beck just downstream. Above the bridge the valley opens out and the waste heaps of the Bonsor Mill can be seen.

The other popular activity at Coniston is Coniston Boatlandings, where boats can be hired and cruises made on Coniston Launch and the National Trust's steam yacht 'Gondola' (see Coniston Water lake description).

The Copper Mines

Numerous and extensive copper ore veins were discovered at Coniston by the 'Company of Mines Royal', formed of miners from Germany, from the late 1590s. The mine reached its peak production of ore in 1856, employing over 500 men with workings down to 488 m (1,600 ft) below the surface, but decline began in the 1860s. The main workings ceased production in 1897, with final robbing of the ore pillars below Deep Level leaving the mine in a dangerous and unrestorable state, and the lower workings flooded below the valley floor. Extraction of any ore left in the higher older workings trickled on until the turn of the century with all the remaining waterwheels, the most visible relics, scrapped by 1939.

Coniston

The Slate Quarries

The Hodge Close group of quarries (or the 'Coniston Green'

Coniston Water

quarries as they became known) located in the Tilberthwaite Valley, 2.5 miles to the north of Coniston, were a major area of slate production, being worked since the mid 19th century when the demand for roofing slate massively increased as a result of the growth of the industrial towns of northern England. The Bursting Stone slate quarry, a former mine, was given permission to re-open in 1959 and is still in operation.

Early Closing- Thursday.

PLACES OF INTEREST
● CONISTON BREWERY - 1B. Started in 1995 in premises behind the 400 year old Black Bull Hotel, this micro-brewery produces around 40 barrels (1440 gallons) a week of Blacksmith's Ale, Old Man Ale, the blended Opium and the award winning Bluebird Bitter, made using water from the high fells (Levers Water). Barrelled on the premises, the brew is distributed to the adjacent Black Bull and other outlets in the local area. Specialised interest by appointment only, limited to a maximum of 5 people per visit. Coniston Brewing Company, The Forge, 'Coppermines Road', r/o The Black Bull Hotel, 1 Yewdale Road. Tel: 015394 41133.
● CUMBRIA WAY - 3B to 1C. (see Ulverston description).
● DONALD CAMPBELL MEMORIAL - 1B. Simple memorial plaque to Donald Campbell, and his chief mechanic and friend Leo Villa, set in a slate wall on the village green. Village Green, Ruskin Avenue / Tilberthwaite Avenue.
● RUSKIN MUSEUM - 1B. Established in 1901 at the back of the Coniston Mechanics Institute as a memorial to John Ruskin, and as a celebration of the area's heritage, by William Gershom Collingwood. A Donald Campbell section has photographs revealing the many facets of the man, including his funeral, the recovery of 'Bluebird K7', and a video showing his two final world water speed record runs. These exhibits are planned to eventually include the restored

craft (recovered from the lake bed in 2001). Outside is the John Usher Miniature Village and a fascinating demonstration of traditional Lakeland dry stone wall constructed of both riven slate and beck cobbles. A V12 Merlin aero-engine from the Halifax bomber that crashed on Great Carrs in 1944 is also on display here. Apart from an internationally significant collection of watercolours, drawings and sketchbooks by John Ruskin, the museum's prize exhibits are William Gershom Collingwood's famous and evocative watercolour of Ruskin at work in his study in his old age, and the large 'Coniston' railway sign and seat. Coniston Institute, 15 Yewdale Road. Tel: 015394 41164.

ENTERTAINMENT
● Libraries - Coniston Institute, 15 Yewdale Road. (Limited opening hours). Tel: 015394 41731.

SPORT and LEISURE
● Activity Centres - Summitreks Adventure Activities, Unit 2, Lake Road Workshops, Lake Road. Tel: 015394 41212.
● Boating / Boats for hire - Coniston Boating Centre, Lake Road. Tel: 015394 41366.
● Bowling Greens - Recreation Ground, Yewdale Road.
● Children's Entertainment - Lake Road Playground, Lake Road.
● Cricket Grounds - Recreation Ground, Yewdale Road.
● Cycle Hire - Summitreks, 14 Yewdale Road. Tel: 015394 41822.
● Horse Riding - Crook Barn Stables, Torver (SW of Coniston). Tel: 015394 41088. Spoon Hall Pony Trekking, Haws Bank. Tel: 015394 41391.
● Tennis Courts - John Ruskin School, Lake Road. Recreation Ground, Yewdale Road.

EGREMONT

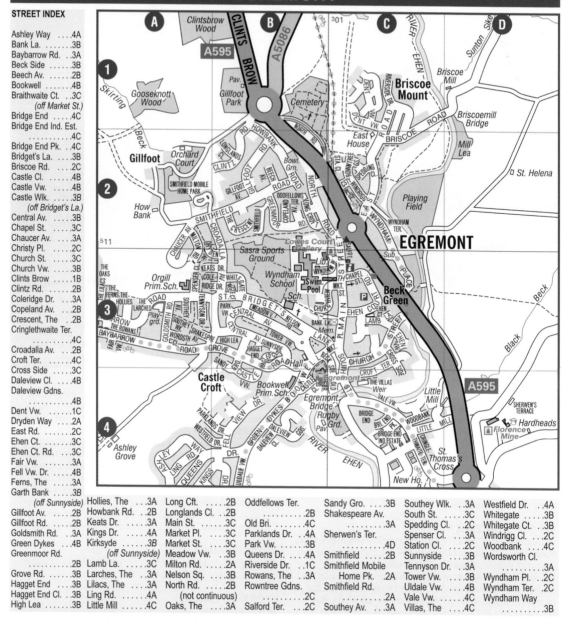

Egremont is a small market town on the River Ehen with a wide Main Street (designed for the market stalls) overlooked at the southern end by the remains of the castle and St Mary and St Michael's church on Church Street. The town was the subject of raids, in 1315, and again in 1322 by marauding Scots under Robert Bruce. By the 1800s Egremont was thriving, with many mills powered by the river. The town from the 1830s onwards was surrounded by extensive iron-ore mines with which it became closely associated. The opening of the Whitehaven, Cleator and Egremont Railway in 1857, did much to facilitate the continued development of this industry, which reached its peak in the 1880s. However, between 1880 and 1890 the USA, led by the giant Carnegie combine, using investment in new technologies led to steel being imported into Britain and produced a progressive economic downturn in iron-ore mining in Cumbria. In the

20th century few new ore-fields were found around Egremont and no mines remained open in the parish after 1943, with the last large scale mine in West Cumbria finally closing in the 1980s. Opposite Lowes Court Gallery are two sculptures commemorating the towns iron-ore mining history.

The town is home to several legends, including that of a lady of the Lucy family, who in 1205 was said to have been devoured by a wolf near the castle.

Egremont is famous for its Crab Fair, first held in 1267 when King Henry III granted a Royal Charter for a weekly market and an annual crab fair, which is now held annually in the second or third week of September. The event has its roots in the distribution of the excess crab apple harvest to the poor by the lord of Egremont, the sharp taste is thought to have originated the gurning competition now embodied in the renowned 'World Gurning Championship', the pulling of ugly faces (gurn) through a horse's braffin or collar, held in the Market Hall on the evening of the fair. The fair now includes traditional sporting events such as Cumberland wrestling and fell running as well as hound trails, animal shows, greasy pole climbing and fun fair.

Early Closing- Wednesday.
Market Days- Main Street (outdoor), Fridays.

PLACES OF INTEREST
Tourist Information Centre (All year) - 3C. Lowes Court Gallery, 12 Main Street. Tel: 01946 820693.
● EGREMONT CASTLE - 4B. A Norman motte castle built by William le Meschin, the first noble of the barony of Copeland created by Henry I, dating from c.1130-40, with further additions in the 13th century. In public parkland on a natural mound overlooking the River Ehen, remains include part of the red sandstone curtain walls, gatehouse in the south-west, part of the Great Hall wall at the end of the outer bailey and well preserved ditches. The much neglected castle, fell (with the exception of the courthouse) into ruins, the stone finding its way into many buildings in Main Street by the mid 17th century. Off Bookwell.

Wast Water

● FLORENCE MINE - 4D. The last deep working iron-ore mine in Western Europe exploiting the rich deposits known as haematite, which are found, in a variety of different forms, in abundance in the Carboniferous limestone strata of West Cumbria. The present shaft (Florence no. 2) was sunk in 1945-6 and was in use by 1951. It was used to extract valuable ore left around Florence no. 1 shaft of 1914, named by the wife of the chairman of the Millom and Askam Mining Company. In 1953 the mine was joined to the Ullcoats system, and in 1970, after a closure and change of ownership in 1968, to the Beckermet Mines creating a 5 mile underground system. In a climate of overseas competition and diminished demand for the premium iron-ore, the mine was taken over by employees as the Egremont Mining

Company in October 1980. Now most of the small amount of ore produced is used in annealing cast iron to extract the carbon, and in the manufacture of pigments for paint and cosmetics as well as for mineral samples and polished haematite jewellery. Underground guided tours are given, commencing with a yard visit showing the crushing machines, the preparation of the haematite, and the shafts and cages that were used to take the men underground. Participants are issued with a miners lamp, safety hat, and boiler suit if necessary, however visitors are advised to bring old clothing and their own wellington boots.
Tel: 01946 820683 / 825830.

● FLORENCE MINE HERITAGE CENTRE - 4D. The heritage centre at Florence Mine operated by the West Cumbria Mines Research Group, houses a mining museum, and geology and mineral room, featuring a display of fluorescent crystals and housing the acclaimed collection of minerals and fossils assembled by Edgar Shackleton. The museum displays cover all the paraphernalia of mining and miners in Cumbria from tools, clothes, lamps and surveying instruments to clay pipes and old drinking flasks. Florence Mine. Tel: 01946 825830.

● LOWES COURT GALLERY - 3C. Gallery opened in 1972 on the upper floor of a restored 18th century building to promote appreciation of the arts in West Cumbria. Displays include contemporary paintings, photography, prints and traditional art and crafts by new and established artists from Cumbria and the bordering counties. There is a changing programme of exhibitions throughout the year. 12 Main Street. Tel: 01946 820693.

ENTERTAINMENT
● Concert Venues - Market Hall, Market Street. Tel: 01946 820254.
● Libraries - Wyndham School, Main Street. 01946 820464.
● Theatres - Wyndham Theatre, Wyndham School, Main Street. Tel: 01946 820356.

SPORT and LEISURE
● Bowling Greens - Copeland Bowls Centre, Wyndham Street, Cleator Moor (indoor) (N of Egremont). Howbank Road.
● Children's Entertainment - Orgill Playground, Goldsmith Road.
● Cricket Grounds - Gillfoot Park, Clints Brow.
● Cycle Hire - Ainfield Cycle Centre, Ainfield, Jacktrees Road, Cleator (N of Egremont). Tel: 01946 812427.
● Golf Courses - St Bees Golf Course, Peck Mill, St Bees (9 hole) (W of Egremont). Tel: 01946 824300.
● Parks and Gardens - Castle Park, Bookwell. Wyndham Place Playing Field, Wyndham Place.
● Swimming Pools - Copeland Pool, Cleator Moor Road, Hensingham (indoor) (N of Egremont). Tel: 01946 695021. Egremont and District Swimming Pool, Main Street (indoor). Tel: 01946 821038.

STREET INDEX

Grange-over-Sands, often referred to as 'Lakeland's Riviera', is a quiet seaside town with an elegant Victorian and Edwardian character. Situated on the Cartmel Peninsula adjacent to the sands of Morecambe Bay and less than 7.5 miles by road from Windermere lake, it is the only south facing northern resort in England. Starting life as a small fishing community, the hamlet was initially only accessible from Lancaster by coach or foot, on a route over the potentially treacherous sands of Morecambe Bay (hence 'over sands') or by a long overland route.

The town's position on the shores of Morecambe Bay with its expansive sands, affords many vantage points for bird watching, however the beach has much mud and common cord-grass , which has colonised in recent years and limits the traditional bucket and spade seaside resort activities. A walk of just over 1 mile along the Promenade, part of the town's historic town trail (marked with black and gold plaques) is recommended.

Each June an Edwardian Festival celebrating the town's Edwardian past is held in Park Road Gardens.
Early Closing- Thursday.

PLACES OF INTEREST

Tourist Information Centre (All year) - 2C. Victoria Hall, Main Street . Tel: 015395 34026.

● BROWN ROBIN NATURE RESERVE - 1D. 23.4 hectares reserve, half grazed pasture and half woodland. Roe deer are prevalent and there are views over Morecambe Bay. Lindale Road.
● BROWN ROBIN NATURE TRAIL - 1D. Waymarked trail clearly marked with white-topped posts and information boards. Brown Robin Nature Reserve, Lindale Road.
● CISTERCIAN WAY - 1D. 33 mile long distance trail from Grange-over-Sands westwards to Roa Island, and Walney Island. The route is waymarked. Station Square.
● CUMBRIA COASTAL WAY - 1D to 3B.
● GRANGE-OVER-SANDS ORNAMENTAL GARDENS - 1D. Showpiece seafront ornamental gardens, described as amongst the best in the North, with a large pond and an exotic collection of wildfowl, rare trees and plants, flowers and shrubs. Main Street.

ENTERTAINMENT
● Concert Venues - Victoria Hall, - 1C. Tel: 015395 32375.
● Libraries- Grange Fell Road. Tel: 015395 32749.

SPORT and LEISURE
● Bowling Greens - Kents Bank Road. Promenade.
● Children's Entertainment - Yew Tree Playing Fields Playground, Yew Tree Road. ● Golf Courses - Grange Fell Golf Course, Grange Fell Road (9 hole). Tel: 015395 32536. Grange-over-Sands Golf Course, Meathop Road (18 hole) (E Grange-over-Sands). Tel: 015395 33180.
● Horse Riding - Lakeland Riding Centre, Lakeland Leisure Park, Moor Lane, Flookburgh (SW of Grange-over-Sands). Tel: 015395 58131.● Parks and Gardens - Ornamental Gardens and the Normandy Veterans Memorial Gardens, Main Street. Park Road Gardens, Park Road. ● Putting Greens - The Promenade. ● Sports and Leisure Centres - Berners, Kents Bank Road. Tel: 015395 38150. ● Swimming Pools - Berners, Kents Bank Road (indoor). Tel: 015395 38150.● Tennis Courts - Yew Tree Playing Fields, Yew Tree Road. Promenade.

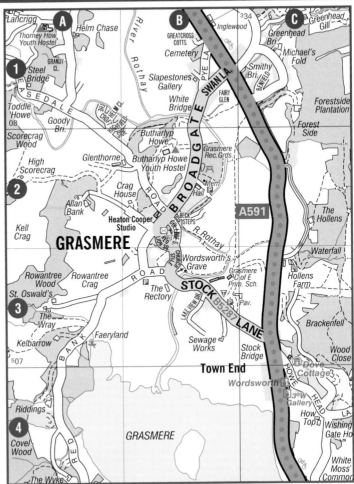

Grasmere, a spread out village on the River Rothay, including the hamlet of Town End to the south-east, is situated at the head of Grasmere lake in a broad vale at the foot of Dunmail Raise, set beneath Yew Crag and Silver Howe to the west and Rydal Fell to the east. Once a quiet part of the local sheep farming community, with a rurality acclaimed by pioneer visitors in the 18th century, it is now absorbed by tourism based on its rich associations with the poet William Wordsworth, having been his home for 14 of his most creative years from 1799 to 1813. Its irregularly arranged streets, with Moss Parrock functioning as the village green, have local grey green stone typical lakeland buildings, most dating from the 19th and early 20th centuries, now housing mainly gift shops, cafes and a disproportionate amount of large hotels.

In 1808, after formatively residing at Dove Cottage, Town End from 1799, Wordsworth and his wife Mary with offspring John, Dora and Thomas, moved to Allan Bank, a larger house set in parkland on the west side of the main village over-looking Grasmere lake. Here they had a daughter Catherine in 1808 and last son William in 1810. However after falling out with the landlord in 1811 they moved to the (Old) Rectory, opposite St Oswald's church, a cold and damp house, where Catherine (age 4) and Thomas (age 6) died within 6 months of each other in 1812. His youngest William survived and lived to age 73, his oldest John to age 72, and his favourite Dora died in 1847, age 43. In 1813 the family moved to Rydal Mount, their last home.

Thomas de Quincey

Thomas de Quincey, born in 1785, the son of a wealthy Manchester merchant, was a gifted scholar until he dropped out of school at age 17. Reduced to begging in London, he recommenced studies at Oxford before dropping out again with a developing opium addiction in 1807. In the same year he met Samuel Taylor Coleridge (see Keswick description), through this association developing a friendship with the Wordsworths', going first to the Lake District in 1807, and later staying with them at Allan Bank. Subsequently falling out with the family, he took on the tenancy of Dove Cottage in 1809. He was famous as a prolific and noted essayist, being regarded as one of the greatest prose writers of the 19th century, in particular for his acclaimed autobiography 'Confessions of an English Opium Eater' in 1821/2 chronicling his struggle with opium addiction. Leaving Grasmere for good in 1830, he died in debt in Edinburgh in 1859, being buried in Greyfriars churchyard.

Grasmere

The outwardly unremarkable St Oswald's church, dating from the 13th century, on a 7th century site, is a literary shrine to more than 100,000 visitors each year. Inside the whitewashed interior are several memorials to the le Fleming family of Rydal Hall, a marble memorial and medallion to William Wordsworth near the altar, and a case containing his prayer book. The massive pillars separating the nave from the late 15th century north aisle, are sections of the original outer wall, the original two hipped roofs were replaced in 1562 by one, hence the unusual roof rafter geometry written about by the poet. In the churchyard, with yew trees planted by Wordsworth, in a railed enclosure on the east side, are the famous graves, marked with simple tombstones, of William Wordsworth (died 1850), and other family members.

Situated by the northern lychgate to the St Oswald's churchyard is the celebrated Grasmere Gingerbread Shop, sole makers since 1854 of Sarah Nelson's original Grasmere gingerbread made to a special recipe. This tiny building was once the village school opened in 1630. Nearly opposite is Church Stile, a 16th century cottage, once an inn, one of the oldest in the village, bought by the National Trust in 1968 and used as an information centre and shop.

A pleasant footpath runs beside the River Rothay from the car park at the Grasmere Recreation Grounds, Broadgate to the church using the east bank crossing on two footbridges.

The Lake Artists Society was founded in 1904, largely on the initiative of William Gershom Collingwood. Annual summer

Grasmere from Red Bank

exhibitions are held in the New Hall on Broadgate showing Cumbrian landscapes, and other subject matter by Cumbrian resident artists. Grasmere's rushbearing ceremony is held on the Saturday nearest St Oswald's Day (5th August).
A procession around the village carrying bearings, symbolic wooden structures wound with rushes, from St Oswald's church is followed by a traditional distribution of Grasmere gingerbread to the participants (a similar rushbearing

ceremony is also held in the neighbouring St Mary's, Ambleside).
Grasmere Lakeland Sports and Show, held at Grasmere Sports Field, near the main car and coach park on Stock Lane, in late August, is one of the oldest and most popular events in the Lake District having been held annually since at least 1852. Traditional events include Cumberland and Westmorland wrestling, fell races and hound trails as well as dog shows, military and pipe bands, and a fairground.

There are several popular medium distance walks from Grasmere.
■ A 3.5 mile circular walk is possible around Grasmere lake.
■ The Coffin Path is a gentle 2 mile low-level route from Grasmere to Rydal, visiting Wordsworth's Dove Cottage and Rydal Mount.
■ Sour Milk Gill falls are reachable by a 1.25 mile uphill footpath along Easedale via Easedale Road.
■ For the well equipped fell walker, there is a 1.75 mile walk to Helm Crag (405 m or 1,329 ft), immediately to the north-west of Grasmere (using a footpath also off Easedale Road). It is famously crowned at its south-east end by the two rock formations known as 'the Lion and the Lamb', a silhouette of a lion couchant and small lamb, when viewed from Grasmere or the east. The north-west end has 'The Howitzer', or 'Old Woman Playing the Organ (or Piano)'.

Alfred Heaton Cooper
Alfred Heaton Cooper is often regarded as the most famous and successful Lake District artist of his time, renowned for his detailed watercolours and guide book illustrations. Born in Manchester in 1864, and brought up in Bolton, Lancashire, he studied art in London where he determined to make a living from drawing and painting, subsequently retracing a tour of the famous beauty spots of northern England taken by J. M. W. Turner. He moved to Norway, writing a guide book illustrated with his own paintings, 'The Norwegian Fjords', but not being able to earn a living there returned to England eventually settling in the Lake District. Here a log cabin studio, known as The Ark, was specially shipped from Norway where it was erected at Coniston and then moved to its current site in Lake Road, Ambleside where it is now 'The Log House' restaurant. From this base he toured the Lakeland valleys and fells painting, whilst his wife opened the studio selling the pictures to wealthy tourists. He was also a prolific illustrator of travellers' guides before the advent of colour photography, notably those produced by A and C. Black Ltd. between 1904 and 1925. His son William (1903-95) continued the family tradition as an artist, moving the studio to Grasmere in 1938 (The Heaton Cooper Studio,

opposite Moss Parrock), where reproduction prints, and originals, by both artists are still sold.

Early Closing- Thursday (most shops stay open).

PLACES OF INTEREST
● 3°W GALLERY - 4C. The Wordsworth Trust's new art gallery at Island View, in a building previously used as a corner shop. The changing contemporary art exhibitions are related to the Lake District's literary and cultural history, linking the visual arts to poetry and prose, both past and present. Island View, Town End. Tel: 015394 35544.

Dove Cottage

● DOVE COTTAGE - 3C. William Wordsworth moved to Dove Cottage, then an empty early 17th century inn called the 'The Dove and Olive' situated on the former Grasmere to Ambleside coach road, on 20th December 1799. Here, with his sister Dorothy, he spent the happiest, and most prolific and productive period of his life, marrying Mary Hutchinson in October 1802 and raising their first 3 children, staying until the family outgrew the house in May 1808 and moved to Allan Bank, Grasmere. Wordsworth described the garden as 'The loveliest spot that man hath ever found'. Dorothy (1771-1855) wrote her famous diary 'The Grasmere Journal' here, between May 1800 and the beginning of 1803, chronicling life at Dove Cottage, as well as providing insights into the different personalities of Wordsworth's circle of friends, daily life and many evocative descriptions of nature. Not intended for publication, her 'Alfoxden Journal' of 1798, the 'Grasmere Journal', and her approximately 30 poems, were published posthumously. Besides being a domestic labourer, and with Mary, transcriber of her brother's drafts into fair copy, she is now recognised as a gifted writer in her own right.
The Wordsworths' created a garden and orchard behind Dove Cottage, which was partly destroyed by Thomas de Quincey after he took on the tenancy of the cottage in 1809, the cause of some acrimony. Bought by the Wordsworth Trust in 1891, who run 'The Wordsworth Museum' adjacent,

the cottage is now a place of literary pilgrimage. Guided tours are given of the cottage which, with its limewashed stone walls, slate roof, and small lattice windows, is furnished with the poet's belongings. There is an oak panelled hall with Westmorland slate floors, kitchen, buttery, downstairs bedroom, houseplace, children's room (papered with newspapers!), upstairs bedroom, study and guest room, all feeling as if Wordsworth had just left on one of his famous walks. The recreated garden and orchard has views over Grasmere and the River Rothay valley. Howe Head Lane, Town End. Tel: 015394 35544.
● WORDSWORTH MUSEUM, THE - 4C. Museum of the Wordsworth Trust, opened in 1981, displaying some of the nation's greatest treasures from the English Romantic movement, interpreting the life and work of Wordsworth, his family and circle, in a 2 storey converted coach house adjacent to Dove Cottage. The displays are grouped into sections on Wordsworth's Life, Life in Grasmere and The Wordsworth Circle (he was connected with over 3,000 writers and artists including Samuel Taylor Coleridge, Thomas de Quincey and Sir Walter Scott). In the displays are some portraits of William and his contemporaries, including Mary, Dorothy and Dora Wordsworth as well as Coleridge, de Quincey and the famous Beauty of Buttermere. There are also many watercolours and landscape drawings (including works by Turner, Constable and Gainsborough) showing the growth of art in the Lake District. A comprehensive collection of 90% of the poets original working manuscripts, many bequeathed by his grandson, has the first complete draft of 'The Prelude' of 1805, hand-written by Mary and Dorothy Wordsworth, Dorothy Wordsworth's 'Grasmere Journal', major manuscripts of Coleridge and de Quincey, the Arnold family notebooks and rare printed book editions. There are also special annual themed exhibitions. Howe Head Lane, Town End. Tel: 015394 35544.

SPORT and LEISURE
● Boating / Boats for hire - Faeryland, Red Bank Road. Tel: 015394 35060.
● Children's Entertainment - Grasmere Recreation Grounds Children's Play Area, Broadgate.
● Parks and Gardens - Grasmere Recreation Grounds, Broadgate. Moss Parrock (village green), College Street.

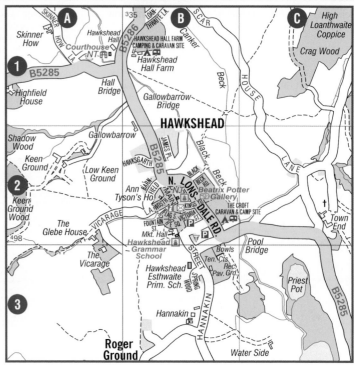

Hawkshead, derived from the name of the Norseman 'Haukr' and once owned by the monks of Furness Abbey, is set in the Vale of Esthwaite, at the head of Esthwaite Water. An historic and picturesque village, it is a cluster of small intimate whitewashed houses with grey slate roofs set within the narrow streets and cobbled alleyways which form the centre of the village, together they create an ambience unique to this Lakeland village. With its strategic location above the Windermere Ferry, Hawkshead was, from the 17th until the early 19th centuries, the centre of the local woollen industry, becoming a prominent and prosperous Lakeland 'market town'. Many of the buildings date from this time, but its importance declined with the growth of nearby railway connected towns, such as Windermere.

Main Street, running north-south past the Red Lion coaching inn, was once the principle thoroughfare and there are many street names with historical connections. Flag Street takes its name from the stream, subsequently covered with flagstones, which once provided water to householders; Leather, Rag and Putty Street (now officially renamed Wordsworth Street) reflected earlier crafts (cobbler, tailor and putty maker). The late 18th century Market Hall overlooking The Square, restored and enclosed in late Victorian times, once had open arched bays used as butchers market stalls, it is now parish rooms. The town trail leaflet gives more information.

Hawkshead has links with Lakeland's two most famous people: Beatrix Potter, and William Wordsworth. Wordsworth attended Hawkshead Old Grammar School here, and lodged at the elderly Ann Tyson's house (now a guest house, on Wordsworth Street). Situated on the highest position in the village, an oval hill at the south end, is the stone church of St Michael and All Angels; with its low squat tower and side aisles, the present building mostly dates from c.1500. The churchyard, which has commanding views over the village and Esthwaite Water, was a favourite of Wordsworth inspiring his verses 'I saw the snow-white church upon her hill, sit like a throned lady, sending out a gracious look all over her domain' ('The Prelude', book IV, published 1850). The 'white' rough cast rendering was removed in the restoration of 1875-6.

The centre of the village is pedestrianised and therefore closed to vehicles, but a large car park is located to the south-east. The Hawkshead Show is held by Hawkshead Agricultural Society in August.

Betty Fold (now a guest house), just over a mile north-west on a minor road between Hawkshead Hill and Knipe Fold, was the villa home, built in 1907-8, of Henry Holiday (1839-1927), and was designed by him. An artist influenced by the Pre-Raphaelite style, many of whose stained glass windows can be seen in churches in America and Britain, including a good selection in Cumbria (see Ambleside and Keswick descriptions).

Hawkshead

PLACES OF INTEREST

Information Centre **NT** - 2B. Red Lion Square, Main Street. Tel: 015394 36319.

● BEATRIX POTTER GALLERY - 2B. Housed in an attractive 17th century building once the office of Beatrix Potter's husband, William Heelis, a local solicitor whom she married in 1913, are rooms displaying an annually changing exhibition of a selection (from a collection of more than 500) of her original sketches, drawings, illustrations and watercolours, noted for their exceptional quality and many familiar from the pages of her children's classic tales. The interior, which has remained substantially unaltered, has a reconstruction of part of William Heelis' office and a section on the life of Mrs Heelis as a member of the local farming community, offering a unique insight into her life and times. Main Street. Tel: 015394 36355.

● HAWKSHEAD COURTHOUSE - 1A. All that remains of the mostly medieval 15th century manorial buildings of Hawkshead 'Old' Hall held, until the Dissolution of the Monasteries, by the monks of Furness Abbey as a centre for the administration of their estates in the area. The building was the gatehouse to the hall, where the bailiff of Hawkshead dispensed justice in the court room over the gate in the name of the abbots. The building was given to the National Trust in 1932. Situated about half a mile north of Hawkshead, there is no parking at the site. To view the interior, a key may be obtained from the National Trust shop at The Corner Shop, The Square, Hawkshead (not to be confused with the National Trust's Hawkshead Information Centre at Red Lion Square, Main Street). Tel: NT shop - 015394 36471.

● HAWKSHEAD OLD GRAMMAR SCHOOL - 2B. The free school attended by William Wordworth and his younger brother John, from age 9 in 1779 to 1787, when he went up to St John's College, Cambridge. William spent the summer months roaming the fells, returning to his lodgings long after dark, and the winter months skating on Esthwaite Water, and it was while here that he first showed a talent for writing poetry (his first surviving poem is dated 1785). The school was founded in 1585 by Edwin Sandys, once a native of the parish, and Archbishop of York (1577-1588), the present building dating from 1675 (and closed 1909); a sundial and tablet were later placed in the wall above the door in his memory. On the ground floor is a classroom with old desks covered in carved graffiti (including William's initials), and on the first floor, the headmaster's study, library and a classroom with an exhibition on the history of the school, its founder and William Wordsworth. Wordsworth's brother, John, died tragically on 5th February 1805, when Commander of one of the East India Company's largest ships 'The Earl of Abergavenny', which sank near Portland in cold seas, and was later the subject of three of William's poems. off Main Street. Tel: curator- 015394 35647.

SPORT and LEISURE

● Activity Centres - Go Ape!, Grizedale Visitor Centre, Grizedale Forest Park, Grizedale (S of Hawkshead). Tel: 0870 4445562.

● Boating / Boats for hire - Esthwaite Water Fishery, The Boathouse, Ridding Wood (S of Hawkshead). Tel: 015394 36541.

● Bowling Greens - Hawkshead Recreation Ground, Main Street.

● Cycle Hire - Grizedale Mountainbikes, Grizedale Visitor Centre, Grizedale Forest Park, Grizedale (S of Hawkshead). Tel: 01229 860369.

● Parks and Gardens - Hawkshead Recreation Ground, Main Street.

● Tennis Courts - Hawkshead Recreation Ground, Main Street.

Langdale Pikes

KENDAL

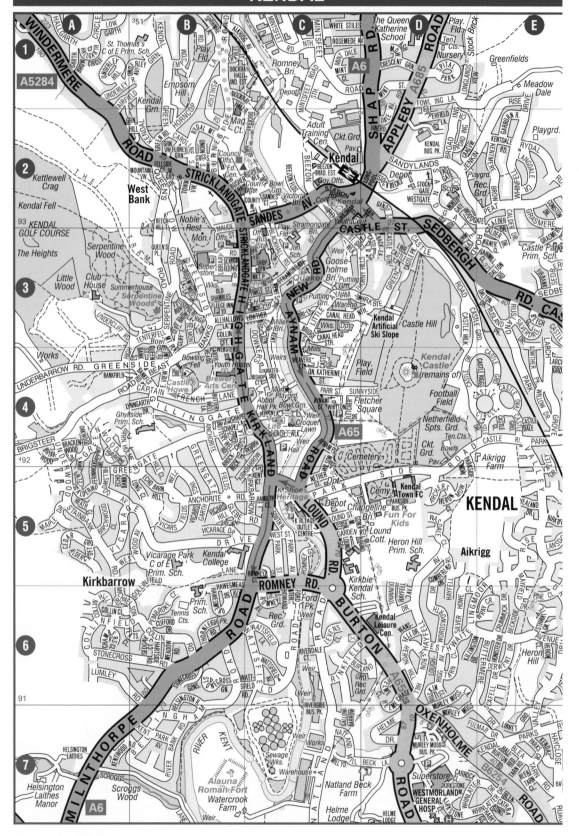

53

F

Cragg View

Jenkincrag

Sandylands

Birds Park Farm

Round Hill Wood

A684

Castlegreen Wood

Castle Green

Birklands

BIRKLANDS OLD MILL

Birk Hagg

Bracken Hill

Kendal Park

High Park Farm

High Park House

The Stables

Oxenholme Wood

STREET INDEX

Aikrigg Av.	1B
Aldercroft	5A
Alderwood	5A
Allhallows La.	3B
Anchorite Flds.	4B
Anchorite Pl.	5C
(off Kirkbarrow)	
Anchorite Rd.	5B
Ann St.	2D
Appleby Rd.	2D
Applewood	4A
Archers Mdw.	5D
Ashleigh Rd.	1B
Ash Mdw.	1D
Aynam Ct.	4C
Aynam Pl.	4C
Aynam Rd.	3C
Back La.	3D
Bankfield	4A
Bankfield Rd.	4B
Bank St.	4B
Barn Holme	4A
Beast Banks	4B
Beckside	6E
Beech Cl.	3E
Beech Hill Ter.	2B
Beezon Flds.	2C
Beezon Rd.	2C
Beezon Trad. Est.	2C
Bellingham Rd.	7B
Belmont	3B
Birchwood Cl.	5A
Birkbeck Cl.	5E
Birklands Old Mill	5F
Bishop Ct.	4C
Blackhall Rd.	3C
Blackhall Yd.	3C
Blea Tarn Cl.	7E
Blea Tarn Rd.	7E
Blencathra Gdns.	7E
Bluebell Cl.	6E
Bowland Dr.	3E
Brackenwood	4A
Branthwaite Brow	3C
Briarwood	4A
Bridge La.	3C
Bridge St.	3C
Brigsteer Rd.	4A
Broad Ing	2D
Broad Ing Cres.	2D
Brockbeck	4B
Broom Cl.	3F
Burland Gro.	6C
Burneside Rd.	2B
Burton Rd.	6C
Busher Wlk.	2B
Buttermere Dr.	6E
Buttery Well La.	4B
Buttery Well Rd.	4B
Calder Dr.	2E
Canal Head Nth.	3C
Canal Head Sth.	3C
Capper Cl.	4B
Captain French La.	4B
Caroline St.	2B
Carrock Cl.	7D
Castle Circ.	4E
Castle Cl.	4E
Castle Cres.	3D
Castle Dale	4E
Castle Dr.	4D
Castle Gdns.	4C
Castle Gth.	3D
Castle Grn. Cl.	4E
Castle Grn. La.	3E
Castle Grn. Rd.	3E
Castle Gro.	4E
(Castle Dale)	
Castle Gro.	3D
(Castle Rd.)	
Castle Oval	4E
Castle Pk.	3D
Castle Riggs	3D
Castle Ri.	4E
Castle Rd.	3D
Castle St.	3C
Castle Vw.	3D
(off Back La.)	
Castle Wlk.	3D
Cedar Gro.	5A
Chambers Cl.	6A
Chapel Cl.	3B
(off Clifbrow Ter.)	
Chapel La.	4B
(not continuous)	
Charles St.	1B
Cherry Tree Cres.	4A
Church Ter.	3B
(off Sepulchre La.)	
Church Wlk.	4C
Cliff Brow	3B
Clifford Dr.	6B
Cliff Ter.	3B
Collin Cl.	6A
Collin Cft.	2C
Collinfield	6A
Collinfield La.	6B
Collin Hill	6A
Collin Rd.	6B
Coniston Dr.	2E
Copperfield La.	2D
County M.	2C
(off Sandes Av.)	
Crag Vw.	2D
Crescent Grn.	1D
Crook Lea	2B
(off Caroline St.)	
Cross La.	4B
Cross St.	2B
Crummock Dr.	6E
Cumberland Dr.	5D
Dale Av.	2D
Dalton Dr.	3E
Dalton Rd.	3E
Derwent Dr.	6E
Dockray Hall Ind. Est.	1B
Dockray Hall Rd.	1B
Dockray Hall Wlk.	2C
Dowker's La.	3C
Dr Manning's Yd.	4C
Dunmail Dr.	6D
Eastgate	2D
East Vw.	4B
East Vw. Ct.	4B
(off East Vw.)	
Echo Bank	5A
Echo Barn Hill	5B
Edgecombe Ct.	3C
(off Gulfs Rd.)	
Elephant Yd.	3B
Eller Raise	2D
Empsom Rd.	1B
Esthwaite Av.	6D
Esthwaite Grn.	6E
Fairfield La.	1A
Fell Brow	4B
Fellside Ct.	2B
Ferney Grn.	2B
Fernwood Dr.	5A
Finkle St.	3C
Firbank	3E
Fleece Inn Yd.	3B
Fletcher Dr.	4C
Ford Ter.	6C
Fountain Brow	3B
(off Middle La.)	
Fowl Ing La.	1D
Fulmar Dr.	7D
Gallowbarrow	7C
Gandy St.	2D
Garburn Rd.	2E
Garden M.	5C
Garden Rd.	5C
Garden St.	5C
Gardiner Bank	2B
(off Caroline St.)	
Garth Brow	1A
Garth Heads	4B
Gawith Pl.	3C
(off Gulfs Rd.)	
Ghyll Side	4B
(off Gillingate)	
Gillinggate	4B
Glebe Rd.	5B
Grasmere Cres.	2E
Greencoats Yd.	3C
(off Blackhall Rd.)	
Greengate	4B
Greengate La.	5A
Green Hill	2B
Green Rd.	2B
Greenside	4A
Green Vw.	2B
Greenwood	4A
Grizedale Av.	3F
Gulfs Rd.	3C
Haliburton Rd.	7E
Hallgarth Circ.	1A
Hamilton Ter.	5C
Hardknott Gdns.	7E
Hartside Rd.	6B
Hawesmead Av.	6B
Hawesmead Dr.	6B
Hayclose Ct.	7E
Hayclose Dr.	7E
Hayclose Rd.	7E
Hayfell Av.	6D
Hayfell Ri.	6D
Haygarth Ct.	4B
(off Highgate)	
Hazelwood	5A
Heath Cl.	5A
Helme Chase Gdns.	6D
Helme Cl.	6D
Helme Dr.	7D
Helme Lodge	7D
Helsington Laithes	7A
Helsington Rd.	7B
Heron Cl.	6E
Heron Hill	6D
High Fellside	3B
Highgate	3B
High Tenterfell	4A
Hill Cl.	4B
Hillswood Av.	5A
(off Back La.)	
Honister Dr.	6E
Horncop La.	2B
Howard St.	6E
Jamieson's Pl.	3B
(off Low Fellside)	
Jenkin Ri.	2D
Jennings Ter.	4C
(off Dowker's La.)	
Kendal Bus. Pk.	2D
Kendal Grn.	1B
Kendal Parks Cres.	7E
Kendal Parks Rd.	7E
Kent Ct.	5C
Kentdale Rd.	2E
Kentmere Brow	2E
Kent Pk. Av.	7B
Kent Pl.	4C
(off Dowker's La.)	
Kent St.	3C
Kentwood Rd.	7A
Killington Dr.	6D
Kilner Cl.	3E
Kirkbarrow	4B
Kirkbarrow La.	4B
Kirkbie Grn.	3D
Kirkland	4C
Kirkstone Cl.	7D
Kirkstone M.	7D
Knott Vw.	3B
(off Low Fellside)	
K Village Outlet Cen.	5C
Langdale Cres.	2E
Lansdown Cl.	5E
Larch Gro.	3E
Levens Cl.	6C
Library Rd.	3B
Lingmoor Ri.	6D
Linnet Gro.	5C
Little Aynam	3C
Littledale	5E
Long Cl.	5B
Longlands Vw.	1D
Longpool	5C
Loughrigg Av.	6D
Lound Rd.	5C
Lound Sq.	5C
Lound St.	5C
Lwr. Castle Pk.	3D
Low Fellside	2B
Low Garth	1A
Low Kirkbarrow La.	4C
(off Kirkbarrow La.)	
Lowther Pk.	4E
Lowther St.	3C
Lumley Rd.	6A
Lynngarth Dr.	4B
Maple Dr.	5A
Market Pl.	3C
Maude St.	3B
Mayfield Dr.	5E
Meadow Rd.	6B
Michaelson Rd.	6A
Middle La.	3B
Mill Yd.	7C
Milnthorpe Rd.	7A
Mint Cl.	1C
Mint Dale	1C
Mintsfeet Rd.	1C
Mintsfeet Rd. Nth.	1C
Mintsfeet Rd. Sth.	1C
Mint St.	1D
Mountain Vw.	2B
Mt. Pleasant	3B
Mount St.	4B
Murley Moss	7D
Murley Moss Bus. Pk.	7D
Murley Moss La.	6D
Natland Mill Beck La.	7C
Natland Rd.	7C
Nether St.	5C
New Rd.	3C
New Shambles	3C
(off Finkle St.)	
Northgate	2D
Nursery Vw.	3D
Oak Tree Rd.	3E
Oakwood	4A
Old Lound	5D
Old Shambles	3B
Oxenholme Rd.	7D
Park Av.	5C
Parkside Bus. Pk.	5D
Parkside Mdw.	4D
Park Side Rd.	5C
(Lound Rd., not continuous)	
Park St.	5C
Parr St.	4C
Peat La.	2E
Pembroke Ct.	6B
Peppercorn La.	4C
Pine Cl.	6E
Prospect Ter.	3B
(off Rosemary La.)	
Queen Katherine St.	4C
Queen's Pl.	3B
Queen's Rd.	2B
Queen St.	4B
Red Tarn Rd.	7E
Rinkfield	6C
River Bank Rd.	7B
Riverdale Ct.	6C
Riverside Bus. Pk.	6C
Rock Vw.	4B
(off Captain French La.)	
Romney Av.	6C
Romney Ct.	5C
Romney Gdns.	5C
Romney Rd.	5C
Rosemary La.	3B
Rosemede Av.	1C
Rowan Tree Cres.	3E
Ruskin Cl.	6D
Rusland Pk.	3E
Rydal Mt.	2B
Rydal Rd.	2E
St George's Wlk.	3C
Sandes Av.	2C
Sandes Ct.	2C
Sandes Hospital Cotts.	3B
(off Highgate)	
Sandgate	2D
Sandylands Rd.	2D
Sawmill Cl.	3E
Sawmill La.	3D
Scafell Dr.	6E
Scroggs La.	7A
Sedbergh Dr.	3E
Sedbergh Rd.	3E
Sedgwick Ct.	6B
Sepulchre La.	3B
Serpentine Rd.	3B
Shap Rd.	2D
Silverdale Dr.	3E
Silver Howe Cl.	6D
Singleton Pk. Rd.	4F
Skye, The	3B
(off Middle La.)	
South Rd.	5C
South Vw. La.	2B
Sparrowmire La.	1B
Spital Pk.	1D
Spital Vw.	3B
(off Low Fellside)	
Spring Gdns.	3B
(off Low Fellside)	
Stainbank Rd.	5A
Station Rd.	2C
Stockbeck	2D
Stockgate	2D
Stonecross Gdns.	6B
Stonecross Grn.	6B
Stonecross Rd.	6A
Stoney La.	3B
Stramongate	3C
Strickland Ct.	2B
(off Windermere Rd.)	
Stricklandgate	2B
Summer Hill Gdns.	4B
(off Greenside)	
Sunnyside	4C
Swallow Cl.	6E
Tanners Yd.	3C
(off Highgate)	
Tarn Cl.	6D
Teal Beck	6E
Tenterfell Ct.	3B
(off Queen St.)	
Thirlmere Rd.	2E
Thornleigh Rd.	6B
Thorny Hills	3D
Tithebarn Cotts.	4B
(off Bankfield Rd.)	
Town Vw.	2B
Tram, The	2A
Ullswater Rd.	2F
Underbarrow Rd.	4A
Undercliff Rd.	3A
Underley Av.	1B
Underley Hill	1A
Underley Rd.	1A
Underwood	4A
Union St.	2B
Valley Dr.	4E
Vicarage Dr.	5A
Vicars Flds.	5B
Vicars Gth.	5B
Vicars Hill	5B
Vicars Wlk.	5B
Vine Rd.	2D
Wansfell Dr.	6D
Wasdale Cl.	5D
Waterside	4C
Wattsfield Av.	6C
Wattsfield La.	6C
Wattsfield Rd.	6C
Weavers Ct.	4C
Websters Yd.	4B
Well Ings	5B
Westgate	2D
West Gro.	2B
Westmorland Shop. Cen.	3C
West St.	5C
Westwood Av.	5A
Whinfell Dr.	2E
Whinlatter Dr.	7D
Whitbarrow Cl.	2F
White Stiles	1C
Whitton Ter.	4C
Wildman St.	2C
Willow Dr.	4E
Wilson St.	4C
Windermere Rd.	1A
Woodgate	2D
Wordsworth Dr.	6D
Wray Cres.	6E
Yealand Dr.	5E
Yeats Cl.	6A

Kendal

Kendal, a large and attractive bustling market town on the River Kent, is historically the southern gateway to the Lake District being less than 1 mile from the national park boundary. Built largely of a uniform grey local limestone, which has given it the nickname of 'the auld grey town', it was the largest town in the county of Westmorland (the county town was Appleby-in-Westmorland), until 1974 when that county was incorporated into the administrative county of Cumbria.

Kendal was granted a Market Charter in 1189. Unlike the towns in the north of the county Kendal did not suffer from Scottish raids, which helped the town's prosperity, initially based on the wool trade using fleeces from the local bred Herdwick sheep. The industry flourished from the 14th century, when Flemish weavers came to the area, through to the 19th century when many mills, weaving shops and dyeing works were built on the banks of the River Kent. From these factories the famous 'Kendal Green', a rough, hardwearing serge material, a sort of denim of its time, was produced in large quantities and helped to make the town one of the most important in northern England
Manufacturing also included such products as snuff and leather, and the famous Kendal Mint Cake, as supplied to the 1953 British Everest Expedition led by Sir Edmund Hillary and his guide Sherper Tensing.

Kendal has connections with several famous people:
■ Sir Arthur Stanley Eddington. The mathematician, physicist and astronomer, regarded as the founder of modern astrophysics, was born in Kendal on 28th December 1882.
■ The painter George Romney (1734-1802), best known for his portraits, especially those of Emma Hart, later Lady Hamilton, mistress of Admiral Lord Nelson. He spent his apprenticeship in Kendal from 1755 to 1757. ·
■ Alfred Wainwright was born in poverty in the industrial landscape of Blackburn, Lancashire in 1907. Having moved to Kendal in 1941, he spent all his spare time walking the Lakeland fells in all weathers, resulting in his famous classic series of 7 'Pictorial Guides to the Lakeland Fells' published between 1955 and 1966. They detail routes to virtually all the 214 Lakeland fells over 305 m (1,000 ft). Beautifully hand-written with maps, and intricate pen and ink drawings taken from photographs he took en-route. Noted for his reclusive personality, he was awarded an MBE and died in 1991. Some of his possessions are in the 'Kendal Museum'.
Early Closing - Thursday (most shops stay open).
Market Days - Market Hall, upper level Westmorland Shopping Centre (indoor), Mondays-Saturdays.
Market Place (and Stramongate) (outdoor), Wednesdays and Saturdays.

PLACES OF INTEREST

Tourist Information Centre (All year) - 3C. Town Hall, Highgate. Tel: 01539 725758.
● ABBOT HALL ART GALLERY - 4C. Fine collection of British art in a small independent gallery managed by the Lakeland Arts Trust, housed in a mansion built in 1759 on the banks of the River Kent. Sold to Kendal Corporation in 1897, whereupon the grounds became a public park, the house was opened as an art gallery in 1962. There is a diverse temporary exhibition programme. Abbot Hall, Kirkland. Tel: 01539 722464.
● ALAUNA ROMAN FORT - 7B. Barely visible earthworks of a 1.5 hectares c.90 AD Roman fort at Watercrook (Farm) on a bend in the River Kent. Abandoned by the 4th century it was built purely for military use, there being no settlement here. Finds from excavations of the site, including domestic and military items, coins, jewellery, shoes and alters, are on display in the Wainwright Gallery of the Kendal Museum. On private land, the only possible views are from the river but there is no public footpath except on the north bank. Exterior view only. Watercrook Farm, Natland Road, Natland.
● BREWERY ARTS CENTRE - 4B. A multi-purpose arts complex run by The Kendal Brewery Arts Centre Trust with a year round programme of theatre, music, films, lectures and exhibitions. The centre, set in a landscaped garden, is situated in the redeveloped buildings of the Highgate Brewery of 1858. 122a Highgate. Tel: 01539 725133.
● CASTLE DAIRY - 2C. Substantially 14th century one storey hall-house with cross-wings, built of rubble walls under a slate roof. Sometimes called 'The Dairy House', the name does not necessarily refer to a dairy for the castle, but is thought to be a corruption of 'Dowery House' or 'Castle Dowry'. It is now leased as a restaurant. 26 Wildman Street. Tel: 01539 730334.
● CASTLE HOWE - 4B. Remains of a motte and bailey castle, on a limestone spur to the west of the town, thought to have been built by the first Norman baron of Kendal c.1087. The earth mound, or motte, now crowned with an obelisk. Bowling Fell, Beast Banks.

Buttermere Pines

● CASTLE HOWE OBELISK - 4B. Monument and steps erected in 1788 on top of the motte of Castle Howe commemorating the 'Glorious Revolution' of 1688-9 when the Protestant William of Orange and Mary II became joint sovereigns forcing the abdication to France of the hugely unpopular Catholic monarch King James II of England. Castle Howe, Bowling Fell, Beast Banks.

Kendal

● FUN FOR KIDS FUN FACTORY - 5D. Indoor soft play centre for children aged 10 and under. Bouncy castle, climbing frames, ball pool etc. Parkside Business Park, Parkside Road. Tel: 01539 735556.
● KENDAL CASTLE - 4D. Remains of castle, on a knoll to the east of the town, built in the 1180s and reconstructed in stone in the early 1200s. It was the home of the barons of Kendal, the best known being the Parr family whose most famous member was Katherine Parr, the sixth wife of King Henry VIII, whom she married in July 1543. Display boards show a plan of the site and Kendal Museum has an exhibition telling the story of the castle together with reconstructions. There are panoramic views. Castle Hill, Sunnyside / Castle Road.
● KENDAL HOLY TRINITY PARISH CHURCH - 4C. 'The Church of the Angels', is Cumbria's largest and England's second largest parish church, and at 43 m (140 ft), one of the widest churches in England. There is a children's trail, and brass rubbing is available. Church Walk, Kirkland. Tel: 01539 721248.
● KENDAL MUSEUM - 2C. One of the oldest museums in the country, founded in 1796 and opened on its present site in 1913, in a former wool warehouse, forming the basis of Kendal's first municipal museum. There are outstanding displays of archaeology, natural history, geology and social history in 3 galleries. There are also children's hands-on activities, temporary exhibitions and a wildlife garden. Station Road. Tel: 01539 721374.
● K SHOES HERITAGE CENTRE - 5C. Small heritage centre in the K Village Outlet Centre on the history of shoe making in Kendal and the Lake District. Exhibits include a reconstructed K Shoe Shop and an X-ray machine formerly used to measure children's feet! There is an audio-visual and a children's play area and picnic area overlooking the River Kent. K Village Outlet Centre, Lound Road, The Lound. Tel: 01539 732363.
● LAKELAND LIFE, MUSEUM OF - 4C. Museum housed in the converted stable block of the Georgian Abbot Hall (Art Gallery), managed by the Lakeland Arts Trust. The permanent collection covers the social history of how people worked, lived and entertained themselves in Lakeland in the changing social climate of the past 200 years. Temporary

displays draw on the large costume collection which dates from the 17th century onwards and craft demonstrations are held on selected days. Kirkland. Tel: 01539 722464.
● QUAKER TAPESTRY EXHIBITION CENTRE, THE - 3C. 77 tapestry embroidered panels (635mm by 533mm or 25" by 21"), in narrative crewel using the unique 'Quaker Stitch' on specially woven wool cloth. Celebrating 350 years of the ideas and experiences of Quakers since the Religious Society of Friends was formed by George Fox in 1652. Embroidery Workshops. Friends Meeting House, Stramongate / New Road. Tel: 01539 722975.
● SERPENTINE WOODS NATURE TRAIL - 3B. 0.5 mile trail through mixed woodland up to the open fell giving views across the River Kent valley. Serpentine Woods are one of the best areas near Kendal for woodland birds and also curlew, wheatear and European little owls. Included in the nature trail is an alpine meadow, known since Victorian times, situated on the steep, north-facing slopes of Kendal Fell between the woods and Windermere Road. There is a Victorian summerhouse, with a permanent display on the history and ecology of the woods. A trail guide is available from the tourist information centre. Serpentine Woods, Serpentine Road.

ENTERTAINMENT
● Cinemas- Brewery Arts Centre, Highgate. Tel: 01539 725133.
● Libraries- Stricklandgate. Tel: 01539 773520.
● Theatres- Brewery Arts Centre, 122a Highgate. Tel: 01539 725133. Kendal Leisure Centre, Burton Road. Tel: 01539 729702.

SPORT & LEISURE
● Activity Centres - Kendal Artificial Ski Slope, Canal Head North. Tel: 01539 732948. Lakeland Climbing Centre (Kendal Wall), Unit 27, Lake District Business Park, Mint Bridge Road (N Kendal). Tel: 01539 721766.
● Bowling Greens - Abbot Hall Park, Dowker's Lane. Mount Pleasant. Netherfield Sports Ground, Parkside Road. Sandes Avenue.
● Children's Entertainment - Abbot Hall Park Playground, Dowker's Lane. Burland Grove Recreation Ground Play Area, Rinkfield. Sandylands Road Recreation Ground Play Area, Sandylands Road.
● Cricket Grounds - Netherfield Sports Ground, Parkside Road. Shap Road.
● Cycle Hire - Askew Cycles, The Old Brewery, Wildman Street. Tel: 01539 728057.
● Golf Courses - Carus Green Golf Course, Burneside Road, Kentrigg (18 hole) (N Kendal). Tel: 01539 721097. Kendal Golf Course, The Heights, High Tenterfell (18 hole). Tel: 01539 733708. Kendal Golf Driving Range, Oxenholme Road (SE Kendal). Tel: 01539 733933.
● Parks and Gardens - Abbot Hall Park, Dowker's Lane. Bowling Fell, Beast Banks. Burland Grove Recreation Ground, Rinkfield. Castle Hill, Sunnyside / Castle Road. Ford Park, Natland Road. Hawesmead Park, Milnthorpe Road. Noble's Rest, Maude Street. Romney Avenue Recreation Ground, Romney Avenue. Sandylands Road Recreation Ground, Sandylands Road.
● Putting Greens - Goose Holme Putting Green, New Road.
● Sports and Leisure Centres- Kendal Leisure Centre, Burton Road. Tel: 01539 729777.
● Swimming Pools - Kendal Leisure Centre, Burton Road (indoor). Tel: 01539 729777.
● Tennis Courts - Appleby Road. Netherfield Sports Ground, Parkside Road.

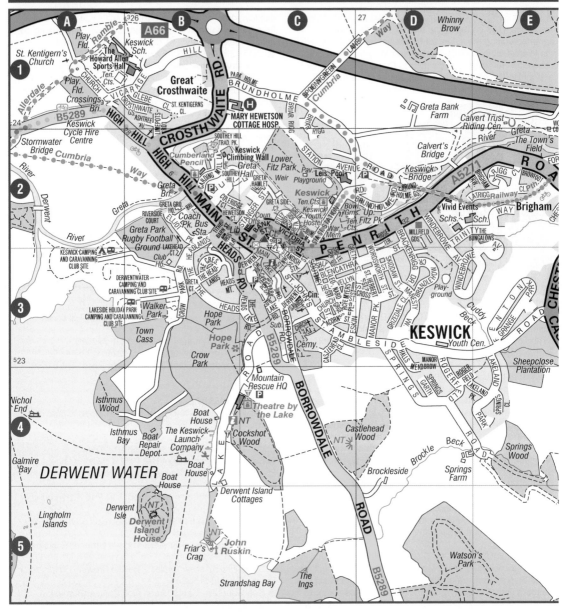

Keswick, pronounced 'kezzick', in a beautiful setting beneath Skiddaw on the north shore of Derwent Water, is the popular main tourist centre of northern Lakeland. Granted a Market Charter by Edward I in 1276, the original settlement was at Crosthwaite on the west side of the town near the site of St Kentigern's (or Mungo's) parish church.

The wool trade flourished for several centuries, then a new period of prosperity began in 1564 when the 'Company of Mines Royal' was created with expert German miners who obtained permission from Queen Elizabeth I to mine in the area. Most mining had ceased by the early 20th century, with the landscape now having been reclaimed by nature. Black lead or natural graphite, known locally as 'wad', now long since exhausted, was discovered c.1500 on the side of Seathwaite Fell in Borrowdale. It was highly valued from the reign of Queen Elizabeth I, being used for moulds in the

manufacture of cannon balls, for medicinal purposes and as a lubricant. About 1558, a cottage industry producing square cased pencils began, with the first local pencil factory recorded in 1832, the first pencil mill in the world, becoming the Cumberland Pencil Company in 1916.

Many people were attracted to Keswick by the writings of the romantic poets Southey, Coleridge and William Wordsworth who had close associations with the town.
After the arrival of the Cockermouth, Keswick and Penrith Railway, opened to passengers from 1865 to 1972, the town became accessible to mass tourism, with much development occurring.

Mainly Victorian in character but beset with hotels, inns, outdoor clothing and sporting equipment shops and restaurants. There are a few buildings of special note:

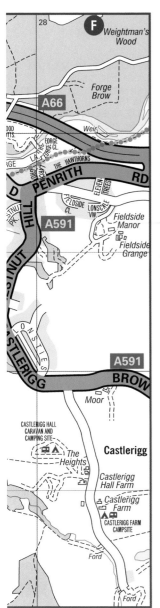

Keswick

Brundholme Gdns.	Forge Cl. 2F	Leonard St. 3C	St Kentigerns Cl. . . .1B
. . . . .2D	Forge La. 2E	Limepost Rd. 2B	Schoolhouse, The . .2B
Brundholme M. 2C	George St. 3C	Little Hills 3C	(off Coleridge Ct.)
Brundholme Rd. . . .1C	Glebe Cl. 1B	(off Lake Rd.)	Scotts Ct. 2B
Bungalows, The . .2E	Grange Pk. 3E	Lonscale Vw. 2F	(off Main St.)
Carding Mill La. . . .2B	Greta Ct. 3B	Lonsties 3E	Seams, The 3C
Castlehead Cl. . . .3C	Greta Gro. Ho. 2B	Low Mill 2C	(off Derwent St.)
Castlerigg Brow . . .3E	Greta Hamlet 2C	(off Greta Side)	Shorley La. 3C
Castlerigg Farm	Greta Side 2C	Luptons Ct. 2C	Shu Le Crow Gdns.
Campsite 5F	Greta Side Ct. 2C	(off Bell Ct.)	. . . . .3C
Castlerigg Hall Cvn.&	Greta St. 3C	Main St. 2B	Skiddaw St. 3D
Camping Site . .4E	Greta Vs. 2C	Manesty Vw. 3D	Southey Hill 2B
Catherine Cotts. . .2D	Grizedale Cl. 3D	Manor Brow 3D	Southey Hill Trad. Pk.
(off Rose Ter.)	Halls Mead 3D	Manor Pk. 3D	. . . . .2B
Central Car Pk. Rd.	Hawthorns, The . . .2F	Market Sq. 3C	Southey St. 3C
. . . . .3C	Headlands, The . . .3B	(off Lake Rd.)	Spoonygreen La. . .1C
Chestnut Hill 3E	Heads, The 3B	Millbank 2C	Springs Gth. 4D
Chestnut Pk. 2E	Heads La. 2B	(off Great Side Ct.)	Springs Rd. 3D
Church La. 1A	Heads Mt. 3B	Millfield Gdns. 2D	Standish St. 3C
Church La. 3C	Heads Rd. 3B	Museum Sq. 3B	Stanger St. 2C
Church St. 3C	Helvellyn St. 3C	(off Heads Rd.)	Station Av. 2C
Coleridge Ct. 2B	Hewetson Ct. 2B	Myers St. 3C	Station Rd. 2C
Crescent, The 3B	High Hill 1A	Myrtle Vs. 2C	Station St. 3C
Cross St. 3D	High St. 3C	New St. 3C	Tithebarn St. 2B
Crosthwaite Gdns. . .1B	Howrahs Ct. 2B	Otley Rd. 2C	Trinity Way 2D
Crosthwaite Rd. . . .2B	(off Elliot Pk.)	Pack Horse Ct. . . .3C	Vicarage Hill 1A
Crow Pk. Rd. 3B	Kenrigg Dr. 3D	(off New St.)	Victoria St. 2C
Derwent Cl. 3C	Keswick Camping &	Park Holme 1B	Wickham Ct. 3C
Derwent St. 3C	Caravanning Club	Park Vs. 2C	(off Central Car Pk. Rd.)
Derwentwater Camping	Site 3A	(off Greta Vs.)	Windebrowe Av. . . .2D
& Caravanning	Kings Head Ct. . . .3C	Penrith Rd. 2D	Wordsworth St. . . .3D
Club Site 3A	(off Main St.)	Police Ct. Yd. 3C	
Derwentwater Pl. . . .3C	Lakehead Ct. 2B	(off Derwent Cl.)	
(off St John's St.)	Lakeland Pk. 3E	Poplar St. 3C	
Eleventrees 2F	Lake Rd. 3C	Ratcliffe Pl. 3C	
Elliot Pk. 2B	(not continuous)	Riverside Ct. 2B	
Elm Ct. 2B	Lakeside Holiday Pk.	Riverside Flats . . .2C	
(off Elliot Pk.)	Camping &	(off Greta Side)	
Eskin St. 3C	Caravanning Club	Rogerfield 3D	
Fenton 3E	Site 3A	Rose Ter. 2D	
Fieldside Cl. 2F	Larch Gro. 2F	St Herbert St. 3D	
Forge, The 2F	Latrigg Cl. 2E	St John's St. 3C	

STREET INDEX

Acorn St. 3C
Ambleside Rd. 3C
Ashtree Av. 1B
Banks Pl. 3C
  (off Standish St.)
Bank St. 2C
Bell Cl. 2C
Blencathra St. 3C
Borrowdale Rd. . . .3C
Brackenrigg Dr. . . .2D
Brandlehow Cres. . .3D
Briar Rigg 1C
  (not continuous)
Bridge Ter. 2B
Brigham Row 2E
Browfoot 2E

■ The central Moot Hall on Market Square (now used as the tourist information centre), of German influence, dating from 1813, has an unusual one-handed clock.

■ St Kentigern's church, on Church Lane, Great Crosthwaite, a late Perpendicular church on the site of one built by St Kentigern in 553 AD, was substantially rebuilt in 1523, and restored in 1844 by the famous architect Sir George Gilbert Scott.

■ The core (nave, tower and spire) of St John's church, on Church Lane, was designed by Anthony Salvin in the late 1830s, with the east window regarded as one of Henry Holiday's (see Hawkshead description) finest works.

Keswick is noted culturally for the Theatre by the Lake (see 'Theatre by the Lake' entry below). A town trail leaflet is available from the tourist information centre.

Keswick has important connections with many of the most famous people associated with the Lake District: George Dixon Abraham (1872-1965) and Ashley Perry Abraham (1876-1951), popularly known as the 'Keswick Brothers', born in Keswick, sons of a studio photographer, were one of the first to venture onto the crags laden with heavy photographic equipment, often in dangerous and difficult conditions, producing some of the most exciting photographs of the period.

There are many escapes to be had from the crowded shopping area. A lake cruise can be taken from Keswick Boat Landings, Lake Road (see Derwent Water lake description). Either Hope Park off Lake Road, or the 11 hectares Fitz Park can be visited. Fitz Park, bought in 1882, with the River Greta flowing along its full length, is considered one of the most attractive urban parks in the United Kingdom. Crow Park, located on the north shore of Derwent Water, given to the National Trust in 1925, is a popular relaxation area.

Friar's Crag is a famous promontory jutting into Derwent Water, a short walk past the Keswick Boat Landings along Friar's Crag Path from the end of Lake Road. This famous spot, best on a still summers evening, gives one of the best views of lower Borrowdale looking across Derwent Water to Derwent Isle, St Herbert's Island, and Brandelhow with Causey Pike behind.

The Keswick Show held on the late August bank holiday Monday off High Hill, includes agricultural events, Cumberland and Westmorland wrestling and fairground rides.

Early Closing- Wednesday.
Market Days- Market Square (outdoor), Saturdays.

PLACES OF INTEREST

Tourist & NP Information Centre (All year) - 3C. Moot Hall, Market Square, Main Street. Tel: 017687 72645.
Information Centre **NT** - 4B. Lake Road. Tel: 017687 73780.
● ALLERDALE RAMBLE - 2A to 1B.
● CARS OF THE STARS MOTOR MUSEUM - 3C. A collection of celebrity cars from film and television, displayed in individual settings with appropriate lighting and sound, in the converted former Royal Oak Garage. The reception area has part of the forecourt building with original petrol pump. Standish Street. Tel: 017687 73757.
● CUMBERLAND PENCIL MUSEUM, THE - 2B. The history of graphite mining in Borrowdale (see above), from the reign of Queen Elizabeth I to the present day, at the Cumberland Pencil Company including displays on the production of pencils. The museum is home to the Guinness world record for the 'Longest Pencil in the World', nearly 8 m (26 ft) long and weighing over 70 stone! There is also a children's drawing corner, brass rubbing section and artist's exhibitions. Cumberland Pencil Co. Ltd., Southey Works, Carding Mill Lane, Greta Bridge. Tel: 017687 73626.
● CUMBRIA WAY - 2A to 1D. (see Ulverston description).
● DERWENT ISLAND HOUSE **NT** - 5B. Derwent Isle, the largest (2.8 hectares), most northerly and only inhabited of the 4 Derwent Water islands was home to workers from the 'Company of Mines Royal' in the late 1560s. In the 1840s the house was sold to the industrialist Henry Marshall, who employing architect Anthony Salvin to create an Italianate house, added a dining room wing, 3 storey tower and refitted the interior in a restrained classical style. Given to the National Trust in 1951, the restored garden and parts of the interior are open to the public by booked timed ticket on 5 days a year, in the months of May-September. By appointment only. Derwent Isle. Tel: 0870 609 5391.
● HOPE PARK GARDENS - 3B. Part of Hope Park with its magnificent mountain backdrop, the landscaped grounds are Keswick's floral showpiece with stream garden, formal bedding, ornamentation and woodland walk. It has been run by a charitable trust since 1974. Hope Park, Lake Road.
● JOHN RUSKIN MEMORIAL - 5B. A tall slate memorial with portrait roundel, amid trees on Friar's Crag, to John Ruskin. Unveiled in 1900, the year of Ruskin's death, by Canon Hardwicke Rawnsley of Crosthwaite. Friar's Crag, Friar's

Ashness Bridge and Skiddaw

Friars Crag, Derwent Water

Crag Path, Lake Road.

● KESWICK MUSEUM AND GALLERY - 2C. A fine small late Victorian purpose built museum of 1897, the only one of its kind in the Lake District, retaining much of its original character, set in the landscaped Fitz Park. The museum covers the local history of the town from Roman times, through the mining industry to its discovery as a tourist destination over 200 years ago.There is an extensive collection of rock and mineral specimens, including Joseph Flintoft's 4 m (13 ft) scale relief model of the Lake District of 1834. The art gallery has monthly exhibitions and Lake District landscape paintings. Fitz Park, Station Road. Tel: 017687 73263.

● KESWICK RAILWAY FOOTPATH - 2D to 1F. 3 mile footpath / cycleway between Keswick and Threlkeld owned by the Lake District National Park Authority on the single track formation of the former Cockermouth, Keswick and Penrith Railway. An extension of the footpath only, off a minor road across the A66, leads to the site of Threlkeld station and Threlkeld Quarry and Mining Museum. Station Road.

● PUZZLING PLACE, THE - 3C. A unique exhibition based on optical illusion. Witness balls rolling uphill in the Anti-gravity Room, visibly grow and shrink in the Ames Room and be amazed by the interactive optical illusion exhibits, artwork and sculptures, as well as the Hologram Gallery. 9a Museum Square. Tel: 017687 75102

● THEATRE BY THE LAKE - 4C. Cumbria's only year round professional producing theatre presenting a range of drama, music, dance, comedy, exhibitions & events. Lake Rd. Tel: 017687 74411.

ENTERTAINMENT

● Cinemas - Alhambra Cinema, St John's St. Tel: 017687 72195.

● Libraries - Heads Lane. Tel: 017687 72656.

● Theatres - Theatre by the Lake. Tel: 017687 74411.

SPORT & LEISURE

● Activity Centres - Derwentwater Marina, Portinscale. Tel: 017687 72912. Keswick Climbing Wall & Activity Centre, Southey Hill Trading Estate, Carding Mill Lane, Main Street.

Tel: 017687 72000. Newlands Adventure Centre, Stair (SW of Keswick). Tel: 017687 78463. Nichol End Marine, Portinscale (W of Keswick). Tel: 017687 73082. Platty+, Lodore Landing Stage / Boat Landings, Lodore, Borrowdale (S of Keswick). Tel: 017687 77282 / 76572. Vivid Events, Denton House, Penrith Road. Tel: 017687 75351.

● Boating / Boats for hire - Derwentwater Marina, Portinscale (W of Keswick). Tel: 017687 72912. The Keswick Launch Company, Lake Road, Keswick CA12 5DJ. Tel: 017687 72263. Platty+, Lodore Landing Stage / Boat Landings, Lodore, Borrowdale (S of Keswick). Tel: 017687 77282 / 76572. Nichol End Marine, Portinscale (W of Keswick). Tel: 017687 73082.

● Bowling Greens - Upper Fitz Park, Station Road.

● Children's Entertainment - Lower Fitz Park Playground, Station Road.

● Crazy Golf Courses - Hope Park Obstacle Golf, Hope Park, Lake Road.

● Cricket Grounds - Lower Fitz Park, Station Road.

● Cycle Hire - Gone Mountain Biking, Portinscale (W of Keswick). Tel: 017687 80812. Keswick Motor Company, Lake Road. Tel: 017687 72064. Keswick Mountain Bike Centre, Units 1-2, Southey Hill Trading Park, Main Street. Tel: 017687 75202.

● Golf Courses - Keswick Golf Course, Thelkeld Hall, Threlkeld (18 hole) (E of Keswick). Tel: 017687 79324.

● Horse Riding - Calvert Trust Riding Centre, Little Crossthwaite, Underskiddaw (caters for disabled). Tel: 017687 72250.

● Parks and Gardens - Crow Park, Lake Road. Lower Fitz Park, Station Road. Upper Fitz Park, Station Road. Hope Park, Lake Road.

● Pitch and Putt Courses- Hope Park, Lake Road.

● Putting Greens - Upper Fitz Park, Station Road. Hope Park, Lake Road.

● Sports and Leisure Centres - The Howard Allen Sports Hall. Keswick School, Vicarage Hill. (evenings and weekends only). Tel: 017687 74929.

● Swimming Pools - Keswick Leisure Pool & Fitness Centre, Station Road (indoor). Tel: 017687 72760.

● Tennis Courts - Lower Fitz Park, Station Road. Upper Fitz Park, Station Road.

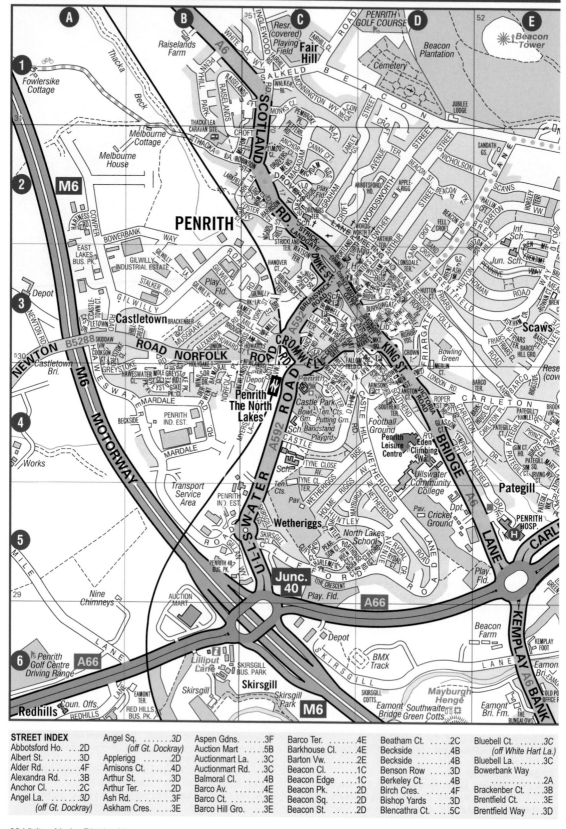

STREET INDEX

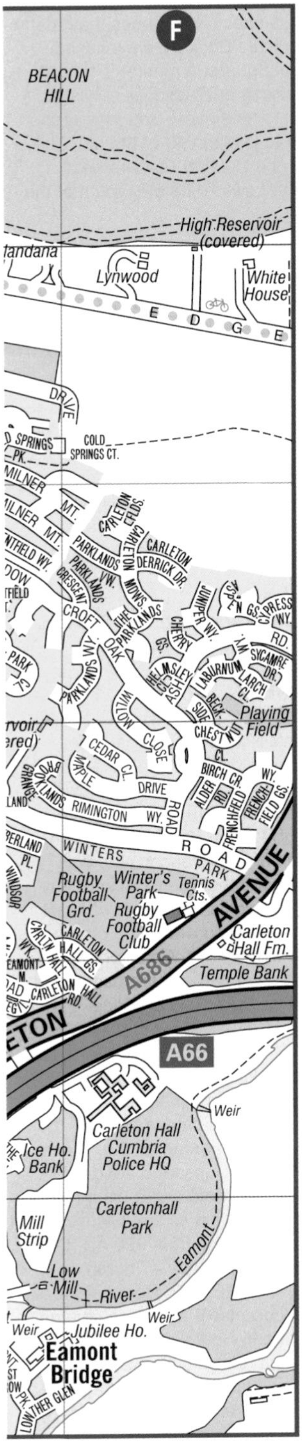

F
BEACON HILL
High Reservoir (covered)
Lynwood
White House
EDGE
COLD SPRINGS CT.
DRIVE
MILNER MT.
CARLETON FLDS.
CARLETON DERRICK DR.
PARKLANDS
CRESCENT
CROFT
THE PARKLANDS
JUNIPER WY.
CYPRESS WY.
SYCAMRE DR.
LABURNUM WY.
LARCH CL.
HELMSLEY
ASH
BECK
CHERRY GS.
OAK
WILLOW
CLOSE
Playing Field
CHESTNUT CL.
CEDAR CL.
MAPLE
DRIVE
BIRCH CR.
ALDER RD.
FRENCHFIELD
FRENCHFIELD GS.
RIMINGTON WY.
ROAD
WINTERS PARK
AVENUE
Rugby Football Grd.
Winter's Park
Tennis Cts.
Rugby Football Club
CARLETON HALL GS.
Carleton Hall Fm.
Temple Bank
A686
A66
Weir
Carleton Hall Cumbria Police HQ
Ice Ho. Bank
Mill Strip
Carletonhall Park
Eamont
Low Mill
River
Weir
Jubilee Ho.
Eamont Bridge
LOWTHER GLEN

Penrith

Penrith is a traditional border market town which grew up on a strategic and accessible site between the Lake District fells, and the Eden Valley and North Pennines. It is located on an important north-south route, a communication corridor since Roman times, subsequently utilised by the modern routes of the West Coast main line, A6 trunk road and M6 motorway. During the 9th and 10th centuries Penrith was the capital of the Kingdom of Cumbria (part of the Kingdom of Scotland and Strathclyde), and remained so until 1070 AD when it was incorporated into England under the Normans.

The town is now an important market place for cattle and other livestock, a centre for the farming community and, as one of the gateways to the Lake District, one of the best known towns in Cumbria.

Aira Force

The town is characterised by its predominant local red sandstone buildings, and narrow streets with many attractive lanes, yards and alleyways, and has at its heart one long north-south street incorporating Middlegate, and the wide Devonshire Street with 'the narrows' at the junction with Burrowgate. Some of the best of the buildings are around the parish church of St Andrew's (off Market Square). Significant buildings include the small Victorian clock tower in Market Square, commemorating the death of Philip Musgrave of Eden Hall, and the Cornmarket, an open sided building situated at the northern end of Great Dockray, where local farmers bought and sold their produce. Hutton Hall, on the corner of Friargate and Benson Row, incorporates a stone 15th century pele tower.

The town, which is noted for its specialised shops, has many pedestrianised areas, notably Little Dockray, Devonshire Arcade, Angel Lane and Angel Square. A market is held in the open triangle of Great Dockray on Tuesdays, whilst a popular large open air market is held every Saturday at the Auction Mart at Skirsgill, next to junction 40 of the M6. The Lowther Horse Driving Trials and Country Fair are held annually in early August on the Lowther Estate, south of the town.

Penrith was the home town of William Wordsworth's mother Ann (who died in 1778 when he was 8), and where the future poet laureate (from 1843-50) and his sister Dorothy attended infants school from 1776 to 1777. The building can still be seen off St Andrew's Place (a footpath adjacent the south side of the churchyard behind King Street). The school was also attended by Mary Hutchinson, whom he later married.

Further information on the history of Penrith can be found in 'The Penrith Millennium Trail' which details 7 walks exploring the town; a leaflet is available from the tourist information centre.

Early Closing- Wednesday.
Market Days- Great Dockray (outdoor), Tuesdays.
Auction Mart, Skirsgill (outdoor), Saturdays.

PLACES OF INTEREST

Tourist Information Centre (All year) - 3C. Penrith Museum, Robinson's School, Middlegate. Tel: 01768 867466.

● BEACON TOWER - 1E. Squat square tower with pyramid roof built, in 1719, of local red sandstone on top of Beacon Hill (286 m, 938 ft). The structure, on an ancient beacon site, was built to warn Penrith and the Eden Valley of any threat to the town by Scottish troops. It was last used in 1805 when it flashed a warning of invasion during the Napoleonic Wars, which proved to be a false alarm! There are panoramic views. A path leads up from Beacon Edge. Beacon Hill, Beacon Edge.

● GIANT'S GRAVE - 3D. Two 3.4 m (11 ft) high Norse (10th century Viking period) sculptured stone cross shafts, with hogback tombstones in-between, situated in the churchyard of St Andrew's parish church, regarded as the traditional grave of Owen Caesarius, King of Cumbria (920 to 937 AD). Also in the churchyard, immediately to the south-west, is the 'Giant's Thumb'- a Norse cross dating from 920 AD. St Andrew's Churchyard, St Andrew's Church.

● LILLIPUT LANE VISITOR CENTRE - 6B. Home of the famous Lilliput Lane range of collectable miniature cottages founded in 1982. A visitor centre in Honeysuckle Cottage, a life-sized thatched building set in gardens, houses a shop (with current cottages) and museum of 'retired' cottages. A bookable studio tour of the adjacent factory shows the processes involved in creating models, from photographs of the original building, through sculpting in wax and making of the silicone 'master' mould, to casting the models in Amorphite and final painting. Honeysuckle Cottage, Skirsgill Business Park, Redhills. Tel: 01768 212692.

● MAYBURGH HENGE - 6D. Impressive late Neolithic to early Bronze age henge. A single circular bank, 4.5 m (15 ft) high and 117 m (394 ft) in diameter, with an entrance in the

Ullswater

east but no internal or external ditch, surrounds a solitary large 2.8 m (9 ft) high stone. The bank is not earthen being built of river cobblestones / pebbles (visible through the turf in places) from the nearby rivers Eamont and Lowther. In the 18th century the noted antiquarian William Stukely recorded 4 standing stones in the centre and 4 at the entrance but these were later destroyed by blasting with gun powder! (see also the younger henge of King Arthur's Round Table nearby). Eamont Bridge.

● NOAH'S ARK SOFTPLAY CENTRE - 3D. Indoor soft play centre for children aged 8 and under. Ball pool, bouncy castle etc. Above Spar stores. 36-40 Burrowgate. Tel: 01768 890640.

● PENRITH CASTLE - 4C. Ruins of a square enclosure castle built c.1399 to repel Scots raiders by William Strickland (later to become Bishop of Carlisle and Archbishop of Canterbury) as an adaptation of an earlier pele tower. At its height the castle was the royal fortress of Richard, Duke of Gloucester, who became the infamous Richard III in 1483. By the late 16th century the castle was partly ruinous, the red sandstone being used for other building in the town. The pronounced motte (surrounded by a wide ditch or dry moat), part of the south wall and two towers remain, together with the foundations of the inner and outer gatehouses and internal buildings. Castle Park, Castlegate.

● PENRITH MUSEUM - 3C. Local history museum in an altered Elizabethan building, originally a charity school for poor girls and still a school until the early 1970s. Exhibits cover the history, geology and archaeology of Penrith and the Eden Valley. There are also changing historical and contemporary arts exhibitions throughout the year. Robinson's School, Middlegate. Tel: 01768 212228.

ENTERTAINMENT
● Cinemas - Alhambra Cinema, Middlegate. Tel: 01768 862400.
● Libraries - St Andrew's Churchyard. Tel: 01768 242100.

SPORT & LEISURE
● Activity Centres - Eden Climbing Wall, Penrith Leisure Centre, Southend Road. Tel: 01768 863450.
● Bowling Greens - Castle Park, Castlegate. Friargate.
● Children's Entertainment - Castle Park Playground and Paddling Pool, Castlegate.
● Crazy Golf Courses - Castle Park, Castlegate.
● Cricket Grounds - Wetheriggs Lane.
● Cycle Hire - Arragons Cycle Centre, Brunswick Road. Tel: 01768 890344.
● Golf Courses - Penrith Golf Centre and Driving Range, Redhills (9 hole). Tel: 01768 892167. Penrith Golf Course, Salkeld Road (18 hole) (N of Penrith). Tel: 01768 891919.
● Horse Riding - Parkfoot Trekking Centre, Howtown Road, Pooley Bridge (SW of Penrith). Tel: 017684 86696. Sockbridge Pony Trekking Centre, The Cottage, Sockbridge, Tirril (SW of Penrith). Tel: 01768 863468.
● Parks & Gardens - Castle Park, Castlegate. Winter's Park, Carleton Avenue.
● Putting Greens - Castle Park, Castlegate.
● Sports & Leisure Centres - Penrith Leisure Centre, Southend Road. Tel: 01768 863450.
● Swimming Pools - Penrith Swimming Pool, Penrith Leisure Centre, Southend Road (indoor). Tel: 01768 863450.
● Tennis Courts - Castle Park, Castlegate. Winter's Park, Carleton Avenue.

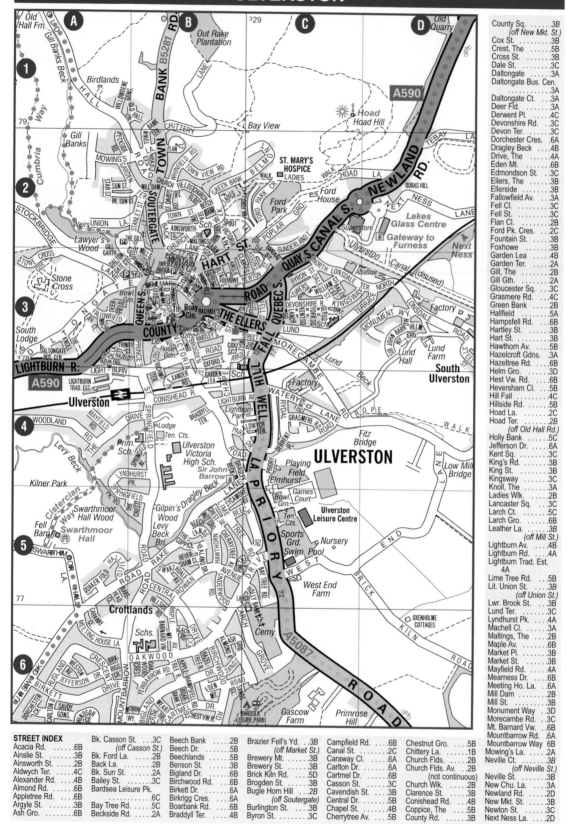

Ulverston, an attractive small market town on the Furness Peninsula, although only 9 miles by road from Windermere lake, is often by-passed by the Lakeland tourist. A quiet town, except on market days, of cobbled streets and ginnels (alleyways). In 1280 Edward I granted the town a Market Charter to hold a Thursday market and annual September fair.

Developing in the 18th century through the exploitation of iron-ore, and its strategic location on the route over the Morecambe Bay sands, its prosperity grew rapidly on the opening of the Ulverston Canal in 1796. For centuries the only direct land route to Ulverston and the Furness Peninsula was across the treacherous sands of Morecambe Bay. Access improved with the arrival of the Furness Railway from Barrow-in-Furness in June 1854.

Ulverston has many fine Georgian and Victorian buildings from its hey-day, many of which are featured on the town's historic town trail (marked with blue and white plaques). Ulverston is associated with several famous people, including Sir John Barrow and Stan Laurel (see Laurel & Hardy Museum), who were both born in the town.

Pole vaulting for height, rather than distance, was pioneered by football and cricket club members in Ulverston; the town is thought to be the origin of pole vaulting as a competitive sport in 1879. Ulverston is home to the spectacular Ulverston Lantern Procession, in early September, hundreds of candlelit lanterns, handmade by local people from willow sticks and tissue paper, are lead in procession to Ford Park where there is an art based display of fire sculptures, music, performance, ingenious structures and effects.

Early Closing- Wednesday.
Market Days- Market Place / Market Street / New Market Street (outdoor), Thursdays, Saturdays. Market Hall, New Market Street (indoor), Monday-Tuesdays, Thursday-Saturdays.

PLACES OF INTEREST

Tourist Information Centre (All year) - 3B.
Coronation Hall, County Square. Tel: 01229 587120.
● CISTERCIAN WAY - 4B to 6A. (see Grange-over-Sands description).
● CUMBRIA WAY - 2A to 1A. 70 mile long distance trail bisecting the heart of the Lake District National Park running south to north from Ulverston on the shores of Morecambe Bay (taking around 5 days), to Carlisle, close to the Scottish border.
● GATEWAY TO FURNESS EXHIBITION - 2D. Displays on the history of the Furness Peninsula, its countryside, coast, market towns and people, and the development of the area as a tourist destination since the arrival of the Furness Railway in 1857. The Lakes Glass Centre, Oubas Hill. Tel: 01229 584400 / 581121.
● HOAD MONUMENT - 1C. Imposing 30 m (100 ft) high stone replica (known as 'The Pepper Pot') of the Eddystone Lighthouse set atop Hoad Hill. Erected by public subscription, to a design by Andrew Trimen in 1850-1, as a memorial to Sir

John Barrow (1764-1848). Restored in the early 1990s, & now reinforced with concrete. The tower is open when the red flag is flying. Hoad Hill, Hoad Lane.
● LAKES GLASS CENTRE, THE - 2D. The combined factories of both Heron Glass & Cumbria Crystal, who used to have individual premises in Ulverston, in a new purpose built building constructed in 1999. Oubas Hill. Tel: 01229 584400 / 581121.
● LANTERNHOUSE (CENTRE FOR CELEBRATORY ART) - 3B. The powerhouse, opened in 1999 in a redesigned building previously used as a Labour Exchange. There are regular exhibitions & performances, together with seminars, arts training in the form of public workshops for local people & artists, & activities for young people. Welfare State International, The Ellers. Tel: 01229 581127.
● LAUREL & HARDY MUSEUM - 3B. World's first museum dedicated to the famous comedy duo of Stan Laurel and Oliver Hardy. An extensive but crowded collection of memorabilia is displayed including photographs, personal items and furniture. 4c Upper Brook Street. Tel: 01229 582292.
● NEXT NESS NATURE RESERVE - 2D. 1.8 hectares reserve of willow & alder carr adjacent to the railway line to Barrow-in-Furness. Next Ness Lane, Next Ness.
● SIR JOHN BARROW COTTAGE MUSEUM, THE - 4B. Small cottage museum at Dragley Beck, the birthplace of the geographer Sir John Barrow in 1764. Sir John Barrow Cottage, Dragley Beck, Priory Road. Tel: 01229 582369.
● SWARTHMOOR HALL - 5A. Elizabethan manor house, built in 1586, the former family home of Judge Thomas Fell, with a fine collection of 17th century period furniture, oak panelling & artefacts. Swarthmoor Hall Lane, Swarthmoor. Tel: 01229 583204.

ENTERTAINMENT
● Cinemas - Roxy Cinema, Brogden Street. Tel: 01229 582340.
● Libraries- King's Road. Tel: 01229 894151.
● Theatres - Lanternhouse, The Ellers. Tel: 01229 581127. Coronation Hall, County Square. Tel: 01229 587140.

SPORT & LEISURE
● Bowling Greens - Church Walk. Queen Street. Ulverston Leisure Centre, Priory Road.
● Children's Entertainment - Lightburn Park Playground, Lightburn Avenue. Pound Playground, Garden Terrace.
● Cycle Hire - Gill Cycles, 1 The Gill. Tel: 01229 581116.
● Golf Courses - Ulverston Golf Course, Bardsea Park, Bardsea (18 hole) (S of Ulverston). Tel: 01229 582824.
● Parks & Gardens - Lightburn Park, Lightburn Avenue. Ulverston Rose Garden, Victoria Road.
● Sports & Leisure Centres - Ulverston Leisure Centre, Priory Road. Tel: 01229 584110.
● Swimming Pools - Ulverston Leisure Centre, Priory Road (indoor). Tel: 01229 584110.
● Tennis Courts - Ulverston Leisure Centre, Priory Road.

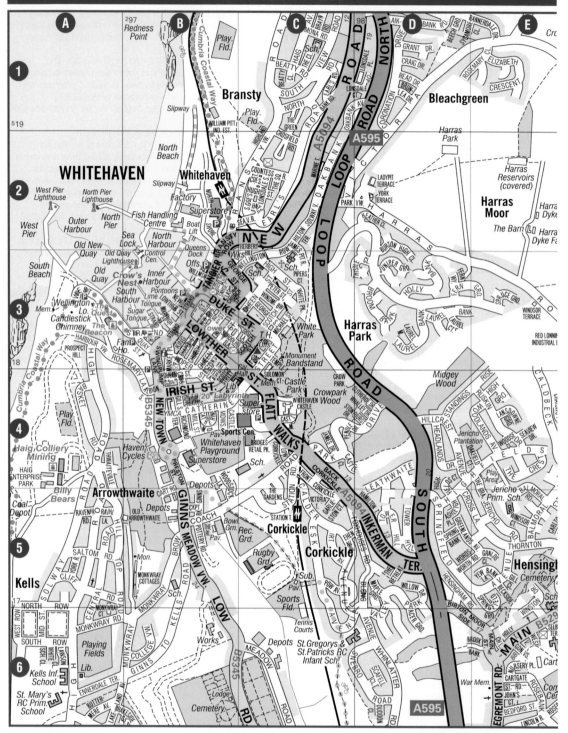

Whitehaven

Whitehaven, situated on the south-east side of the Solway Firth, was once a small coastal fishing village, but was transformed by coal mining beginning in 1634 when the landowner Sir Christopher Lowther built a stone quay (Old Quay, subsequently extended but still one of the oldest remaining coal wharves in England), to ship coal to Ireland.

He started the building of the present layout of the town from the original settlement around Market Place, which was continued by Sir John Lowther (1642-1705), with the principal roads constructed between 1640 and 1680. This was the earliest post Renaissance planned town in England. Inspired by the designs of Sir Christopher Wren, in a grid pattern, with St Nicholas' Church in the middle.

By the mid 18th century Whitehaven was a thriving town, having become the third largest port in the country, after London and Bristol, and remained so until the development of the port of Liverpool. There are around 250 listed buildings in the town, many Georgian, dating from the 18th century, with the best in the Scotch Street and Roper Street area.

The main activity of the port was the export of coal and iron-ore and the import of molasses, rum and sugar from the West Indies, tobacco from Virginia and Maryland, and cotton, with many bonded warehouses constructed to store the goods. The Jefferson family, connected with the rum trade ('the dark spirit of Whitehaven'), traded with the West Indies for over 200 years from 1785.

Around 1650 shipbuilding started in earnest at Whitehaven. The harbour expanded rapidly, the West Pier was completed in 1838, whilst North Pier was completed in 1841. In 1876, the final phase, Queens Dock, once gated, was opened. This prosperity continued until the late 19th century when the decline of the iron-ore industry, and the coal industry conspired to cause the decline of the port and its shipbuilding industry, with the last shipyard closing in 1889.

The West Cumberland Coalfield, with workings up to 4 miles out beneath the Solway Firth, although small by national standards, produced coal of a very high quality. It was, however, highly geologically faulted, and was also notorious for a high concentration of 'firedamp' (methane), causing many problems for the miners, and resulting in many violent explosions leading to the deaths of over 1,200 men, women and children during the operational life of the Whitehaven pits. The most famous mine was Wellington Pit, above The Beacon on the south side of the harbour, sunk in 1838 (and closed 1932).

Whitehaven has connections with several notable people: A plaque on 25 Roper Street marks the former family home of Captain Daniel Brocklebank (1741-1801). Initially establishing a shipbuilding concern in America, he returned to Whitehaven and in 1782 set up a yard at North Shore. Officially incorporated in 1801 as 'Thos and Jno. Brocklebank' trading mostly in coal, he became Whitehaven's most successful shipbuilder. In 1819 the main company business moved to Liverpool, and was acquired by the Cunard Line in 1911, who, due to this connection claim to be the world's oldest registered shipping line.

On 23rd April 1778 Whitehaven was the subject of a famous raid on the town led by John Paul Jones, an American naval officer and privateer, now regarded as the founder of the American Navy, who was born in Scotland in 1747 and had served an apprenticeship as a seaman in Whitehaven. The intention of the raid, during the American War of Independence, was to set fire to the large fleet of merchant ships at anchor in the harbour. In his ship 'The Ranger' he managed to torch 3 ships and take Whitehaven fort before being repelled. 3 of the original cannons used to repel the attack, with a bronze statue of a sailor, can be seen on West Strand. The scant triangular ruins of the fort (with large anchor in the centre) can be found between Old Quay and Old New Quay off West Strand.

'The Renaissance of Whitehaven' project, part funded by the Millennium Commission and other grants, has seen a complete renovation of the historic harbour area; completed in spring 2001 at a cost of over £50 million. It has funded the construction of the sea-lock (allowing a complete loop of the

Inner Harbour to be walked) resulting in the creation of a 100 berth marina and protection from tidal flooding, unique seating and sculptures, The Hub, an open-air tented public meeting area, Crow's Nest (see below), and on Lime Tongue a 'fluorescent light sculpture' called The Wave, reflecting green light in the sea on one side and blue on the other, whilst Sugar Tongue is lit with fluorescent columns.

Today the main trade of the port is leisure craft and the fishing industry, principally prawns and scallops handled by the new Fish Handling Centre constructed on North Quay. The harbour is sometimes visited by tall ships, notably during Whitehaven's Maritime Festival, held normally bi-annually in June. All these new developments have enhanced the harbour and town as an historic, attractive and rewarding place to visit.

Whitehaven

Whitehaven is also noted as the beginning of the 140 mile long coast to coast (C2C) cycle route. Situated on the slipway at the harbour is a sculpture marking the starting point of the route to Sunderland or Tynemouth, running through Lorton, Keswick and Penrith, and initially following the Whitehaven to Ennerdale Cycle Path (a 10 mile long route largely on the disused Whitehaven to Rowrah railway line). There is also the option of starting at Workington passing through Cockermouth. The Whitehaven to Ennerdale Cycle Path is part of the 72 mile West Cumbria cycle network, partly on disused railway lines.

Early Closing - Wednesday.
Market Days - Market Place (outdoor), Thursdays, Saturdays.

PLACES OF INTEREST

Tourist Information Centre (All year) - 3B. Market Hall, Market Place. Tel: 01946 852939.

● 19/20 IRISH STREET - 4B. Listed building of an imposing Italianate design by Sydney Smirke. Private residence. Exterior View only. 19/20 Irish Street.

● BEACON, THE - 3A. Purpose built circular building on the harbour, opened in 1996, telling the story of Whitehaven's social, industrial and maritime heritage. There are 4 levels, recommended to be viewed from the top down. Level 4, The Met. Office Weather Gallery, has interactive computer systems and satellite links connected to the Met. Office with information on clouds, weather patterns, the seasons and global warming. There are panoramic views of the harbour. Level 3, Whitehaven Looking Out, covers The American Connection, George Washington and John Paul Jones, sailors lives on board ship, smuggling, and the tobacco, sugar, rum and slave trades. Level 2, Whitehaven Looking In, covers the social heritage of the area, showing Whitehaven past and present, with original 1920s and 30s newsreel cinema footage. Also the development of coal mining, and its disasters, iron-ore mining, pottery and shipbuilding connections, and the Lowther family history. Level 1, The Harbour Gallery, on the ground floor, houses a venue for the visual arts with an annual programme of exhibitions and events. West Strand. Tel: 01946 592302.

● BILLY BEARS FUN CENTRE - 4A. Indoor soft play centre for children aged 5 and under. Ball pool, bouncy castle, slides, bikes etc. Unit B1, Haig Enterprise Park. Tel: 01946 690003.

● CROW'S NEST - 3B. 40 m (131 ft) high illuminated concrete mono-pile tower on Lime Tongue based on the design of a tall ship's mast, a focal point for the harbour regeneration. The 11 m (36 ft) diameter domed platform at the base provides views of the harbour area. Lime Tongue, South Harbour, Inner Harbour, West Strand.

● CUMBRIA COASTAL WAY - 5A to 1B.

● HAIG COLLIERY MINING MUSEUM - 4A. Haig Pit, situated on a clifftop site 0.5 miles south of Whitehaven harbour, was sunk for the Whitehaven Colliery Co. Ltd. between 1914 and 1918 to exploit reserves between the Ladysmith Pit to the south and Wellington Pit to the north. 3 disasters occurred at Haig Pit during the life of the mine, the pit closing in March 1986, after a major geological fault was encountered in 1983, Cumbria's last deep working coal mine. Solway Road, Kells. Tel: 01946 599949.

● RUM STORY, THE - 3B. The story of rum housed in Jeffersons, the oldest family-owned business of rum traders and importers in the United Kingdom, in the original 18th century bonded warehouses with original Georgian wine merchant's shop front. Inside are the original Victorian office and cellar barrel stores, and displays, dioramas and audios. 27 Lowther Street. Tel: 01946 592933.

● WHITEHAVEN LABYRINTH, THE - 4B. A stone paved labyrinth, some 11.5 m (38 ft) across with 11 circuits (based on the design of a labyrinth in Chartres Cathedral, France), constructed at the end of 2000 as a monument to the millennium, together with a commemorative plaque and inscribed rock, in the grounds of the former Holy Trinity church, demolished in 1949. Trinity Gardens, Irish Street / Scotch Street.

● WHITEHAVEN NORTH PIER LIGHTHOUSE - 2A. 8m (26 ft) high white round tower set with the date 1841 at the top, at the head of Whitehaven's North Pier. The disused lighthouse tower has been castellated and converted to a beacon with a range of 9 miles. Exterior view only. North Pier Head, Outer Harbour, North Shore.

● WHITEHAVEN OLD QUAY LIGHTHOUSE - 3B. Disused stone built lighthouse on Whitehaven's Old Quay, refurbished externally under the harbour regeneration project. A sundial dated 1730 is attached to the side. Exterior view only. Old Quay, Inner Harbour, West Strand.

● WHITEHAVEN QUEST - 3A. Family orientated prize-winning trails exploring Whitehaven and its history. 10 town trails can be followed by purchasing a 'Quest Box' at The Beacon (look for the big yellow 'Q'), or the tourist information centre. The Beacon, West Strand. Tel: 01946 852920.

● WHITEHAVEN ST JAMES' CHURCH - 3C. A fine example of Georgian architecture, built 1752-3 with commanding views down Queen Street, to designs by Carlisle Spedding, it is regarded as having the best Georgian church interior in the county. There are upper galleries on 3 sides, together with an alter picture portraying 'The Transfiguration' at the east end by Giulio Cesare Procaccini. (1574-1625). High Street.

● WHITEHAVEN ST NICHOLAS' CHURCH TOWER - 3B. The tower and entrance of a Perpendicular Gothic style church, built 1881-3 at the centre of Whitehaven's grid pattern of streets, as a replacement for a church erected by Sir John Lowther in 1693. The grounds contain the (now unmarked) grave of Mildred Gale, grandmother to the first U.S. President George Washington. The floor of what used to be the church has a pebble mosaic dedicated to the miners that were lost in the local pits. St Nicholas' Gardens, Lowther Street. Tel: 01946 62572.

● WHITEHAVEN WEST PIER LIGHTHOUSE - 2A. 14 m (46 ft) high white round tower with a range of 13 miles built, at the head of Whitehaven's West Pier, in 1832 after the completion of this part of the Outer Harbour. Exterior view only. West Pier Head, Outer Harbour, West Strand.

ENTERTAINMENT

● Concert Venues - Whitehaven Civic Hall, Lowther Street. Tel: 01946 852821.

● Libraries - Lowther Street. Tel: 01946 852900. Richmond Hill Road, Hensingham. Tel: 01946 852921. High Road, Kells. Tel: 01946 852922.

● Theatres - Rosehill Theatre, Moresby (NE of Whitehaven). Tel: 01946 692422.

SPORT & LEISURE

● Bowling Greens - Corkickle Recreation Ground, Coach Road.

● Children's Entertainment - Castle Park, Lowther Street.

● Cricket Grounds - Whitehaven Playground, Richmond Terrace.

● Cycle Hire - Haven Cycles, Preston Street Garage, Preston Street, Whitehaven, CA28 9DL. Tel: 01946 632630.

● Golf Courses - St Bees Golf Course, Peck Mill, St Bees (9 hole) (S of Whitehaven). Tel:01946 824300. Whitehaven Golf Course, Red Lonning (18 hole). Tel: 01946 591177.

● Parks & Gardens - Castle Park, Lowther Street. Corkickle Recreation Ground, Coach Road. Rosebank Recreation Ground, Rosebank. St Nicholas' Gardens, Lowther Street / Duke Street. South Beach Recreational Area. Trinity Gardens, Irish Street / Scotch Street.

● Sports & Leisure Centres - Whitehaven Sports Centre, Flatt Walks. Tel: 01946 695666.

● Swimming Pools - Copeland Pool, Cleator Moor Road, Hensingham (indoor) (SE Whitehaven). Tel: 01946 695021.

WINDERMERE

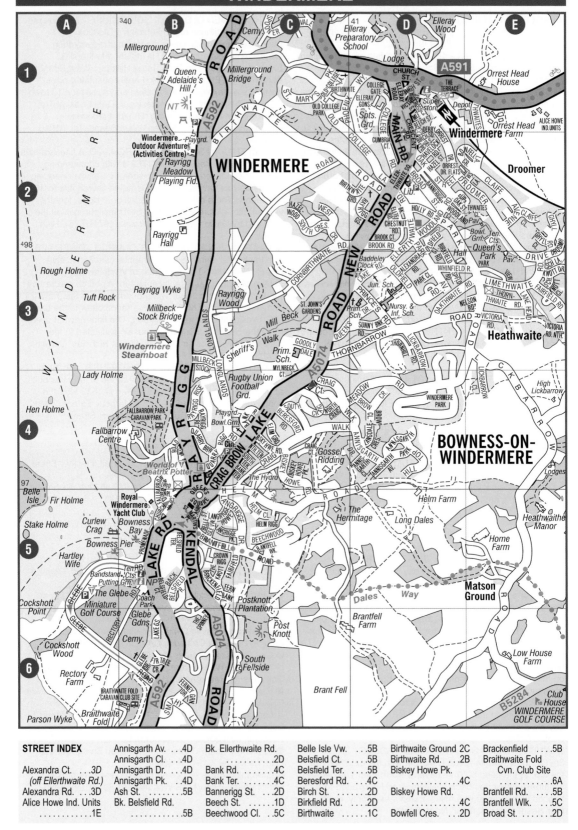

Bowness-on-Windermere

Windermere

Windermere, perhaps the best known of Lake District names, grew up around the desire of wealthy 19th century industrialists from Lancaster and the North West to have residences here. Mansions, many now converted to hotels, such as the Old England Hotel (on Church Street) and the Belsfield Hotel (on Kendal Road) were built. The area, which had previously been confined to this wealthy elite, was made accessible to the mass tourism of the less prosperous middle classes by the arrival in 1847 of the Kendal and Windermere Railway (later absorbed by the London and North Western Railway, (L.N.W.R.)). A branch of the Lancaster and Carlisle Railway from Oxenholme, which had

suprisingly initially avoided the major town of Kendal on its rush northward, was the first incursion of a railway into the heart of Lakeland.

The railway was opposed by the 'Lakeland Poet' William Wordsworth, one of the principal exponents of English Romanticism in literature, and the first writer to promote and extol the natural beauty of the Lakeland landscape. Unfortunately his vision was enthusiastically embraced by the educated classes, in part as a substitute for the European 'Grand Tour' of classical sites, and he thereby helped create the influx of visitors and development that he discouraged.

Nearly 50 years later building on both sides of the lake was effectively stemmed by the beginnings of the conservation movement and fledgling National Trust. The station was actually sited in Birthwaite, some 1.5 miles from the most accessible point on the lake at Bowness Bay (Bowness-on-Windermere), but was given the more desirable name of Windermere, which was subsequently applied to the large Victorian village which developed around the station, whilst the older Bowness-on-Windermere was to become one of the most popular of Lakeland destinations.

There are few buildings of note, however St Martin's parish church (off Church Street), consecrated in 1483, and restored in 1870, is the most historic, with beautiful late 15th century glass believed to be from Cartmel Priory, set in its east window. Behind, leading to the prestigious Royal Windermere Yacht Club, is the area of Lowside with its narrow streets and former residences of the local boat and fishermen. Between the two villages is a prominent slate clock erected in 1907 as a memorial to M. J. B. Baddeley.

Nowadays Bowness-on-Windermere is a large and busy seasonal tourist orientated shopping area, whilst Windermere has most notably Lakeland Limited, a large commercial outlet sited beside the station. Escapes can, however, be made by taking one of the popular lake cruises from Bowness Bay (see Windermere lake description) or

largest iron-ore deposit in Britain (Park Mine) at what is now Askham in Furness. He subsequently erected blast furnaces at Barrow, which by 1876 was the biggest steel works in the world. Schneider epitomised the nouveau riche of the period, wealthy industrialists who built many of the fashionable mansions and villas bordering Windermere to escape the very industrial landscape of the North West which they had in fact helped to create. A statue of Lord Henry Schneider can be found in Schneider Square, Barrow-in-Furness.

Thomas Hayton Mawson

Thomas Hayton Mawson was one of the foremost landscape architects of the Edwardian era. Born at Scorton in Lancashire in 1861 into a poor family, he studied technical drawing and first worked in the building trade. In 1885 he established a successful nursery and landscaping business, Lakeland Nurseries in Windermere. In his lifetime, Mawson undertook at least 160 major garden commissions in England, Scotland and Wales, his archive comprising an estimated 9,600 plans and drawings, with his greatest achievement, the publication in 1900/1 of 2 large volumes entitled 'The Art and Craft of Garden Making'- now widely accepted as a foundational work for modern landscape architecture. He died in 1933 and is buried at Bowness Cemetery, off Rectory Road, Bowness-on-Windermere.

Early Closing- Thursday.

Windermere lake

walking to one of several nearby viewpoints overlooking Windermere. Biskey Howe viewpoint off Biskey Howe Road, and Post Knott viewpoint off Brantfell Road, on National Trust land below Brant Fell, are both a short walk from the centre of Bowness-on-Windermere.
Public access to the east shore of Windermere is limited, however Millerground (off Rayrigg Road) is a traditional bathing beach, and the shingle beach of Bowness Bay next to the cruise piers is popular for feeding the waterfowl.

Henry William Schneider

In 1839 Schneider, a young speculator and dealer in iron, came to Barrow and by 1850 had discovered the second

PLACES OF INTEREST

Tourist Information Centre (All year) - 1D. Victoria Street, Windermere. Tel: 015394 46499.
Tourist and NP Information Centre (All year) - 5B. Glebe Road, Bowness Bay, Bowness-on-Windermere. Tel: 015394 42895.
● DALES WAY, THE - 5B to 6E. 81 mile long distance trail finishing at Bowness-on-Windermere. Devised by the Ramblers' Association in 1968, the trail starts at Ilkley and follows a waymarked fairly easy and predominantly low-level valley and riverside route north-westwards through the Yorkshire Dales National Park, exiting it north-west of Sedbergh, then crossing the M6 and passing north of Kendal

via Burneside and Staveley, now in the Lake District National Park, to Bowness-on-Windermere. Kendal Road, Bowness-on-Windermere.

● WINDERMERE STEAMBOATS AND MUSEUM - 3B. Unique and historic collection of Victorian and Edwardian steam and motor boats dating from 1850-1911, owned by the Windermere Nautical Trust, covering all the key stages in the development of steam launches on Windermere. These sleek boats, with their tall narrow funnels, were the preserve of enterprising engineers and entrepreneurs of the industrial revolution creating a world of elegant fashion centred on weekend steamer trips and tea parties. Many historic boats are included. S.S. Raven (built 1871), was a steam cargo boat used by The Furness Railway Company. T.S.S.Y. (Twin Screw Steam Yacht) Esperance (built 1869 for Henry William Schneider, see above), is the oldest boat on the Lloyds Register of Yachts. Esperance was the inspiration for Captain Flint's houseboat in Arthur Ransome's classic 'Swallows and Amazons' children's book series. In the Windermere building is Beatrix Potter's rowing boat, which she used on Moss Eccles Tarn, together with photographic displays illustrating the history of Windermere lake and the vessels in the collection. 50 minute steamboat cruises operate daily throughout the season, weather permitting, making a trip around Belle Isle, using S.L. Swallow (built 1911) or M.L. Water Viper (built 1907). Rayrigg Road. Tel: 015394 45565.

● WORLD OF BEATRIX POTTER ATTRACTION, THE - 4B. Scenes from all 23 of the Lakeland tales of Beatrix Potter are brought to life in an enchanting series of indoor 3D tableaux, complete with sights, sounds and even smells of the countryside and including characters such as Peter Rabbit™, Jemima Puddle-duck™, Tom Kitten, Pigling Bland, Mrs Tiggywinkle™, Squirrel Nutkin and Benjamin Bunny™. The interactive Virtual Walks display allows visitors to explore in the footsteps of Miss Potter and learn about her work as a children's author, artist, farmer and pioneer conservationist. The Old Laundry Theatre is housed in the same building. The Old Laundry, Crag Brow, Bowness-on-Windermere. Tel: 015394 88444.

Windermere Boats

ENTERTAINMENT

● Cinemas - Royalty Cinema, Lake Road, Bowness-on-Windermere. Tel: 015394 43364.
● Libraries - Ellerthwaite Road. Tel: 015394 62400.
● Theatres - The Old Laundry Theatre, The Old Laundry, Crag Brow, Bowness-on-Windermere. Tel: 015394 88444.

SPORT & LEISURE

● Activity Centres - Windermere Outdoor Adventure, Leigh Groves Building, Rayrigg Road. Tel: 015394 47183.
● Boating / Boats for hire - Shepherds (Windermere) Ltd., Glebe Road, Bowness Bay, Bowness-on-Windermere. Tel: 015394 44031 / 45395. Windermere Lake Cruises Ltd., Bowness Pier, Promenade, Bowness Bay, Bowness-on-Windermere. Tel: 015395 31188.
● Bowling Greens - Longlands Road. Queen's Park, Park Road.

● Children's Entertainment - Longlands Road Playground, Longlands Road. Queen's Park Playground, Park Road. Rayrigg Meadow Playground, Rayrigg Road.
● Cricket Grounds - Queen's Park, Park Road.
● Cycle Hire - Country Lanes, The Railway Station. Tel: 015394 44544.
● Golf Courses - Windermere Golf Course, Cleabarrow (18 hole). Tel: 015394 43123.
● Horse Riding - Lakeland Pony Trekking, Limefitt Park, Patterdale Road, Troutbeck (N of Windermere). Tel: 015394 31999.
● Parks & Gardens - Glebe Gardens, Rectory Road. Queen's Park, Park Road. Rayrigg Meadow Playing Field, Rayrigg Meadow, Rayrigg Road.
● Pitch & Putt Courses - The Glebe, Glebe Road.
● Putting Greens - The Glebe, Glebe Road. The Lake District Visitor Centre at Brockhole, Troutbeck Bridge (NW of Windermere). Tel: 015394 46601.
● Tennis Courts - The Glebe, Glebe Road. Queen's Park, Park Road.

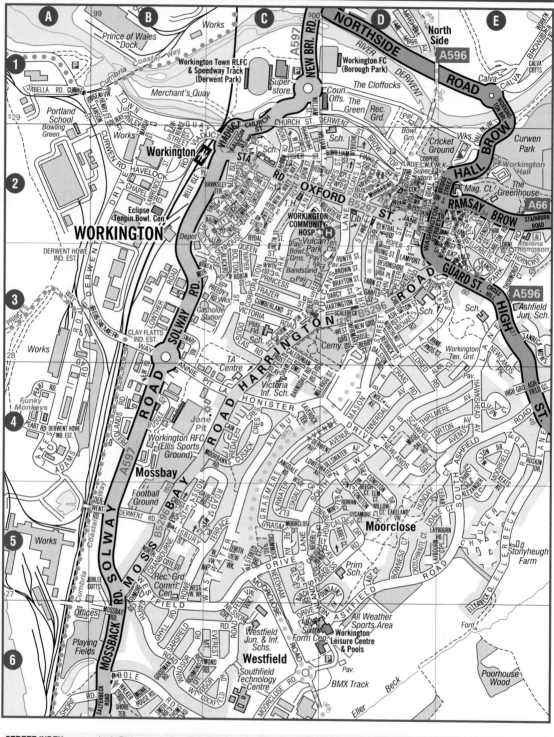

Workington

Workington, situated at the mouth of the River Derwent where it flows into the Solway Firth, and conveniently situated on the Cumbrian Coast Railway, developed from the late 18th century, with the exploitation of the local iron-ore and coalfields. With the first colliery opening in 1780, and the Lonsdale Dock built in 1865 facilitating trade with Ireland and America, it grew to become a major industrial town and port, achieving the height of its prosperity in the second half of the 19th century.

Promoted by the local landed gentry, the Curwen family of Workington Hall (see below), in the same way that rival mine owners the Senhouses' and Lonsdales' created the ports of Maryport and Whitehaven respectively, it developed an iron and steel manufacturing industry, with the first iron works, the Workington Haematite Iron Company Ltd., one of 6 to eventually be built in the area, opening on 6th November 1856. In 1882/3, the Derwent Iron and Steel Company and its port facilities, situated south of the River Derwent, was acquired by the well known Charles Cammel and Company.

All these developments resulted in a southwards urban expansion of the town to house the workers, however in the second half of the 20th century a period of decline began, with in 1981 the Derwent blast-furnaces being demolished, following closure of the iron manufacturing part of the Moss Bay Ironworks, marking the end of 125 years of iron-making in the town.

Although the blast furnaces have long disappeared and steelmaking has now also ceased, railmaking using reheated imported 4.4 tonne steel blooms continues at the CorusRail plant. For a short time in the mid 19th century Workington was also a centre for shipbuilding.

Workington has in more recent times diversified into light and service industries and has a small marina at Harrington to the south. The harbour area has recently become the subject of a rejuvenation bid, with the best view in the north-west along the north bank of the River Derwent at Oldside picnic site (next to the Oldside wind turbine cluster), off Northside Road.

The town has many associations with the Curwen family, with Curwen Street, and the elegant Portland Square, built in the 18th century, previously a focal point of the town, named after John Curwen's political allies. Workington is a busy shopping centre, with a pedestrianised shopping precinct, and is culturally represented by the Carnegie Theatre and Carnegie Arts Centre on Finkle Street. An exploration of the town can be made by using the town trails available from the tourist information centre.

Workington is a start point (see also Whitehaven description) of the 'Coast to Coast' cycle route (which runs to Sunderland or Tynemouth), and is also on the Cumbria Cycleway, linked with the West Cumbria cycle network using routes on disused railway lines. The 'medieval' Curwen Fair is held annually in May at Workington Hall.

Early Closing- Thursday (most shops stay open).
Market Days- St John's Precinct (outdoor), Wednesdays, Saturdays.

PLACES OF INTEREST
Tourist Information Centre (All year) - 2D. 21 Finkle Street. Tel: 01900 606699.
● CUMBRIA COASTAL WAY - 6A to 3A, and 1A to 1C.
● CURWEN PARK MINIATURE RAILWAY - 2E. Miniature railway operated by the West Cumbria Guild of Model Engineers, usually on Sundays in season, located at the side of Workington Hall in Curwen Park. Curwen Park, Hall Brow.
● FUNKY MONKEYS FUN FACTORY - 4A. Indoor soft play centre for children aged 10 and under. Slides, ball pool, trampolines, play house etc. Unit 12, Peart Road, Derwent Howe Industrial Estate. Tel: 01900 64222.
● HELENA THOMPSON MUSEUM - 2E. A small local history museum for Workington, in a fine Georgian house bequeathed in 1940 to the people of Workington by Helena Thompson, a local philanthropist, whose family were connected with the building since the late 18th century. Many of the displays reflect the interests of the family and their way of life with family possessions, portraits, collections of pottery, silver and glass and period furniture from Georgian to Victorian times. Also information on the Curwen family of Workington Hall (see below), with a large scale model of the hall, displays on social and industrial history covering coal-mining, shipbuilding, railways and the town's iron and steel industry. Park End Road. Tel: 01900 326255.
● JANE PIT - 4C. Roofless steam powered beam winding engine house and chimney of a coal-mine built in the 19th century by the wealthy landowner Henry Curwen of Workington Hall (see below). A scheduled ancient monument, it is the best surviving example of the ornate

castellated style of colliery architecture . With the circular earthwork remains of a horse gin, south of the winding engine house, it is also a rare example of a coal mine that demonstrates the evolution of horse-powered winding to steam power, the transition taking place here in 1843. The pit closed in 1875 when pumping was discontinued after the sea disastrously broke into the mine workings. The remains were the subject of a drawing by L.S. Lowry. Annie Pit Lane / Mossbay Road.
● WORKINGTON HALL - 2E. Ruins of the ancestral seat of the Curwen family, lords of the manor of Workington. Started as a defensive pele tower c.1362, battlemented walls and a stone gatehouse were added in the late 14th and early 15th centuries, being developed in the 1780s into a beautiful and large manor house. Occupied by the Curwens up until 1929, in WW2 it was badly damaged by fire.
The ruins of what is now the most important secular historic building in Workington, include the 15th century Justices Hall, banqueting hall, family chapel, kitchens, cellars and the room in which Mary Queen of Scots sought refuge. The house was the main home of Fletcher Christian's cousin Isabella and her husband (and another of Fletcher's cousins) John Curwen. Closed to the Public, External view only. Curwen Park, Hall Brow.

ENTERTAINMENT
● Cinemas - The Plaza Cinemas, Dunmail Park Shopping Centre, Maryport Road (N Workington). Tel: 01900 870001.
● Libraries - Vulcan's Lane. Tel: 01900 325170. Workington Sixth Form Centre, Needham Drive, Moorclose. Tel: 01900 325190.
● Theatres - Carnegie Theatre, Carnegie Arts Centre, Finkle Street. Tel: 01900 602122. Theatre Royal, Washington Street. Tel: 01900 603161.

SPORT & LEISURE
● Bowling Greens - The Cloffocks, Brow Top. Vulcan Park, Vulcan's Lane.
● Children's Entertainment - Vulcan Park, Vulcan's Lane.
● Cricket Grounds - The Cloffocks, Brow Top.
● Golf Courses - Workington Golf Course, Branthwaite Road (18 hole) (SE of Workington). Tel: 01900 603460.
● Parks & Gardens - Curwen Park, Hall Brow. Vulcan Park, Vulcan's Lane.
● Pitch & Putt Courses - Siddick Pond, Northside (N Workington).
● Sports & Leisure Centres - Workington Leisure Centre & Pools, Newlands Lane South, Moorclose. Tel: 01900 61771.
● Stadiums - Workington Speedway, Derwent Park Stadium, New Bridge Road. Tel: 01900 608071 (race days) / 01943 878448 (office hours).
● Swimming Pools - Workington Leisure Centre & Pools, Newlands Lane South, Moorclose (indoor). Tel: 01900 61771.
● Tennis Courts - Vulcan Park, Vulcan's Lane. Workington Tennis Ground, Newlands Lane.
● Ten Pin Bowling - Eclipse Tenpin Bowling Centre, 4 Derwent Howe Industrial Estate, Derwent Drive. Tel: 01900 872207.

GUIDE TO PLACES OF INTEREST

HOW TO USE THE PLACE OF INTEREST GUIDE

Places of interest are represented by the appropriate symbol on the map together with red text in a yellow box. The index reference is to the square in which the symbol (or its pointer) appears, not to the box text; e.g. **Calder Abbey -3D 21**, is to be found in square 3D on page21.

Entries shown without a main map index reference have the name of the appropriate town plan on which they appear, with an index reference for that plan.
The extent of these town plans are indicated on the main map by a blue box.

Terms such as 'museum', 'country park' etc are omitted from the text on the map.
Entries in italics are not named on the map but are shown with a symbol only.

Entries in italics and enclosed in brackets are not shown on the map.
For both these types of entry the nearest village or town name is given, where that name is not already included in the name of the place of interest.

Places of interest that are open for the summer season only are shown with an S symbol after the index reference.

Opening times for places of interest vary considerably depending on the season, day of the week or the ownership of the property. Please check opening times before starting your journey.

EH, English Heritage Site.
NT, National Trust Property - Always open.
NT, National Trust Property - Restricted opening.
NP, National Park Property - Always open.

Tourist Information Centre

Ambleside -see Ambleside plan -2B, Tel: 015394 32582.
Appleby-in-Westmorland -see Appleby-in-Westmorland plan -3B, Tel: 017683 51177.
Arnside -3D 37, Tel: 01524 761228.
Bowness-on-Windermere -see Windermere plan -5B, Tel: 015394 42895.
Broughton in Furness -1C 35, S, Tel: 01229 716115.
Cockermouth -see Cockermouth plan -2C, Tel: 01900 822634.
Egremont -see Egremont plan -3C, Tel: 01946 820693.
Grange-over-Sands -see Grange-over-Sands plan -2C, Tel: 015395 34026.
Kendal -see Kendal plan -3C, Tel: 01539 725758.
Keswick -see Keswick plan -3C, Tel: 017687 72645.
Killington Lake Services, M6 (Southbound), Killington -3D 33, S, Tel: 015396 20138.
Maryport -1A 12, Tel: 01900 813738.
Millom -2B 34, S, Tel: 01229 774819.
Penrith -see Penrith plan -3C, Tel: 01768 867466.
Redhills (Rheged), Penrith -2D 17, Tel: 01768 860034.
Sellafield, Calder Bridge -3C 21, Tel: 019467 76510.
Ullswater, Glenridding -1B 24, Tel: 017684 82414.
Ulverston -see Ulverston plan -3B, Tel: 01229 587120.
Whitehaven -see Whitehaven plan -3B, Tel: 01946 852939.
Windermere -see Windermere plan -1D, Tel: 015394 46499.
Workington -see Workington plan -2D, Tel: 01900 606699.

Abbey / Friary / Priory

See also Church / Chapel
Calder Abbey -3D 21. First founded in 1134 for monks from Furness Abbey, situated on the north bank of the River Calder, it is regarded as one of the most beautiful of ruins. With a turbulent early history, being attacked on more than one occasion by Scottish border raiders, the monastery surviving until the Dissolution which occurred here c.1536, when Henry VIII dissolved 380 of the lesser monasteries. The sandstone ruins date from the 13th century and include a substantial part of the abbey church tower, chapter house and dormitories. The ruins are on private land and are difficult to see, although they may be glimpsed from a public footpath which runs just north of the church in Calder Bridge. By appointment only.
Shap Abbey EH -1A 26. Former Premonstratensian abbey founded here c.1199, home to 12 canons, in a remote and

isolated location by the River Lowther. The monks were also known as 'White Canons' from the colour of their habits. The imposing west tower, dating from c.1500, and ruins of the mainly 13th century abbey church remain, in a delightful peaceful rural location.

Animal collection

See also Farm Park, Wildlife Park, Zoo
Alpaca Centre, The -2D 17, Tel: 01768 891440. Working farm breeding, rearing and selling Peruvian alpacas. View Information on their fibres, history and first introduction to this country. Alpacas are related to llamas, the fibre being valued for its soft but hard wearing nature.
Eden Ostrich World -1B 18, S, Tel: 01768 881771. Large collection of ostriches including African Blacks with opportunities to see eggs hatch. Maze, tractor rides, outdoor and undercover adventure play areas. Riverside walk alongside River Eden.
Knoxwood Wildlife Rescue Trust -1B 10,
Tel: 016973 43812. Specialising in the rescue, rehabilitation and release of all British wild and domestic birds, mammals, amphibians and reptiles, the centre opened in 1981. The only one of its kind in Cumbria, seeing around 2,000 casualties yearly. The work of the centre can be viewed at weekends.
Lakeland Wildlife Oasis -3A 38, Tel: 015395 63027. Animal collection of exotic wildlife with interactive 'hands-on' exhibits, computer displays and projection microscopes, used to view marine life, and fossils. Animals include monkeys, leaf cutter ants, molluscs and snakes. The butterfly house and tropical halls have butterflies, birds, bats, fish, reptiles and mammals.

Aquarium

Aquarium of the Lakes -1B 36, Tel: 01539 530153. Naturally themed habitats of the Lake District featuring the UK's largest collection of freshwater fish. Discover the underwater tunnel featuring giant carp and amazing diving ducks. Learn about the mysterious life of a river after dark and encounter a variety of British mammals including harvest mice, bank voles and brown rats. Visitors can also see playful otters, British sharks and rays. There are breathtaking views across Lake Windermere from the coffee shop.

Lake District Coast Aquarium, The -1A 12,
Tel: 01900 817760. Medium sized aquarium comprising 2,000 specimens of around 200 different species of local marine and freshwater life displayed in 45 different marine habitats filled with local sea water. Displays include a Deep Reef with large cod, Conger Eels and 'Fletcher Christian' Shipwreck. Handling of creatures is allowed at The Rock Pool display, as is gentle stroking of rays at the Ray Pool. Fish feeding takes place 3-4 times daily and there is an adventure playground adjacent.

Arboretum / Botanical Garden

See also Garden
Gowbarrow Park Arboretum, Dockray NT **-3C 17.**
Arboretum, created in 1846 at the lower end of Aira Beck, with over 200 specimen conifers (firs, pines, spruces and cedars) from around the world. It is part of a former Victorian landscaped park, or pleasure garden, set out by the Howard family of Greystoke Castle. They planted a sylvan Victorian glade, landscaped the area around the falls with ash, oak, willow, beech, and alder, and established a network of footpaths and bridges. Away from Aira Beck to the east, the majority of Gowbarrow Park was used as a deer park, with Yew Crag giving views over Ullswater to Place Fell. The 305 hectare park was bought by public subscription by the National Trust in 1906.

Art Gallery

3°W Gallery -see Grasmere plan -4C.
Abbot Hall Art Gallery, Kendal -see Kendal plan -4C.
Beatrix Potter Gallery NT -see Hawkshead plan -2B, S.
Blackwell, The Arts & Crafts House -3A 32, Tel: 015394 46139. Housed in Blackwell (see 'Historic Building and garden' section entry), in the main rooms downstairs are displays of Arts and Crafts furniture, objects and works of art, complementing the original decoration of the house. In the bedrooms upstairs are changing exhibition spaces of the best quality historic and contemporary applied art and craft items.
Brewery Arts Centre -see Kendal plan -4B.
Homes of Football, The, Ambleside
-see Ambleside plan -3B.
Lowes Court Gallery -see Egremont plan -3C.
Theatre by the Lake -see Keswick plan -4B.

Aviary / Bird Garden

Lakeland Bird of Prey Centre -3A 18, S, Tel: 01931 712746. Large collection of over 150 eagles, hawks, falcons and owls from around the world in aviaries, located within a walled garden in the parkland of Lowther Park. Flying displays at 12 noon, 2pm and 4pm.
Leighton Hall Birds of Prey -3D 37, S, Tel: 01524 734474. Small collection of birds of prey in the Aviary Garden of Leighton Hall, including a Russian steppe eagle, saker falcon, owls and harris hawk, some of which have lived at the hall for nearly 20 years. Flying displays at 3.30pm, weather permitting, with information on their breeding, hunting and feeding habits.

World Owl Centre -2C 29, Tel: 01229 717393. Set in the grounds of Muncaster Castle this is the headquarters of the World Owl Trust, a charity dedicated to worldwide owl conservation and whose primary aim is to ensure the survival of all species of the world's owls. The centre is home to one of the most comprehensive collections of owls in the world with over 100 birds of more than 50 different species. A closed circuit tv link in the observation unit enables owls in their nests, and rearing young in the breeding season, to be seen. (see also 'MeadowVole Maze' entry).

Bridges

Ashness Bridge -1D 23. One of the most photographed bridges in the Lake District and England, famous for its views to Derwent Water and the Skiddaw range. The bridge carries the narrow no-through road to the popular hamlet of Watendlath, over the tumbling rock strewn course of Barrow Beck which rises on Bleaberry Fell. Probably a former packhorse bridge, it carries a heavy burden of traffic over its narrow width.
Birks Bridge -2A 30. A narrow single segmental arch of around 3.5 m (11.5 ft) span crossed by a bridleway, scenically bridging a natural rock gorge on the River Duddon. Forest Commission walks, car park and picnic site ensure the popularity of this location.
Boot Packhorse Bridge -1D 29. 17th century or early 18th century stone built packhorse bridge of roadway width, leading to Eskdale Mill, crossing Whillan Beck in an 8 m (27 ft) span.
Eskdale (Doctor) Bridge -1D 29. An original narrow packhorse bridge of some 10 m (33 ft) width spanning the River Esk, remodelled in the first half of the 18th century by a local doctor (hence the name) from Penny Hill to provide access for horse drawn carriages. The original upstream version can be seen by looking underneath the arch.
Monks Bridge -2D 21. Ancient narrow turf covered packhorse bridge crossing the River Calder in remote countryside 3 miles upstream of Calder Abbey. Spanning a small gorge with no parapets this listed structure has a pointed arch, not the most stable of structures, spanning about 6 m (20 ft).
Sedgwick Aqueduct -1A 38. Short but massive listed stone aqueduct on the 'Northern Reaches', the disused section, of the Lancaster Canal. Engineered by John Rennie, the 57 mile long canal was begun in Preston in 1792 and finally reached Kendal in 1826, the bridges and aqueducts being typical of his usual massive classical scale. Steps lead up to the canal where the towpath and dry aqueduct trough can be seen. The former towpath can be followed southwards, or the 4 miles north to Kendal.
Slaters Packhorse Bridge -1C 31. Extremely picturesque footbridge over the River Brathay (Little Langdale Beck) just downstream from Little Langdale Tarn, the most famous packhorse bridge in Cumbria. The bridge consists of a two span clapper bridge followed by a shallow rustic arch, with untrimmed arch stones projecting above the rough surface of

the roadway, all guarded by a crooked iron handrail on one side. A model of the bridge can be found at the Lakeland Miniature Village.

Sosgill Packhorse Bridge -3A 16. Little visited stone packhorse bridge with segmental arch over St John's Beck in the quiet of St John's in the Vale.

Stockley Packhorse Bridge NT -2C 23. Packhorse bridge, with an arch of around 5 m (16 ft) span, across Grains Gill on the old packhorse route from Seathwaite (in Borrowdale) over the Sty Head pass to Wasdale. Widened in 1887 to nearly 2 m (6.5 ft), the bridge was restored in the same style, after it was badly damaged in the severe Borrowdale floods of August 1966. 'Stockley' means a 'woodland clearing', much of the district having been heavily forested until the late Middle Ages. The bridge, with its distant view of Taylorgill Force, is a landmark today as the gateway to popular high level walks on the fells starting from Seatoller and Seathwaite Farm.

Throstle Garth (Lingcove) Packhorse Bridge -1A 30. Beautifully sited former packhorse bridge across Lingcove Beck just before its confluence with the River Esk with its series of cascades and waterfalls. The 6.5 m (21 ft), 1.2 m (4 ft) wide span provides access into Upper Eskdale and is a good stopping off place if heading to Sty Head.

Wasdale Head Packhorse Bridge -3B 22. Crossing Mosedale Beck behind the Wasdale Head Inn, this narrow bridge, with no parapets, has a shallow span of approximately 8 m (26 ft).

Watendlath Packhorse Bridge -1D 23. Much photographed like Ashness Bridge this is a fine (foot only) packhorse bridge spanning Watendlath Beck at the outfall of Watendlath Tarn, just downstream of a shallow ford, connecting Rosthwaite and Wythburn (Thirlmere). With a width of approximately 1 m (3.3 ft) and span of 7 m (23 ft) the parapets were added in the early 20th century.

Castle

See also Castle and Garden
Appleby Castle -see Appleby-in-Westmorland plan -4C, S.
Brougham Castle EH -2A 18, S, Tel: 01768 862488. Ruins of a castle constructed on the site of a former Roman fort (see 'Brocavum Roman Fort' entry). Rebuilding work, notably the tower, was undertaken by Henry II in the early 13th century. Vital during the protracted Anglo-Scottish border wars and subsequent skirmishes, and also during the Wars of the Roses, its military usefulness diminished after medieval times with consequent periods of neglect. Although the 4 storey keep is now open to the elements, it may be climbed to the small private chapel, or oratory, on the top floor. Introductory exhibition.

Castle Howe -see Kendal plan -4B.
Cockermouth Castle -see Cockermouth plan -2C.
Dacre Castle -see Historic Building section.
Dalton Castle NT -3C 35, S, Tel: 01524 701178. Situated on one side of the former market square Dalton Castle was built to defend Dalton-in-Furness and the approaches to Furness Abbey, the present 14th century building being basically a rectangular 14 m (46 ft) by 9 m (30 ft) non-domestic pele tower with limestone walls up to 1.8 m (6 ft) thick. It is thought to have been built at the instruction of the abbot of the nearby Furness Abbey, one of the most powerful, landowners of the time. Its main use was however as a prison and courthouse which it remained until 1774 and 1925 respectively. Extensively altered inside in the 18th and 19th centuries resulting in only 2 floors from the original 4, it was given to the National Trust in 1965 by the 8th Duke of Buccleuch.

Egremont Castle -see Egremont plan -4B.
Greystoke Castle -see Historic Building section.
Kendal Castle -see Kendal plan -4D.
Lowther Castle -see Historic Building section.

Millom Castle -2B 34. Originally a manor house, the Huddleston family were granted a license to crenelate and fortify by King Edward III in 1335. A massive tower, 15 m (49 ft) square with 2 m (6.5 ft) thick walls, was added in the 16th century and is part occupied by the present house, approached by a noticeable wide flight of steps on the east front. Exterior view only.

Penrith Castle EH -see Penrith plan -4C.

Castle & Garden

See also Castle
Appleby Castle -see Appleby-in-Westmorland plan -4C, S.
Muncaster Castle -see Historic Building and Garden section.
Sizergh Castle -see Historic Building and Garden section.

Children's Play Centre

Billy Bears Fun Centre -see Whitehaven plan -4A.
Clown About -1C 15, Tel: 017687 76239. Indoor soft play and climbing area for 4-12 year olds. 2 levels of interconnected padded walkways, rope bridges, slides, steps and ball pools. Dedicated under 4's area. Housed within Trotters World of Animals.
Fun For Kids Fun Factory -see Kendal plan -5D.
Funky Monkeys Fun Factory -see Workington plan -4A.
Giddy Kiddy's Fun Factory -3C 33, Tel: 01539 741377. Indoor soft play centre for children aged 10 and under. Dual level play structure including a rope bridge, slide, ball pool and bouncy castle. Dedicated under 4's area.
(Noah's Ark Softplay Centre, Penrith) -see Penrith plan -3D.
(Rheged Indoor Play Centre, Penrith) -2D 17, *Tel: 01768 868000. Indoor soft play area for children under 1.37 m (4 ft 6"). Small ball pool for under 1 year olds and separate under 5s area. Housed within Rheged.*

Church / Chapel

See also Abbey
Brougham St Ninian's Church -2B 18. Small low edifice (known as 'Ninekirks') in a lonely situation on the south bank of the River Eamont, on the site of former Saxon and Norman churches. Unusual as it has remained virtually unchanged since 1660 when it was rebuilt by Lady Anne Clifford. Access via a 1 mile long signposted track across fields from the Appleby road.
Brougham St Wilfred's Church -2A 18. Simple low buttressed sandstone building with bellcote, nave and chancel built by Lady Anne Clifford in the mid 17th century when she inherited the Brougham estate. Inside exceptional medieval and continental woodwork and carvings can be found. Connected by a small bridge over road from Brougham Hall.
Caldbeck St Kentigern's Church -3C 11. St Kentigern's (begun in 1112) is noted for its churchyard which famously holds, close to its west wall, the plain grave of Mary Harrison (maiden name Robinson), the celebrated 'Beauty of Buttermere', and the elaborate white tombstone, decorated with hunting horns and whips of John Peel, the celebrated huntsman. Also to be seen is the well / spring of St Mungo (or Kentigern), used for baptisms in the 6th century, which can be found near the churchyard on the banks of Cald Beck.
Cartmel Priory Church -3B 36, Tel: 015395 36261. Remaining part of a priory founded in 1188 by Augustinian canons and built between 1190 and 1220, regarded as one of the finest ecclesiastical buildings in the north of England and known as 'The Cathedral of the Lakes'. The towers top stage is uniquely set on the diagonal. Inside the plain massive arches of the nave lead to a fine 17th century Renaissance screen, magnificent Perpendicular east window containing 15th century

stained glass. Regular tours are held every Wednesday from May to the end of October at 11am and 2pm.

Dacre St Andrew's Church -2D 17. Church dating from the 12th century, with some Viking fragments, on site of a Saxon monastery. The church is famous for its 4 curious ancient carved stone 'bears', of unknown origin, within the churchyard.

Eskdale St Catherine's Church, Boot -1D 29. Typical small dale chapel in an isolated and picturesque setting by the River Esk with ancient stepping stones, and Scafell Pike as a backdrop. Built of local Eskdale granite in the 12th century and extensively rebuilt in 1881, this beautiful building contains interesting stained glass and an octagonal font decorated with 14th century St Catherine's wheel and pagan motifs.

Greystoke St Andrew's Church -1C 17. Large late Perpendicular style church with massive squat tower begun by the 14th Baron of Greystoke Castle. A church was first recorded here in 1255, with the present building begun in 1382 and finished in the 15th century. In the chancel is a tomb on which reclines 2 alabaster effigies of knights in armour, barons of Greystoke Castle, whilst the east window is notable for its fine medieval stained glass. There is a 900 year old yew in the churchyard and a 'Sanctuary Stone' on the approach road (Church Road).

Keld Chapel NT -2B 26. Tiny medieval chantry chapel thought to date from c.1350, initially a part of Shap Abbey. Chantry chapels were where prayers were said for the departed souls of rich patrons. Given to the National Trust in 1918, the simply furnished building is still consecrated and used for the occasional service. Key in village; notice on chapel door.

Kendal Holy Trinity Parish Church -see Kendal plan -4C.

Lowther St Michael's Church, Askham -3A 18. Isolated, originally early 13th century church, rebuilt to a more elegant plan by Sir John Lowther in 1696. Inside the church are memorials to Sir John and other members of the Lowther family. The sizeable mausoleum of William Lowther, the second Earl of Lonsdale, who died in 1844, is also situated in the churchyard.

Martindale St Martin's Church -1C 25. Typical small 17th century dale chapel set in peaceful and isolated countryside on the dead-end road to Bannerdale east of Ullswater. Rebuilt in 1633, this simple building with combined nave and chancel, porch, low roof, simple bellcote and plain leaded glass has a sparse interior with a combined lectern and pulpit of 1634. This church is known for its strikingly colourful contemporary stained glass windows (15 in all) of 1975 by Jane Gray (born 1931). Behind St Martin's is the Martindale Yew.

Morland St Laurence's Church -3B 18. Medieval church (mainly 13th-15th centuries) with Early English transepts and notable 1920s east window. The church is unique in having the only 11th century Anglo-Saxon church tower in Cumbria.

Rydal St Mary's Church -3B 24. Built on the site of an orchard beneath Nab Scar in 1824 by the le Fleming family of Rydal Hall (see 'Rydal Hall Gardens' entry), this small church has close links with William Wordsworth, who helped in its location and design when he lived at nearby Rydal Mount. He was Church Warden from 1833-4, worshipping here regularly until his death in 1850. Built on rocky ground, no burials could take place here, the churchyard having been recently made into the Rydal Millennium Garden. A gate from here leads into Dora's Field.

St Bees Priory Church -2B 20. The priory church of St Mary and St Bega is all that remains of a small Benedictine monastery on a Christian site reputed to have been established by St Bega, an Irish princess, said to have fled here in the mid 7th century to escape an arranged marriage to a Norse prince. The superb Norman west doorway with its 5 concentric zig-zag carved arches and Norman nave arcades

are of note. The priory church is famous for the discovery by archaeologists in 1981 of the extremely well-preserved body of 'St Bees Man'. Found in a vault, the body, thought to have been buried here between 1290 and 1500, was enclosed in a parcel of bees-wax treated cloth within a lead wrapper. The priory church is also known for its organ built in 1899, the last major instrument made by the famous organ builder 'Father' Henry Willis who was responsible for, amongst many others, those in the Royal Albert Hall and St Paul's Cathedral.

Torpenhow St Michael's Church -3A 10. Small church, with bellcote, built in 1120 of very simple construction with aisleless nave and chancel separated by an arch, a rare survival being one of the few remaining unspoilt 12th century churches. Thought to date back to a Saxon foundation, and carefully restored.

Troutbeck Jesus Church -1A 32. Situated by the busy main road from Patterdale to Windermere in the Trout Beck valley bottom a quarter of a mile remote from the current village, this

church, with its yew trees and rebuilt building dating from 1736, would be unremarkable if it were not for its east window of 1873. Its exceptionally clear and colourful stained glass is a notable example of the Pre-Raphaelite style and was designed by the famous painter and illustrator Sir Edward Burne-Jones.

Wasdale St Olaf's Church, Wasdale Head - 3B 22. Small unadorned church probably of 16th century date hidden amidst yew trees. Said to be the third smallest church in England, which prior to restoration in 1892 had earthen floors and no glass in the windows, some of the roof beams are reputed to come from a Viking longship. The churchyard has the graves of climbers who died on the local fells. A south window has in one of its small leaded diamond shaped panes a memorial by the Fell and Rock Climbing Club with an image of Napes Needle. Founded in 1906-7, the club was formed to encourage rock climbing and fell walking in the English Lake District, Wasdale Head being the birthplace of rock-climbing as a sport in 1886 .

Whitehaven St James' Church -see Whitehaven plan -3C.

Country Park

Bardsea Country Park -3A 36. 32 hectare coastal country park, with oak-beech woodland and picnic areas, and 1.5 miles of shoreline. Sea views over Morecambe Bay. The Cumbria Coastal Way long distance footpath runs through the site.

Fell Foot Park NT -1B 36, Tel: 015395 31273. 7 hectare landscaped gardens and parkland (given to the National Trust in 1948) of a long demolished house dating back to the 1780s. Restored to their former glory, the typical formal late Victorian gardens have impressive spring and early summer displays of daffodils, followed by rhododendrons, whilst oaks and pines inhabit the lake shore. The park offers an adventure playground, rowing boat hire and lake swimming as well as extensive picnic areas with views of the Lakeland fells. A short 5 minute ferry crossing to Lakeside Pier (see Windermere lake description) opposite is also possible in the summer season.

Farm Park / Open Farm

See also Animal Collection, Wildlife Park, Zoo
Abbott Lodge Jersey Ice Cream Farm -3A 18, S, Tel: 01931 712720. A working dairy farm set in spectacular scenery which produces over 30 flavours of high quality delicious homemade ice cream. Tearoom, indoor and outdoor play areas and calf viewing. Function room for hire by group visits or meetings. Disabled facilities, ample parking.
Thornby Moor Dairy -1C 11, Tel: 016973 45555. Cumbria's only specialist cheesemaker making handmade Cumberland cheese, using milk from a local herd of Diary Shorthorns, and smaller quantities of goats' milk cheeses. Cheesemaking was first started in 1979. The processes whereby the cheese is made can be seen. Sample tasting.

Forest Park / National Park

Grizedale Forest Park -3C 31. Tel: 01229 860010. Located between Lake Windermere and Coniston Water (near to Hawkshead) this is the largest forest in the Lake District, covering almost 2,500 hectares. It is a working forest run by the Forestry Commission and the majority is planted with spruce and larch, although over 15% is broad-leaved woodland and this is increasing. The forest is home to wildlife such as red squirrel, red and roe deer. There are many visitor facilities (see 'Grizedale Visitor Centre' entry) such as walking and cycle trails. Grizedale is also one of the country's best sites for outdoor sculpture with over seventy site inspired works being scattered throughout the forest.
Lake District National Park -3D 23, Tel: 01539 724555. Established as a national park in 1951, one of currently 13 national parks in Britain. The Lake District National Park in Cumbria, overseen by the Lake District National Park Authority, covers an area of 885 square miles stretching from the west coast, between Ravenglass and Silecroft, to the M6 in the east. It possesses a unique combination of the highest mountain in England (Scafell Pike), rugged fells, lakes, numerous tarns, and pastoral and wooded valleys. Mostly Forestry Commission owned, with National Trust land comprising nearly a quarter of the park. The Lake District holds the record for the wettest inhabited place in England! Its landscape, with numerous fell walking opportunities, history, natural history and cultural associations attracts around 12 million visitors per year, placing great pressure on the environment in the peak tourist season.
Whinlatter Forest Park -2C 15, Tel: 017687 78469. England's only true mountain forest, 1,200 ha, rising to 791 m (2,595 ft) above sea level (at Grisedale Pike), located on 2 separate sites, Thornthwaite Forest at the east end of the Whinlatter Pass, and Dodd Wood, north-west of Keswick above Bassenthwaite Lake. One of the Forestry Commission's oldest forests planted just after WW1. The forest is home to wildlife such as badgers, foxes, roe deer and the increasingly rare red squirrel and includes the waterfall of Spout Force.

Forest Walk / Nature Trail

See also Nature Reserve
Arnside Knott Nature Walk NT -3C 37. 2.5 mile circular trail over 43 hectare hill. Arnside Knott is known for its mixture of southern and northern plant species at the edge of their ranges. Woodland birds and red squirrel may also be seen.
Ash Landing Nature Trail NT -2D 31. Nature trail from National Trust car park on Ferry Hill exploring Ash Landing Nature Reserve opposite.
Blengdale Forest Walks -3D 21. Informal Forestry Commission walks in quite, mature conifer forest plantation adjacent to the River Bleng. Access is on foot from the village of Gosforth.
Bogle Crag Walk -3C 31. Forestry Commission waymarked walk starting at Bogle Crag car park- long walk (3 miles) and short walk (2.5 miles). The trail starts in ancient broad-leaved woodland and then passes through mixed coniferous woodland with ancient beech trees. One of the most well-known forest sculptures- 'Taking a Wall for a Walk' can be seen.

Brantwood Nature Trail -2C 31, Tel: 015394 41396. Over 3 miles of varied walks around the Brantwood estate including a nature walk through woodland to the south of the house, joining onto the estate walk which leads over moorland to the summit of Crag Head.
Broughton Moor Forest Walks -3A 30. Informal Forestry Commission walks in a remote fellside conifer forest either side of Appletree Worth Beck on an unclassified road from Torver to Broughton Mills. The ancient settlement of 'The Hawk' is at the south-west end of the forest and there are views south to the Duddon Estuary.
Brown Robin Nature Trail
-see Grange-over-Sands plan -1D.
Comb Forest Trails -3C 15. 2 Forestry Commission waymarked walks starting at the Whinlatter Visitor Centre car park- the Comb Forest Trail (1.75 miles, marked in red) and Comb Gill Trail (1.75 miles, marked in blue).
Crosscanonby Carr Nature Trail -1B 12. 370 m (405 yds) 6 point nature trail around Crosscanonby Carr Nature Reserve, part on boardwalks, starting from the toilets.
Dodd Wood Forest Walks -2C 15. 3 Forestry Commission waymarked walks starting at Dodd Wood car park. Also here is a picnic site and the Old Sawmill Tearoom, with the history of the building and area outlined on the walls, and displays of old photographs and forest tools. Dodd Wood, leased from the Mirehouse Estate, is part of Whinlatter Forest Park. Guides are available from the tearoom and Whinlatter Visitor Centre.
Dorothy Farrer's Spring Wood Nature Trail -2B 32. Waymarked path around Dorothy Farrer's Spring Wood Nature Reserve with information boards.
Dowpitts Wood Nature Trail -see Appleby-in-Westmorland plan -4A.
Eaves Wood Nature Trail NT -3D 37. 2 mile nature trail leading to the plateau summit of Castlebarrow Head (marked by the Pepper Pot, a tiny stone round tower with conical roof, built as a jubilee memorial), running through a 43 hectare mixed woodland of oak, ash, small-leaved lime, beech and yew. Great spotted woodpecker, woodcock and red squirrel may be seen. Areas of limestone pavement.
Ennerdale Forest Trails -1A 22. 3 Forestry Commission waymarked walks starting at Bowness Knott car park. A guide map can be obtained from Whinlatter Visitor Centre.
Gait Barrows Nature Trail -3D 37. 1.5 mile nature trail along permitted paths through Gait Barrows National Nature Reserve. Trail leaflets on site, signs and interpretation panels. There is no car park or other facilities.

Grizedale Forest Walks -3C 31. *Five waymarked trails start from the Grizedale Visitor Centre (see separate entry). These range from the one mile long Ridding Wood Trail (blue markers) along a surfaced route suitable for wheelchairs, to the ten mile Silurian Way (green markers) which covers a large part of the forest and takes in many of Grizedale's famous sculptures. Intermediate walks include the Carron Crag trail (red markers) which climbs to the highest point in the forest (314m, 1,030 ft) with panoramic views to Morecambe Bay and The Old Man of Coniston. Three different trails start from other forest car parks. A guide is available from the Visitor Centre.*

Hardknott Forest Forest Walks -2A 30. Series of Forestry Commission waymarked walks of varying lengths in Hardknott (or Dunnerdale) Forest. A footpath from the car park crosses Birks Bridge and follows the west bank of the River Duddon southwards below Long Crag through the scenic Wallowbarrow Gorge to Seathwaite.

High Bowkerstead Walk -3C 31. Forestry Commission waymarked walk starting at Blind Lane car park- long walk (4 miles) and short walk (2 miles). The trail passes Force Falls, gives views across the village of Satterthwaite, the Grizedale valley and surrounding fell tops, and takes in the quiet valley of Dale Park.

Launchy Gill Forest Trail -1A 24. Starting beside the minor road half way along the west side of Thirlmere. Included is the Tottling Stone, a 2.75 m (9 ft) high boulder, thought to have been deposited by a retreating glacier. A leaflet should be available from a box at the start or from Swirls car park (see 'Swirls Forest Trail' entry).

Leighton Moss Bird Sanctuary Nature Trails -3D 37. 2 nature trails (short trail of 0.5 miles and long trail of 2 miles) around Leighton Moss Bird Sanctuary.

Machell's Coppice Walk -2C 31. Forestry Commission waymarked walk starting at Machell's Coppice car park. The route passes through mixed broad-leaved and coniferous woodland. There are views over Coniston Water, with boat launching facilities.

Miterdale Forest Walk -1C 29. Informal Forestry Commission walks from Eskdale Green or the car park in Miterdale Forest through extensive areas of native oakwoods and mature mixed conifers beside the River Mite. Miterdale opens up at its upper end into a quiet little visited valley with small waterfalls. It is followed by a bridleway to the bleak Burnmoor Tarn with Wasdale beyond.

Noble Knott Forest Walks, Braithwaite -3C 15. *2 Forestry Commission waymarked walks starting at Noble Knott car park- (1 mile, marked in yellow and 1.75 miles, marked in white). Conifers planted in the late 1950s can be found here with ancient oaks along Masmill Beck. Grisedale Pike (791 m or 2,595 ft) can be reached from here. Opposite are views to Dodd Wood and Skiddaw.*

Revelin Moss Trail -3C 15. Forestry Commission waymarked walk starting at Revelin Moss car park (1.75 miles, marked in yellow). At the foot of Grisedale Pike, this is the easiest trail in the Whinlatter Forest. Also running from here is the Grisedale Pike (High Level) Walk (3-3.5 miles), unwaymarked, but junction marked, to the summit of Grisedale Pike (791 m or 2,595 ft). Revelin Moss is home to Europe's first permanent Trail Orienteering Course (The trail 'O'), using an easy terrain route along forest roads and paths for the less mobile.

Serpentine Woods Nature Trail -see Kendal plan -3B.

Setmurthy Forest Walks -1B 14. Informal Forestry Commission walks in developing woodland, with views north over the Derwent Valley.

Swirls Forest Trail -1A 24. Starting from Swirls car park on the east side of Thirlmere, this 0.75 mile interpretation trail explains the forestry practice and natural history of the area. A leaflet should be available from the information board. Swirls

car park is popular as a starting point for a relative safe route to the summit of Helvellyn.

Garden

See also Arboretum, Historic Building and Garden

Acorn Bank Garden NT -2C 19, S, Tel: 01768 361893. Tranquil garden (of 1 hectare), surrounded by a high sandstone wall, idyllically situated in the Eden Valley and Pennine foothills, above Crowdundle Beck. Home to the north of England's largest collection of culinary and medicinal plants (over 250 species) in a herb garden which reaches its peak in late June. Two adjacent orchards have a varied collection of rare and regional species of fruit, including old species of apple, damson, pear, quince and medlar. Outside the walled garden, the wild garden has a large display of different varieties of daffodils and wood anemones in early spring, through which paths give access to Acorn Bank Watermill.

Brockhole Gardens -1D 31, Tel: 015394 46601. 12 hectare garden of 1900 to the designs of Thomas Hayton Mawson, around an Edwardian country house built for the Gaddum family by architect Dan Gibson in 1899. Much of Mawson's work remains comprising his west and south facing terraces, undergoing a transition from formal to informal planting as they slope gently to the Windermere shoreline. The lower end of the garden has a lakeshore walk, wildflower meadow, croquet and putting lawns, picnic areas, and there are outdoor trails for children around the grounds, involving searching and navigation skills, together with a large woodland adventure playground. Ferries (see Windermere lake description) run from a jetty to Waterhead Pier, Ambleside (see also 'The Lake District Visitor Centre at Brockhole' entry).

Giggle Alley Japanese Garden -1C 29. Created by Lord James Hall Rea, the owner of the adjacent Gate House mansion, which he built in 1896 as a secluded retreat set above a small tarn, from 1901 the surrounding gardens were set out by the renowned landscape garden architect Thomas Hayton Mawson to rival those at Muncaster Castle. The jewel in the crown of the estate horticulturally was the Japanese Garden at Giggle Alley to the north of the lawns.

Grange-over-Sands Ornamental Gardens -see Grange-over-Sands plan -1D.

Graythwaite Hall Gardens -3D 31, S, Tel: 015395 31248. Former Elizabethan house (not open), surrounded by a 2.5 hectare garden laid out in 1889 by the renowned landscape garden architect Thomas Hayton Mawson. One of his earliest large garden designs it is considered a fine example of his work. Its mostly unaltered rose garden, small Dutch garden, yew hedges and terraces are typical of his style, the rhododendrons, azaleas and other shrubs placing the garden at its height in the spring. There is also a stream, pond and arboretum.

Holehird Gardens -1A 32, Tel: 015394 46008. West facing 4 hectare garden at the southern end of the Troutbeck Valley. The garden occupies the formal garden of the listed Victorian house (not open to the public) and some of the adjoining woodland. The gardens, maintained entirely by volunteers, have been run by the Lakeland Horticultural Society since 1969 with the aim of growing, trialing and selecting plants which are suited to the Lakeland conditions. The rhododendrons and maples are particularly fine in season and the Victorian walled garden has outstanding herbaceous borders and island beds. The garden is home to three national collections; Astilbe, Hydrangea and Polystichum.

Hope Park Gardens -see Keswick plan -3B.

Rydal Hall Gardens -3B 24, Tel: 01539 432050. Rydal New Hall, with views down the Rothay valley, was built by the le Fleming family between the 16th and early 19th centuries. They owned it for nearly 400 years from 1595 to 1970

developing it from a modest farmhouse, extended by Daniel le Fleming around the 1650s, into the current mansion. The formal garden with geometric beds on two levels was designed in 1909 by the renowned landscape garden architect Thomas Hayton Mawson (see Windermere description). The formal garden leads to the surrounding more natural planting and rocky ravine of Rydal Beck with Rydal Falls (Low Fall).
Stagshaw Garden NT -1D 31, S, Tel: 015394 46027. 3.25 hectare woodland garden in the picturesque style created between 1957 and 1978 by the National Trust's former regional agent for the area, Cubby Acland. A fine collection of flowering shrubs, best in the spring, including rhododendrons, azaleas, camellias, magnolias, embothriums, eucryphias and ericaceous trees. It is best to park at Waterhead main car park and walk to the site via Skelghyll Wood.
Winderwath Gardens -2B 18, S, Tel: 01768 88250. 2 hectare plantsman's garden originally laid out at the beginning of the 20th century. There is a Victorian kitchen garden and pond, rockeries and herbaceous borders, and a large collection of Alpine and Himalayan plants including Himalayan poppies, as well as Wellingtonia, cut leaf beech and cedar specimen trees.

Wray Castle Grounds NT -1D 31. One of the most extravagant of the Lake District mansions, built in 1840-7 for the wealthy Liverpool surgeon Dr James Dawson. In 1882, when Beatrix Potter was 16, her family rented the castle on their first visit to the Lakes. The castle, with 34 hectares of surrounding land, was given to the National Trust in 1929 'to preserve the beauty of the shore'. The grounds (but not the castle, except on some pre-arranged open days), with many specimen trees, including a mulberry tree planted by William Wordsworth, are open to the public and are best reached by Windermere Lake Cruises via a jetty on the lake, a walk south through Claife Heights (or Woodland) often being undertaken.

Hill Fort

See also Prehistoric Monument
Carrock Fell Hill Fort -1A 16. Cumbria's largest hill fort atop the flat summit of the remote Carrock Fell (661 m or 2,169 ft). The foundations of the collapsed outer walls, once part of massive oval ramparts, enclose the highest part of the ridge which forms an excellent defensive position with commanding views.
Dunmallard Hill Fort -3D 17. Undistinguished small oval Iron Age hill fort with a deep ditch and rampart, atop a conspicuous wooded concentric hill immediately west of the bridge at Pooley Bridge. 'Dunmallard Hill' means 'hill of slaughter'. A permitted footpath skirts the hill base and from the north side ascends to the top where there are views down Ullswater from the south side (236 m or 774 ft) of the summit fort.
Maiden Castle -3D 17. A circular defended settlement, or fort, of the first millennium BC, 65 m (213 ft) in diameter, built on the side of a hill in a poor defensive position. There is an

information panel. Reached by permitted footpath from Pooley Bridge.

Historic Building

See also Historic Building and Garden
19/20 Irish Street -see Whitehaven plan -4B.
Arnside Tower -3D 37. Ruins of 15th century defensive pele tower, the oldest building in the parish of Arnside, erected to defend Morecambe Bay from marauding Scots. Exterior view only.
Belle Isle -2D 31. Circular neo-classical house designed by the architect John Plaw in 1774 for Mr English, one of the first circular houses in Britain. Built using stone from quarries in the grounds of Cragwood House near Brockhole, it is set on a wooded island on Windermere. Formerly known as the Great Island, in 1781 Mr English sold the house and land for £1720 to John Christian Curwen, who presented it as a present to his wife Isabella, renaming the island in her honour. Both Isabella and her husband were first cousins to Fletcher Christian, the notorious mutineer of 'Mutiny on the Bounty' fame. Exterior view only (from lake)- no landing.
Bridge House NT -see Ambleside plan -2B.
Brougham Hall -2A 18. Fortress-style perimeter walls of the former country mansion of the Brougham family. Repaired in the 17th century by the ubiquitous Lady Anne Clifford, the house was extended by Lord Bougham, Lord Chancellor of England, and became known as the 'Windsor of the North', being visited by King Edward VII and the future King George V on many occasions. Still under restoration, the site contains a craft centre and a museum within its outer walls.
Cartmel Priory Gatehouse NT -3B 36, Tel: 015395 36874. Gatehouse, built c.1330, once the fortified entrance through the medieval walls of Cartmel Priory, providing some protection from Scots border raiders. It successively served as a manorial court, village grammar school and merchant's store. Given to the National Trust in 1946, it is now leased by the Cartmel Village Society as the Cartmel Gatehouse Heritage Centre .
(Castle Dairy, Kendal) -see Kendal plan -2C.
Clifton Hall Pele EH -2A 18. Surviving 3 storey, plus roof, 10 m (33 ft) by 8 m (26 ft) pele tower, of a 15th century manor house, built for protection from Scots border raiders. Interpretation panels. Situated in a farmyard, the keys can be obtained from the adjacent Clifton Hall Farm.
Dacre Castle -2D 17. Good example of a near original rectangular 14th century pele tower, with 20 m (66 ft) high walls, 2 m (7 ft) thick, built for protection against the marauding Scots. Private residence. Exterior view only.
Greystoke Castle -1C 17, Tel: 017684 83722. Greystoke Castle was initially one of the border chain of pele tower fortifications and was crenellated in 1353 by William de Greystoke. The estate of over 1214 hectares is now an outdoor activity centre and venue for corporate and private functions. By appointment only.
Hawkshead Courthouse NT -see Hawkshead plan -1A, S.
Hazelslack Tower -3D 37. Ruins of 14th century defensive pele tower, built to provide protection for farmers and their livestock from raiding Scots. Exterior view only.
Lowther Castle -3A 18. Magnificent façade and shell of a castellated (decorated with turrets and battlements) mansion, set in 200 hectares of landscaped parkland. The mock 'castle' was built between 1806 and 1811. By 1936 the building was in decline, and having become too expensive to maintain, the interior was dismantled in 1957. Exterior view only.
Workington Hall -see Workington plan -2E, S.
Yanwath Hall Pele -2A 18. Low 14th century pele tower, once used as a defence against Scottish border raids, attached to a 15th century hall forming part of a 3 sided farm courtyard. The tower, with its battlements stepped up at the corners, is very well preserved and has changed little since Tudor times. Reached by footpath. Exterior view only.

See also Historic Building, Garden

Blackwell, The Arts & Crafts House -3A 32, Tel: 015394 46139. Blackwell is a rare and important example of an Arts and Crafts house built 1897-1900 to designs by Mackay Hugh Baillie Scott, complete with rich interiors that have survived almost entirely intact. Built, overlooking Windermere as a holiday home for wealthy Manchester brewer Sir Edward Holt, his wife and 5 children, Blackwell represents the crossroads between Victorian and Modern architecture. The now grade I listed house became a girl's preparatory school after WW2, which closed in 1976 after which it was leased to English Nature, until bought and restored by The Lakeland Arts Trust and opened in 2001.

Brantwood -2C 31, Tel: 015394 41396. Brantwood, the home of John Ruskin, one of the greatest figures of the Victorian age, was famous as an intellectual powerhouse, one of the greatest literary and artistic centres in Europe. The house is filled with Ruskin's drawings and watercolours and much of his original furniture, books and personal items. With a unique position high above the eastern shore of Coniston Water, it is one of the most beautifully situated houses in the Lake District. Adjacent to the house are over 100 hectares of gardens, lakeshore, meadows, woodland and moorland including the summit of Crag Head (233 m or 764 ft) with its magnificent views. The Harbour Walk and Trellis Walk welcome visitors arriving by boat at Ruskin's Harbour. This is undoubtedly the best approach, either by Coniston Launch or S.Y. Gondola from Coniston (see Coniston Water lake description). Ruskin's coach and his boat the 'Jumping Jenny' are also preserved in the original coach house and there are other exhibitions in various garden buildings.

Conishead Priory -3A 36, S, Tel: 01229 584029. Built on the site of an Augustinian priory of 1188, itself the site of a leper and poor hospital of 1160, the original ecclesiastical priory was dismantled in 1537 under the Dissolution of the Monasteries, whereupon some of the masonry was used to construct a mansion on the same site. In 1976, the house became the Manjushri Kadampa Meditation Centre, an international residential Buddhist college and the mother centre of New Kadampa Tradition, complete with Buddhist temple in the grounds. Visitors are given an audio-visual show and guided tour by the residents of the restored house.

Dalemain -2D 17, S, Tel: 017684 86450. Mansion with pink ashlar façade, home to the Hasell family since 1679. Inside are grand Georgian public rooms, Tudor passages, a Victorian nursery and housekeeper's room (complete with hiding hole), fine furniture, family portraits, ceramics, dolls' houses and old toys. The gardens include terrace and rose walks, Tudor knott garden and a wild garden with huge Himalayan Poppies in early summer. Parkland with fallow deer and red squirrels surrounds the house, whilst a short woodland walk exits from the garden through Lob's Wood above Dacre Beck. A public footpath provides a 1 mile walk to Dacre Castle and church.

Derwent Island House NT -see Keswick plan -5B, S.

Dove Cottage -see Grasmere plan -3C.

Hill Top -2D 31, S, Tel: 015394 36269. Hill Top, a small 17th century stone farmhouse, was bought by the famous children's author Beatrix Potter in 1905 with the royalties from her first books. Six subsequent 'Tales' contain illustrations based on the farm and surrounding countryside - the scenes are similar today. Traditional cottage garden and Beatrix Potter themed shop. Timed tickets. House is closed on Thursdays and Fridays. Original illustrations are displayed at the Beatrix Potter Gallery nearby.

Holker Hall -3B 36, S, Tel: 015395 58328. Victorian sandstone red rose coloured neo-Elizabethan style house, one of the finest in Lakeland. Still home to the Cavendish family, hence some of the house remains private. Rooms on view include the library, drawing room, dining room and carved cantilevered staircase, filled with a fine collection of European furniture, paintings, sculpture, carvings, carpets, tapestries, fireplaces and ornate ceilings. Surrounding the house is a large 50 hectare deer park and 10 hectare part woodland, part formal gardens. There are also woodland walks, one of the largest and finest common limes in Britain, with massive fluted trunk of 8m (26 ft) girth, thought to have been planted as part of a formal garden in the early 18th century, as well as an adventure playground and the Lakeland Motor Museum, containing The Campbell Legend Bluebird Exhibition.

Hutton-in-the-Forest -1D 17, S, Tel: 01768 484449. Historic house based on a medieval pele tower with substantial additions in the 17th, 18th and 19th centuries. Fine collections of furniture, tapestry, portraits and ceramics. Beautiful walled garden with herbaceous beds and trained fruit. Extensive topiary on terraces overlooking surrounding woodland. Home of the Inglewood family since 1605.

Isel Hall -1B 14, S, Tel: 01900 821778. Early 15th century 4 storey pele tower, set above a bend in the River Derwent. The windows at the top of the fortified tower date from the Henry VIII period. Guided tours (very limited opening) are given around all the main rooms of the still inhabited house displaying rich furniture, paintings and textiles, and there are formal gardens with planted south facing terraces overlooking the river.

Leighton Hall -3D 37, S, Tel: 01524 734474. The grey limestone home of the renowned Gillow furniture making family. Rooms on show include the Gothic hall, principal bedroom, drawing room and library. There is also a 19th century walled garden planted in a wild cottage garden style with roses, fragrant herb patch, herbaceous border, caterpillar maze and formal ornamental vegetable plot, as well as the Aviary Garden (see also 'Leighton Hall Birds of Prey' entry) and a large landscaped park with woodland walks.

Levens Hall -1D 37, S, Tel: 015395 60321. Elizabethan grey stone mansion built by the Bellingham family around a defensive pele tower of c.1350. Inside are fine panelling and plasterwork ceilings and Jacobean furniture. The main attraction of Levens, however, are the world famous formal topiary gardens. The gardens also contain the earliest known example in England of a 'ha-ha' (an inconspicuous sunken ditch boundary) dating from 1694, a rose garden, herbaceous borders, nuttery and fountain garden. There is also a steam collection with Fowler showman's road locomotive, and half size traction engine giving rides around the grounds on selected days.

Mirehouse -2C 15, S, Tel: 017687 72287. Family home of the Spedding line since 1802, in a house built by the Earl of Derby in 1666, facing Bassenthwaite Lake beneath Dodd and Skiddaw. Inside are furniture and portraits, and a display of manuscripts. Ground floor rooms, including a Victorian schoolroom and nursery, are shown accompanied by live piano music. The gardens include the Bee Garden, with orchard and heather path maze, and Poetry Walk, whilst along the drive are Scots pines planted in 1786 with a collection of rhododendrons and hydrangeas beneath. The grounds are home to 4 large woodland adventure playgrounds, and a 1 mile circular walk passes through parkland, woods, and along the shores of Bassenthwaite Lake with St Bega's church. Dodd (managed by the Forestry Commission) forms part of the estate where the Old Sawmill Tearoom is located (see 'Dodd Wood Forest Walks' entry).

Muncaster Castle -2C 29, Tel: 01229 717614. The 'castle', set against a backdrop of Lakeland mountains and fells, consists of a late 13th, early 14th century defensive pele tower incorporated in the south-west of a building substantially reconstructed in 1862 for the fourth Lord Muncaster. The rooms on show are filled with fine furnishings and portraits. Muncaster is remarkable for having been in the same family line for more than 7 centuries. Muncaster is also renowned for its formal and informal gardens, covering over 28 hectares. The half mile long Georgian Terrace with its summer houses, laid out by the first Lord Muncaster in the 1780s, is an outstanding feature giving views of lower Eskdale. Muncaster is also one of Britain's most haunted buildings, mostly through its association with Thomas Skelton, the 'fool' or jester of the castle in the late 16th century, reputedly a murderer, whose antics gave rise to the phrase 'tom-foolery' (see also 'World Owl Centre' and MeadowVole Maze' entries).

Rydal Mount -3B 24, Tel: 015394 33002. Rydal Mount was William Wordsworth's last home, where he lived, cared for by 3 admiring females for 37 years. The property became a place of pilgrimage even in his lifetime, with his poems becoming more popular from around 1815-20 onwards, and his work universally praised. Originally a 16th century yeoman's cottage, enlarged during 1750, the house, with views over Rydal Water and the surrounding fells, has little changed since Wordsworth's time and now belongs to descendants of the poet. Outside is the 1.6 hectare garden designed by Wordsworth with fell side terraces, 'Dora's terrace', rock pools, rare shrubs and summerhouse.

Sizergh Castle NT -1D 37, S, Tel: 015395 60951. Fortified mansion containing an exceptional series of oak panelled interiors, some of the finest Elizabethan carved overmantels in the country, a collection of good English and French early oak furniture, family portraits and the magnificent Inlaid Chamber. Sizergh was given to the National Trust in 1950. Fine landscaped gardens surround the 'castle' including the National Trust's largest limestone rock garden, which includes part of the National Collection of Hardy Ferns.

Swarthmoor Hall -see Ulverston plan -5A, S.

Townend NT -1A 32, S, Tel: 015394 32628. Largely 17th century house of solid whitewashed stone with a slate roof, mullioned windows and traditional stout round chimneys typical of the area, a very fine example of Lakeland vernacular architecture. Built c.1626 by George Browne, a wealthy yeoman farmer, the property being transferred to the National Trust in 1948. The dark dimly lit interior is full of period atmosphere and is a fascinating reflection of the domestic life of the period. The surrounding garden has been laid out as close as possible to its 19th century appearance.

Wordsworth House NT -see Cockermouth plan -2B, S.

Horse Racecourse

Cartmel Racecourse -3B 36, S, Tel: 01539 536340. Horse racing, as Cartmel Steeplechases, has been held here since at least 1845. The course is England's smallest National Hunt racecourse, but has superb scenery. Flat racing here is thought to have begun around the middle of the 15th century, with the course becoming a jump only venue by the start of the

20th century. On race days cars can be parked right next to the course, ideal for picnics.

Industrial Monument

See also Mine

Acorn Bank Watermill NT -2C 19, S, Tel: 01768 361893. Mid 19th century two storey water powered corn mill on Crowdundle Beck. A working pitchback waterwheel turns a pair of millstones for demonstrations. The mill once also served as a sawmill and powered a local gypsum mine. Reached from Acorn Bank Garden by a short circular walk through woodland alongside the mill leat and beck.

Brampton Watermill -3D 19, Tel: 01768 353302. Partially restored watermill, with external mid-breastshot waterwheel, containing original machinery. By appointment only.

Crosscanonby Salt Pans -1B 12. The best preserved example of a salt works in West Cumbria. The last remnants of the salt works are the ground features such as the kinch (a circular pit). This large, circular, elevated structure, was filled with salt laden sand (sleech) and water sprinkled over the top, producing a strong salt solution which trickled into a lagoon. After being left to stand, the brine was boiled in large deep iron pans resulting in crystals of bay salt. On site information panels give more details of how the process worked.

Cunsey Beck Forge -3D 31. Important remains of one of the earliest of the few surviving bloomery forges (water-powered iron-smelting furnaces) in the country. On-going conservation at the overgrown site, rediscovered in 2003, has shown evidence of the forge itself, the wheelpit, associated buildings and slag heaps. A public footpath crosses the site. Exterior view only.

Duddon Ironworks -1B 34. One of the best preserved charcoal-fired blast furnaces in Britain, Duddon Ironworks and Furnace were established in 1736 close to abundant supplies of iron-ore, charcoal and water power. Remains include the ore store, charcoal barn, furnace, charging house and water leats. Iron production switched to coal producing areas and the ports such as Barrow-in-Furness, Millom and Workington. Duddon Ironworks operated until 1867 and the site is now preserved by the National Park Authority. Situated on a minor road off the A595 west of Duddon Bridge, there is an information panel.

Eskdale Mill -1D 29, S, Tel: 019467 23335. Situated in Boot village, the oldest working watermill in England. 18th century machinery housed in a medieval building. Oatmeal machinery and stones working daily from an overshot wheel driven by Whillan Beck as it descends spectacularly from the Scafell basin. A second wheel, installed in 1740, has been restored recently, running in stone bearings. The mill grounds, with waterfalls, provide a delightful picnic area. Small admission charge, guided tours.

Heron Corn Mill -3D 37, S, Tel: 01539 565027. Working corn mill dating from the 1740s on the west bank of the River Bela on a site occupied by a mill from at least 1096. With 3 floors, and 4 pairs of mill stones raised on a 'lowder frame', powered by an internal 4.3 m (14 ft) diameter high breast shot waterwheel. Close to the Lancashire border, it is one of the few working mills in the area. The mill contains a permanent '900 Year' exhibition, celebrating over 900 years of milling on the site.

Howk Bobbin Mill, The -3C 11. Preserved and picturesque ruins on Cald Beck of the mill buildings and drying houses of The Howk Bobbin Mill, built in 1857, which produced wooden bobbins and other turned goods (see' Stott Park Bobbin Mill' entry). Closed in 1924, this important remnant of Cumbria's industrial heritage has in recent years been preserved by the National Park Authority; an information board describes the site. The path through the site continues on to The Howk gorge .

Jane Pit -see Workington plan -4C.

Priests Mill -3C 11, Tel: 016974 78267. Converted watermill whose only surviving machinery is a 4 m (14 ft) diameter undershot waterwheel in working order. The mill was built by the rector of Caldbeck in 1702 in a secluded position on the riverbank just below Caldbeck St Kentigern's Church where it ground corn until 1933. A restaurant and small shops now occupy most of the early 18th century stone building.

Rusland Tannery -1A 36. Rare example of a Lake District tannery, opened in 1762 complete with 18th century flint tannery building, much of the original yard and tan pits. An interpretative panel details how leather was produced for saddles, shoes, hats and upholstery, using readily available local oak bark, lime and livestock.

Saltom Pit -1B 20. Saltom Pit, sunk in 1729, with a pioneering use of gunpowder, was the world's first large scale mine to work coal from under the sea. Only 6 m (20 ft) above sea level in a dramatic setting on a small area of flat land below the cliffs, under what was later to become Haig Colliery (see 'Haig Colliery Mining Museum' entry), the coal was raised by horse gin to the surface at Saltom, and then pulled on trams through a tunnel to Ravenhill Pit for lifting to the top of the cliff. Reached by a footpath from the Cumbria Coastal Way.

Stott Park Bobbin Mill EH -1B 36, S, Tel: 01539 531087. A working Victorian bobbin mill situated in an idyllic woodland setting at the southern end of Windermere. Built by John Harrison in 1835, the mill created the wooden bobbins vital to the cotton spinning and weaving textile industry of Lancashire in the 19th century. Although relatively small, with only 25 employees, it produced a quarter of a million bobbins a week from locally grown coppiced timber, until its closure in 1971. Stott Park Bobbin Mill retains its original Victorian machinery and appearance with steam engine, belts and pulleys, but is also fully functional. Entry is by guided tour lasting 45 minutes during which visitors can see the production of bobbins. An exhibition describes the story of the cotton industry, wooden bobbin making and the people who worked the mill.

Watermill, The -1B 18, Tel: 01768 881523. Working water powered red sandstone corn mill, with two 3.6 m (12 ft) diameter cast iron overshot waterwheels. The mill, which was built c.1750, exclusively produces organic stoneground flour from selected British wheats. Mill tours.

Wetheriggs Country Pottery -2B 18, Tel: 01768 892733. Only steam powered 'country pottery' in British Isles. Working since 1855 and a scheduled industrial monument since 1973, the pottery occupies a 3 hectare site. Demonstrations of Potters at work. Children's play areas. Large pottery shop. The 'Pots of Fun' studio allows visitors to throw a pot, or paint a pot, plate or figurine in acrylics or ceramic glazes (which are fired later). Also 'Designer Makers At Work' area includes glassblowers, artists and other craft makers.

Lighthouse

Hodbarrow Lighthouse, Millom -3B 34. Empty narrow rusty steel tower approximately 9 m (30 ft) high on current sea wall, with a hemispherical roof and lantern structure intact. Known as the 'tin' or 'steel' lighthouse. Exterior view only.

Hodbarrow Point Lighthouse, Millom -3B 34. Empty stone tower approximately 10.5 m (35 ft) high on mound just inland of Hodbarrow Point. Known as the 'old' or 'stone' lighthouse or 'Hodbarrow Beacon' it marked Hodbarrow Point at the time of the first sea wall. The disused tower had a concrete extension and balcony fitted in 1941 for use by the Royal Observer Corps until 1950. Exterior view only.

Maryport Lighthouse -1A 12. Disused 14 m (46 ft) high white hexagonal iron tower on stone base at landward end of South Pier, South Quay. Erected in 1846, it is one of the oldest of its type surviving. Exterior view only.

St Bees Head Lighthouse, Sandwith -2A 20. 17 m (56 ft) high white round tower set back from cliffs at 102 m (335 ft) above sea level with a range of 21 sea miles, on the promontory of St Bees Head, a danger to vessels heading for the Solway Firth. The tower was built in 1823, replacing a previous lighthouse with a coal fire on top which was frequently obscured by thick smoke and eventually burnt down. It was the last coal-fired lighthouse in Britain, being replaced by oil. The current electric light was automated in 1987. Exterior view only.

Whitehaven North Pier Lighthouse
-see Whitehaven plan -2A.

Whitehaven Old Quay Lighthouse
-see Whitehaven plan -3B.

Whitehaven West Pier Lighthouse
-see Whitehaven plan -2A.

Long Distance Footpath

Allerdale Ramble -2C 23 to 1B 12. 54 mile waymarked long distance trail forming a connecting route over very varied terrain running south to north from Seathwaite Farm at the head of Borrowdale. With an alternative low level route to avoid ascending Skiddaw, the trail then runs mostly concurrent with the Cumbria Coastal Way north-eastwards along the coast to Grune Point, north-east of Silloth.

Cistercian Way -3C 37 to 3B 36, and 3D 35 to 3C 35 (see Grange-over-Sands plan).

(Coast to Coast Walk, St Bees -2B 20). 190 mile long distance trail running from St Bees, Cumbria to Robin Hoods Bay, North Yorkshire. Devised by Alfred Wainwright after he had walked The Pennine Way in 1968, his classic book 'A Coast to Coast Walk, A Pictorial Guide' was published in 1973 describing a now extremely popular high level route linking the Irish Sea and the North Sea via the hills, moors and valleys of northern England. Wainwright's immaculately hand-written guidebook, revised in 1998 to include essential changes to the original route, is essential as this is not an official long distance path. Even the village sign proclaims the start of the walk!, which begins with an ascent and traverse of St Bees Head; there is a plaque giving details at the north end of Beach Road.

Cumbria Coastal Way -3D 37 to 1B 12. 150 mile waymarked long distance trail established by Cumbria County Council in the late 1980s along the entire Cumbria coast from the boundary with Lancashire at Silverdale (joining with the Lancashire Coastal Way), around the Cartmel Peninsula, through Barrow-in-Furness, Whitehaven, Workington, Maryport and Silloth on the Solway Firth to Grune Point, before continuing to near Gretna on the Scottish border. The Cumbria Coastal Way does not use the dangerous Cross Bay routes (see Grange-over-Sands description).

Cumbria Way -3D 35 to 1D 11 (see Ulverston plan).
Dales Way, The -2A 32 to 2D 33 (see Windermere plan).
Keswick Railway Footpath -3D 15 to 3A 16 (see Keswick plan).
Lancashire Coastal Way -3D 37. 137 mile waymarked long distance trail established by Lancashire County Council along

the Lancashire coast. From Freckleton east of Lytham St Annes, through Blackpool, to Silverdale (in the Arnside and Silverdale Area of Outstanding Natural Beauty) where it joins the Cumbria Coastal Way.

Limestone Link -3D 37 to 3B 38. 13 mile waymarked long distance trail between Arnside and High Biggins, just west of Kirkby Lonsdale, running west to east through the limestone country of south Cumbria from the wooded Arnside and Silverdale Area of Outstanding Natural Beauty, past the Fairy Steps, over limestone pavement, the flat open mosses of Holme Moss and the rocky fells of Clawthorpe and Hutton Roof Crags.

Pennine Way -2D 19 to 1D 19. 268 mile long distance trail designated by the Countryside Agency in 1965 as Britain's first and probably most famous National Trail. The route follows the Pennine Hills along the backbone of England through 3 national parks (the Peak District, Yorkshire Dales and Northumberland). Regarded as one of the toughest long distance trails in Britain, and only intermittently waymarked, it is traditionally walked south to north taking around 19 days. The route runs from Edale, Derbyshire in the Dark Peak, west of Sheffield, immediately crossing Kinder Scout, to Kirk Yetholm just across the Scottish border, north of the Cheviot Hills, with the highest point being Cross Fell.

Mine / Cave

See also Industrial Monument

Florence Mine -see Egremont plan -4D, S.

Honister Slate Mine -2C 23, S, Tel: 017687 77230. Situated at The Hause, at the top of the Honister Pass, at the head of Gatesgarthdale, the glaciated valley forming the west side of the pass, slate quarrying on a large scale has taken place here from the 1750s, with from 1833 onwards underground mines as well as open quarries in operation. Slate mining at Honister ceased in 1986, but restarted in February 1997 under the Buttermere and Westmorland Green Slate Company Ltd., a working and heritage enterprise. There is a visitor centre with displays of artefacts, a series of information panels telling the history of the mine, its characters, triumphs and disasters, and a Slate Stone Garden. Guided tours of the mine illustrate how slate is extracted using gunpowder, and is finished by, sawing, docking, riving (splitting down the grain) and dressing.

Rydal Cave NT -3B 24. A large cavern (the 'Great Cave') with large entrance portal on the north side of Loughrigg Fell, part of the disused Loughrigg Slate Quarries overlooking Rydal Water. With a pool inside fed by a spring, the cave is popularly entered using the stepping stones or over the rocks to the right.

Threlkeld Quarry Underground Experience -3A 16, S, Tel: 01768 779747 / 01228 561883. 40 minute tour through replica mine built underground in Threlkeld Quarry and Mining Museum illustrating mining techniques over different periods from the 1560's to 1960's.

Monument / Folly

Beacon Tower -see Penrith plan -1E.

Brandelhow Memorial NT -3C 15. A stone plaque commemorating the acquisition by public subscription of the Brandelhow estate by the fledgling National Trust in 1902, their first tract of land in the Lake District. The 44 hectares of wood, parkland and pasture on the west shore of Derwent Water were up for sale for housing development. The opening ceremony was marked by the planting of 4 oak trees. The memorial can be reached by ferry to Low or High Brandelhow, or walking from the car park at Hawes End.

Britannia Column -3B 26. Also known as the Queen's Monument, a 7 m (23 ft) high octagonal pillar erected in 1841-2, with an inscription celebrating Victoria's accession to the throne, is topped by a sculpture of Britannia. On a hillside, just north of Shap Wells Hotel the column is visible in the distance from an adjacent public footpath. Permission is required for a closer inspection. Exterior view only.

Castle Howe Obelisk -see Kendal plan -4B.

Centenary Stone, Keswick NT -3D 15. Large circular stone, split in half with two smooth matching carved surfaces placed to mark the centenary of the National Trust in 1995. Situated on the foreshore of Derwent Water beneath a wooded headland at Calf Close Bay, the site looks across Derwent Water to the National Trust's first property in the Lake District, Brandelhow. Reached via ferry to Ashness Gate, or using the car park beneath Walla Crag.

Charles Gough Memorial -2A 24. Upright rectangular stone inscribed tableau, erected on 18th June 1891, near the path that comes up from Striding Edge, commemorating Charles Gough, a 21 year old aspiring artist and former Quaker, who on 17th April 1805 set off with his dog from Patterdale to Grasmere via Striding Edge and Helvellyn. His body, still guarded by his faithful but emaciated dog Foxie, was found on 20th July, over 3 months later. He was thought to have slipped on ice and fallen into the corrie of Red Tarn.

Countess Pillar EH -2A 18. Pillar (in railed enclosure) erected in 1656 by Lady Anne Clifford to mark her last parting with her mother in April 1616. Alms were distributed annually to the poor from here. Situated to south of the Penrith to Appleby road near Brougham.

Donald Campbell Memorial -see Coniston plan -1B.

(Eden Millennium Monument, Eamont Bridge -2A 18). 30 ton block of granite from Shap quarry, carved with the Greek alpha and omega symbols on its west and east faces. The stone was placed here in the year 2000 on a site chosen to celebrate 2000 years of Christianity in a locality noted for its two pagan henges.

Elba Monument -2B 32. Obelisk erected by James Bateman in 1814, in the grounds of Tolson Hall on a prominent site overlooking the River Kent valley, to celebrate the statesmanship of William Pitt and the abdication and exile of Napoleon Bonaparte of France to the island of Elba after his defeat in Paris. Exterior view only.

George III Jubilee Obelisk -1C 35. 6 m (20 ft) high obelisk on square plinth with steps, also known as the Gilpin Obelisk, erected in 1810, to celebrate the Golden Jubilee of King George III. Adjacent are the stocks and fish slabs used to weigh, price and sell fish caught in the River Duddon.

Greystoke Pillar -2D 17. Octagonal obelisk built by Charles Howard, 11th Duke of Norfolk, of Greystoke Castle in the late 18th century (private, but visible from the B5288 west of the Newbiggin junction).

Halifax Bomber Memorial NT -1B 30. Poignant memorial cairn and cross just below the summit of Great Carrs. On 22nd October 1944 Handley Page R.C.A.F. Halifax bomber no. LL505, on a night navigation exercise, crashed on Great Carrs whilst attempting to drop below thick cloud to get a ground positional fix. 8 young crewmen, mostly Canadian, lost their lives. One of the 4 Rolls Royce V12 Merlin engines, is on display at the Ruskin Museum.

Hoad Monument -see Ulverston plan -1C, S.

Hospice, The -3B 36. Well preserved plain, stone square plan building on the 240 m (787 ft) high summit of Hampsfell, with a precarious external staircase to a roof top direction indicator and chart. Erected by Thomas Remington, the vicar of Cartmel in 1846. There are panoramic views across the Cartmel Valley, Morecambe Bay and to the Lakeland fells.

John Ruskin Memorial NT -see Keswick plan -5B.

John Wilkinson Obelisk -2C 37. Black painted iron-plate obelisk on a small mound with an inscription to John 'Iron-Mad' Wilkinson who died on 14th July 1808. Born in 1728 and initially working at Backbarrow Ironworks near Newby Bridge

he owned or founded many ironworks, earning the reputation and name the 'King of the Ironmasters'. The obelisk was subsequently finally moved to its present site in 1863.
(King Edward VII Memorial, Grange NT -1D 23). A memorial plaque to King Edward VII who died in 1910, set on King's How, the western top of Grange Fell, by his sister Princess Louise, daughter of Queen Victoria and a president of the fledgling National Trust. It was placed after the purchase by public subscription of a large part of the fell, including the Bowder Stone, for the National Trust in 1910.
Pennington Tower -1B 36. Tower, also known as Finsthwaite Tower, on a 185 m (607 ft) high wooded national park owned hill overlooking Newby Bridge and the southern end of Windermere. Erected in 1799 by James King of Finsthwaite House, it is inscribed in honour of the officers, seamen and marines of the Royal Navy who 'decisively defeated the fleets of France, Spain and Holland'.
Storrs Temple (Temple of Heroes) NT -3D 31. A naval monument, basically a folly, at the end of a short pier jutting out into Windermere from the end of Storrs Point promontory. A small octagonal building, it was built in 1804, in honour of 4 Admirals of the Fleet: Duncan, Howe, Nelson and St Vincent. Given to the National Trust in 1965, there is no right of access by land; the monument is best viewed from one of the Windermere Lake Cruises from which the temple is clearly visible.
Three Shire Stone NT -1B 30. A limestone monolith on the north side of the road atop the Wrynose Pass (393 m, or 1289 ft) inscribed with the name 'Lancashire' set at the meeting point of the traditional counties of Lancashire, Westmorland and Cumberland which were incorporated in the administrative county of Cumbria in 1974. The restored monument, re-erected by the National Trust, now has flat marker stones set in the turf with the initial letters of the 3 counties marking their directions.

Museum

Alice's Wonderland, Ivegill -2D 11, Tel: 016974 73552. A celebration of childhood comprising over 2,000 dolls, teddies, dolls' houses and toys. The collection is popular with both young and old alike and spans 200 years to the present day. Highly recommended by the local education department. Located within the High Head Sculpture Valley.
Beacon, The -see Whitehaven plan -3A.
Brougham Hall Museum -2A 18, S. History of Brougham Hall and its environs. Scale model of hall in its heyday.
Campbell Legend Bluebird Exhibition, The -3B 36, S, Tel: 015395 58509. Exhibition, housed within the Lakeland Motor Museum, paying tribute to world land and water speed record breakers Sir Malcolm Campbell, and his son Donald Campbell who died on Coniston Water in 1967, who between them captured 21 official world land and water speed records for Britain (10 on land, 11 on water). There are detailed replicas of the famous record breaking 'Bluebird 1935' car and 'Bluebird K7' Hydroplane.
Cars of the Stars Motor Museum, Keswick -see Keswick plan -3C, S.
Cartmel Gatehouse Heritage Centre -3B 36, Tel: 015395 36874. Heritage centre in Cartmel Priory Gatehouse managed by the Cartmel Village Society. The displays cover the history of Cartmel Priory, the gatehouse and development of Cartmel village and the surrounding Cartmel Peninsula. Includes local photographs and maps, brass rubbing plates, costumes and interactive displays.
Countryside Museum -2D 17, S, Tel: 017684 86450. Agricultural and countryside collections, on upper floor of the 16th century Great Barn adjoining the courtyard of Dalemain mansion. There are exhibits on dairying, cheese and butter

making, haytime and harvest, sheep and wool clipping as well as the work of the farrier, saddler, smithy and wheel hooping.
Cumberland Pencil Museum, The -see Keswick plan -2B.
Fell Pony Museum -2D 17, S, Tel: 017684 86450. Displays, artefacts and information on Fell ponies, on the upper floor of the 16th century Great Barn adjoining the courtyard of Dalemain mansion. Fell ponies are a hardy semi-wild breed found on the Cumbria fells, they were essential for the transportation of goods and commodities such as iron, lead or copper ore, coal, slate, lime or wool.
Florence Mine Heritage Centre -see Egremont plan -4D.
Gateway to Furness Exhibition -see Ulverston plan -2D.
Haig Colliery Mining Museum -see Whitehaven plan -4A.
Hawkshead Old Grammar School
-see Hawkshead plan -2B, S.
Helena Thompson Museum -see Workington plan -2E.
Helly Hansen National Mountaineering Exhibition, The -2D 17, Tel: 01768 868000. Britain's only permanent national exhibition dedicated to mountains and mountain adventure; a fascinating exhibition with John Peel and Sir Chris Bonington as virtual guides. Displays include Major British successes in the Himalayas, including the 1953 ascent of Everest by Edmund Hillary and Tensing. The 'Story of Everest', by a member of the 1953 expedition, George Band, is told in film footage in the Summit Theatre. Housed within Rheged.
Kendal Museum -see Kendal plan -2C.
Keswick Museum and Gallery -see Keswick plan -2C, S.
K Shoes Heritage Centre -see Kendal plan -5C.
Lakeland Life, Museum of -see Kendal plan -4C.
Lakeland Motor Museum -3B 36, S, Tel: 015395 58509. Housed in a former shirehorse stable and its courtyard, the museum, with interpretative displays, houses around 20,000 exhibits, with approximately 100 vintage and classic vehicles dating from the early 1900s to 1950s, part set in a 1920s garage recreation.
Lakes Discovery Museum @ the Armitt, The -see Ambleside plan -2B.
Laurel and Hardy Museum, Ulverston
-see Ulverston plan -3B.
Maryport Maritime Museum -1A 12, Tel: 01900 813738. Maryport's maritime history, including displays on Maryport's industrial history, including the Elizabeth and Senhouse docks, the history of Maryport's shipbuilding industry on the River Ellen, and Maryport's social history, with its long association with lifeboats. One of the most notable items in the collection is a scrimshaw work sperm whale's tooth.
Millom Folk Museum -2B 34, S, Tel: 01229 772555. Housed in the railway station, this is a local history museum for the town of Millom with over 10,000 artefacts depicting subjects such as the development and decline of the iron-ore mining industry and iron production, with which Millom was heavily connected from the mid 19th century onwards. With an area devoted to the writer and poet Norman Nicholson (1914-1987) who was born and lived in Millom and chronicled much of the local life of the time.
Paper Making, Museum of -3D 37, S, Tel: 01539 565027. Housed in a converted 18th century 'carter's barn', near and associated with Heron Corn Mill, the historical production of paper, an important local industry established on this site over 250 years ago. There are displays, diagrams, and artefacts including hand paper making moulds.
Penrith Museum -see Penrith plan -3C.
Printing House Working Museum of Printing, The, Cockermouth -see Cockermouth plan -2B.
Quaker Tapestry Exhibition Centre, The -see Kendal plan -3C, S.
RAF Millom Museum -3A 34, Tel: 01229 772636. Small museum housed in an old 1941 building and former officers mess on part of the site of RAF Millom. RAF Millom was

opened in January 1941 as no. 2 Bombing and Gunnery School, the base trained aircraft crews in WW2 using training planes such as Avro Ansons, with the last operational flight in 1953. There is an archive of over 5,000 photographs as well as many relics recovered mainly from WW2 aircraft crash sites. The RAF Mountain Rescue Service started in 1941 at RAF Millom, initially to rescue training crews who had crashed on the Lakeland mountain fells.

Ravenglass Railway Museum -2B 28, Tel: 01229 717171. Detailed history of the Ravenglass and Eskdale Railway and its part in the life of the Eskdale valley community in a building situated in Ravenglass Station yard. Railway artefacts, photographs, models of stations, iron ore mining and audio-visual. The 4-4-2 Bassett-Lowke locomotive 'Synolda' of 1912 is exhibited in the building.

Rum Story, The, Whitehaven -see Whitehaven plan -3B.
Ruskin Museum -see Coniston plan -1B.
Senhouse Roman Museum -1A 12, Tel: 01900 816168. A former battery overlooking the coast, built by the Admiralty in 1885 for the Royal Naval Artillery Volunteer Reserve, houses the largest collection of Roman military alters and inscriptions from a single site in Britain. Begun by John Senhouse of Netherhall in the 1570s.
Sir John Barrow Cottage Museum, The -see Ulverston plan -4C, S.
Threlkeld Quarry and Mining Museum -3A 16, S, Tel: 01768 779747 / 01228 561883. Developing mining museum in

Threlkeld Quarry, a former quarry opened on the lower slopes of Clough Head in the 1860s, closed in 1982, supplying granite for railway ballast and road making as well as producing granite setts and masonry stone. On display are excavators, mine tubs and several of the original buildings including the locomotive shed, weighbridge, explosives store and quarrymen's canteen, now the museum. There is a fine collection of small quarrying and mining artefacts. The Vintage Excavator Trust is based at the quarry with a collection of over fifty cable excavators from the early 1900's to more recent times. Working weekends in May and September. Excavations from 7 tons to 78 tons.

Westmorland and Cumberland Yeomanry Museum -2D 17, S, Tel: 017684 86450. One room in the original pele tower at the core of Dalemain house containing uniforms, photographs, prints, weapons, regalia and memorabilia relating to the yeomanry between 1819 and 1919.
Wetheriggs Country Pottery Museum -2B 18, Tel: 01768 892733. In former drying room of Wetheriggs Country Pottery. Displays on beginnings of the pottery as a brick, pipe and tile works and its development into houseware production from the 1860s followed by decorative and art wares after WW2. Family history. Beehive kiln.
Windermere Steamboats and Museum -see Windermere plan -3B, S.
Wordsworth Museum, The -see Grasmere plan -3C.

Natural Attraction

Aira Force NT -3B 16. Famed beauty spot on Aira Beck, which rises on Matterdale Common and flows into Ullswater, within the landscaped Gowbarrow Park (see 'Gowbarrow Park Arboretum' entry), reached by a short uphill walk from the easily accessible but often busy National Trust car park on the A592, or from a car park on the Troutbeck road. The 21m (70 ft) high falls are situated in a narrow oak wooded ravine. Landscaped paths ascend either side of the beck with narrow single arched stone footbridges both above and below the falls.
Barrow Falls -1D 23. Waterfall, c.33 m (108 ft) high, on Barrow Beck in the 6 hectare grounds of the large whitewashed Barrow House built in the 1790s now used as a youth hostel.
Birker Force -2D 29. 100 m (328 ft) tumbling cascade on Low Birker Pool, down the side of the plateau edge of Ulpha Fell. When in flood, the fall is visible as a white flash on the fellside for some distance from the north side of the River Esk.
Birk Hagg Waterfall -3B 24. Falls situated high up in woodland above Rydal Hall on Rydal Beck. Reached by a path east off the 'Fairfield Horseshoe' walk path on the west side of the beck. The falls, above a footbridge crossing, are spectacular especially after heavy autumn or winter rainfall.
Birks Bridge Rapids -2A 30. Described as a 'sunless cleft' by William Wordsworth, this beautiful natural miniature gorge, with deep silent pools of clear water, on the River Duddon is crossed by Birks Bridge. Just upstream of the bridge is a rock cleft barely 0.6 m (2 ft) wide, where the river is forced into a narrow torrent.
Bowder Stone, The NT -1D 23. A massive roughly cube shaped boulder, over 9.5 m (31 ft) high, perched precariously on one edge with steps running to the top, the Bowder Stone is perhaps the most famous of all the Lake District's natural features. It is estimated to weigh between 1,970 and 2,000 tons. Made of a metamorphic rock not present locally, the boulder appears not to have fallen from the fell above, but have been carried here by glacial action in the Ice Age. The Bowder Stone was acquired by the National Trust by subscription in 1910, and is reached by footpath from a car park a third of a mile to the north.
Colwith Force -1C 31. 15 m (50 ft) high falls on River Brathay (Little Langdale Beck) with viewpoints from the National Trust's High Park woodland south of the river. A dramatic lead-in rapid, leads to a final fall of 7-8 m (23-26 ft) in height split in two by a large central rock outcrop.
Duddon Valley (Dunnerdale) -2A 30. The section of the Duddon Valley from just south of Cockley Beck, between the busy passes of Hardknott and Wrynose, southwards to Ulpha is often referred to as Lakeland's best kept secret. The attraction of the valley does not lie in the dramatic or spectacular but rather in the uncrowded solitude of the gentle unspoilt sheep-farming landscape. There are only two tiny hamlets in the valley, Seathwaite and Ulpha, with perhaps the most photographed post office in the Lake District.
Dungeon Ghyll Force NT -3D 23. A well known fall on the route up to the Langdale Pikes from car parks at the New Dungeon Ghyll Hotel in Great Langdale. The lower fall has a spectacular drop of over 50 m (164 ft). The falls are popularly viewed using the main footpath leading to Loft Crag to the south-west of the Dungeon Ghyll ravine.
Force Falls -1A 38. (Sedgwick). Shallow but wide, and often vigorous, falls on the River Kent, one of the fastest flowing rivers in the country, known for its powerful rapids and weirs. Set in asmall shallow rocky gorge, initial falls above and below the road bridge are followed by an approximately 3 m (10 ft) plunge either side of a central rocky island frequently run by kayaks.

Force Falls -3C 31. Low tumbling cascade at Force Mills, in a woodland setting, on Force Beck (leading from Grizedale Beck). In the 19th century the beck was used to power a bobbin mill downstream. On the High Bowkerstead Walk.

Galleny Force -2D 23. Over 6 m (20 ft) high fall on Stonethwaite Beck, just downstream of the confluence of Langstrath Beck and Greenup Gill, on the Cumbria Way. he water enters a clear pool on a short scenic tree-lined section of the beck, the pools in this area being popular for swimming.

Gill Force -1D 29. Scenic small rapid on the River Esk where the water tumbles through a deep narrow rocky channel into an emerald pool beneath the old girder bridge (now a footbridge) that carried a tramway branch from the 'main-line' of the Ravenglass and Eskdale Railway.

Hardknott Pass NT -1A 30. Perhaps not as fearful a route as it was in the past, the notoriously steep and narrow single-track Hardknott Pass road has sections of 1 in 3 (30%) gradient hairpin bends; although not the highest road pass in the Lake District (see 'Kirkstone Pass' entry), at 393 m (1289 ft) it still provides a motoring challenge over a spectacularly scenic route. It is the same height as the summit of its sister the Wrynose Pass to the east with some equalling difficult 1 in 4 gradients. Not to be attempted in severe winter conditions.

High Force NT -3C 17. Set on Aira Beck, a third of a mile above Aira Force, High Force is a spectacular waterfall in its own right, but is overshadowed by its more famous counterpart below. High Force is unmistakable, situated just before the footpath on the eastern bank, exits the National Trust's Gowbarrow Park estate (see 'Gowbarrow Park Arboretum' entry).

Howk, The -3C 11. Reached by footpath from the car park in Caldbeck, past the popular village duck pond a quarter of a mile west along the north bank of the river Cald Beck. The Howk is a deep limestone gorge of sheer to overhanging sides, with a waterfall in a narrow cleft tumbling around 18 m (60 ft) into a large basin. With moss banks and alder woodland, a rich variety of ferns thrive in every crevice of this damp sheltered environment.

Humphrey Head -3B 36. Steep west-facing limestone promontory, the sea cliff being the tallest in Cumbria, and one of only two sea cliffs in Cumbria (the other is at St Bees Head). Jutting out for over 0.5 mile into Morecambe Bay, and rising steeply 45 m (148 ft) above high tide mark in some places, the promontory gives panoramic views. The cliffs are a famous geological locality, being the finest example of lower Carboniferous rock exposures in north-west England, rich in coral fossils (fossil collecting is however not allowed). The last wolf in England was reputedly killed at Humphrey Head in the 15th century.

Jaws of Borrowdale NT -1D 23. A dramatic natural feature, the Jaws of Borrowdale are high wooded crags squeezing the road and River Derwent together for about half a mile in the Borrowdale valley. The Allerdale Ramble long distance footpath passes the summit where there was once an Iron Age hill fort. There are fine views north and south and a WW1 memorial to fallen Borrowdale men.

Kirkstone Pass -3C 25. The highest and longest road pass in the Lake District at 455 m (1493 ft), named after the Kirk Stone, a rock resembling a church (kirk) steeple towards the top of the pass on the west side. Overshadowed by the dramatic Red Screes and Raven Crag on the west side at the top, there are gradients steeper than 20 % (1 in 5) on the final section from the north and on 'The Struggle' a useful minor road route descending steeply into Ambleside. Just over the summit at 447 m (1468 ft) is the Kirkstone Pass Inn, the highest public house in Cumbria. Once a severe test for horse and coaches, the pass is easier now but should not be attempted in severe winter conditions.

Launchy Gill Force -1A 24. Impressive in spate, this often overlooked cascade on Launchy Gill drops on a precipitous course 150 m (492 ft) down the fellside into Thirlmere. Footpaths ascend both sides to a footbridge which crosses the fall about a third of the way up over one of the most impressive sections; above this point the path ascends on the south side only (see also 'Launchy Gill Forest Trail').

Levers Waterfall -2B 30. Series of cascades (with an initial fall of around 40 m (131 ft)) on Levers Water Beck descending steeply from just below Levers Water reservoir into the Coppermines Valley below. Due south is the famous massive rectangular 11 m (36 ft) high boulder known as the 'Pudding Stone', popular for climbing practice since Victorian times.

Lodore Falls -1D 23, Tel: 017687 77285. Situated on Watendlath Beck, in woodland behind the Victorian Hilton Keswick Lodore Hotel, the falls are spectacular after heavy or prolonged rainfall, the water tumbling over huge boulders with a main descent of 27-30 m (90-100 ft); they are conversely only a trickle in dry periods. On private land, but with allowed access via a gate behind the hotel, there is no parking for the falls at the hotel itself. By car, use the Kettlewell car park adjacent Derwent Water to the north, or take the Keswick Launch service to Lodore. Nearby, north of the footpath to the 'Chinese Bridge', is Cannon Dub, the site in the late 1780s of a cannon which visitors could pay to fire and then count the echoes. Shepherds Crag immediately south-west of the falls is a popular rock climbing area.

Moss Force NT -1B 22. Situated at the top of the quiet Newlands Valley on Moss Beck the fall, dropping over 100 m (328 ft) from Buttermere Moss fed by the runoff of Robinson, can be viewed as comprising of 3 sections, a dramatic top section, split by a rock outcrop, leading into central and lower sections. It is clearly visible from the minor road between Buttermere and Braithwaite.

Rutter Force -1D 27. Also known as Rutter Falls. A scenic, approximately 6 m (20 ft) high waterfall, on Hoff Beck, a tributary of the River Eden, which it joins just west of Appleby. Situated at the end of a short country lane, with footbridge and a ford immediately downstream. A non-working watermill with pitch-back waterwheel (now a gallery shop), adjacent to the falls, completes the picture.

Rydal Falls (Low Fall) -3B 24. Cascading through a rocky ravine in the grounds of Rydal Hall Gardens on Rydal Beck, these falls were much visited in Victorian times, until losing out in popularity to Stockghyll Force. They were painted by many 19th century landscape artists from the building of the Grotto sited below the falls, built in 1669 and thought to be the oldest 'viewing house' in the country (see also 'Birk Hagg Waterfall' entry).

St Bees Head -2A 20. St Bees Head forms part of the designated St Bees Head Heritage Coast. The red sandstone headland with its sheer, fissured cliffs 91 m (300 ft) high, is the most conspicuous natural feature on the entire west coast between Anglesey and the Scottish border, Cumbria's most westerly point and the highest sea cliff in north-west England.

The headland continues to rise to 141 m (463 ft). The Cumbria Coastal Way runs along the cliff top, with its many ledges and grassy tops with gorse patches and good views. The cliff is separated into two headlands by Fleswick Bay (where the shingle beach is reachable by footpath), once used by smugglers. Gem-stones can be found on the beach.

Scale Force NT -1B 22. The highest single vertical drop in the Lake District, in a deep wooded cleft on Scale Beck, Scale Force plunges over 37 m (120 ft) into a small pool before dropping a further 6 m (20 ft) in another split cascade. Foliage partly obscures the falls in the summer. Reached by a 2.5 mile walk from Buttermere via the footpath to the west end of Buttermere lake. Stained red by iron ore, with superb views over Buttermere, Crummock Water and Ennerdale Water.

Sharp Edge -2A 16. Sharp Edge is the finest approach to the summit of Blencathra (868 m or 2848 ft) and the most challenging walk in Lakeland. A sharp, high and exposed ridge with vertiginous sheer drops on either side, but with tremendous views, it is set above Scales Tarn which, rarely seeing the sun, is described as the coldest tarn in Lakeland. Sharp Edge is for the experienced well equipped fell walker only and should not be attempted when frosty, slippery, in windy weather or in poor visibility. There are other safer approaches to the summit of Blencathra.

Skelwith Force -1C 31. 4 m (13 ft) high waterfall on River Brathay below Elter Water. There are viewpoints from adjacent footpaths on the north bank, nearest the Elterwater road, and south bank from National Trust land. Easily accessible but poorly signposted, like Stockghyll Force, Skelwith Force is very different in character having a much lower drop and a less wooded aspect, however after heavy rain this relatively placid waterfall transforms into a powerful and spectacular thundering torrent crossing the rocks on the north side. Do not park at Kirkstone Galleries (customer parking only) but use a car park situated in a disused quarry east off the Elterwater road.

Sour Milk Gill -1B 22. (Nr. Buttermere). Continuous tumbling rocky cataracts of around 300 m (984 ft) descent fed by Bleaberry Tarn (488 m or 1600 ft) set in a glaciated corrie below Red Pike and Chapel Crags. The cascade is clearly visible from Buttermere.

Sour Milk Gill NT -3A 24. (Nr. Grasmere). White churning water falling over 50 m (164 ft) on a series of joining cascades, most prominent lower down the slope, the outfall of Easedale Tarn. The falls are reached by a popular 1.25 mile uphill footpath (from a small car park on Easedale Road, Grasmere). Above the falls is Easedale Tarn, set in its quiet glaciated valley, once popular with the Victorians.

Sour Milk Gill NT -2C 23. (Nr. Seathwaite). Probably named after its white frothing appearance the fall, with its steepest section at the top, is clearly visible from Seathwaite Farm below. The cascade tumbles over 200 m (656 ft) to the River Derwent from the quiet hanging valley of Gillercomb. A steep footpath ascends the south side of the gill and traverses Gillercomb to the summit of Green Gable.

Spout Force -2B 14. As its name suggests a spout of water shoots out and drops around 9 m (30 ft) into a narrow rocky wooded defile. A viewpoint overlooking the falls is accessible via a public footpath a third of a mile from Scawgill Bridge, using a lay-by, or Forestry Commission car park at Darling How nearby to the east.

Stanley Force (Stanley Ghyll Force / Dalegarth Falls) -2D 29. 18 m (60 ft) high waterfall in a deep wooded ravine, one of the Lake District's loveliest. A narrow and steep unfenced path clings to the west side of Birker Beck before crossing it 3 times on wooden bridges as the fall is finally approached. The national park car park is at Trough House Bridge situated south-east of Beckfoot Bridge.

Stickle Ghyll NT -3D 23. Far more easy to get closer to than Dungeon Ghyll Force, Stickle Ghyll follows a narrow tumbling course of a uniform character from Stickle Tarn (470 m or 1542 ft above sea level), 0.75 miles down the fellside to the New Dungeon Ghyll Hotel below. Stickle Tarn (with its brown trout) is famous for the dramatic rock wall of Pavey Ark behind, and is popular as a stopping off point along the principal route to Harrison Stickle (the highest point of the Langdale Pikes). The tarn was dammed in the 19th century so that its water could be channelled, via Great Langdale Beck, to power the gunpowder mill at Elterwater; consequently the beck was often called Mill Ghyll.

Stockghyll Force -see Ambleside plan -2C.

Striding Edge -2B 24. One of Lakeland's most celebrated mountain routes, Striding Edge is regarded as the most popular walk in the Lake District and possibly Britain. Forming the extremely attractive eastern approach to Helvellyn, it is a 1 mile long arete separating Nethermost Cove to the south from Red Tarn to the north, leading directly west onto the Helvellyn summit. There are significant drops on either side, however there is an easier route slightly beneath the main ridge mostly on the north side, which still has the benefit of striking views over Red Tarn. The final ascent over badly eroded ground onto the Helvellyn plateau passes the Charles Gough Memorial on the way. Striding Edge should not be attempted when frosty,

slippery, in windy weather or in poor visibility. Starting at Glenridding car park there are initially a choice of routes, with one of the most popular being a 7.5 mile circuit from the south side of Glenridding Beck.

Tarn Hows NT -2C 31. Perhaps Lakeland's best known beauty spot, this outstandingly beautiful and tranquil lake, surrounded by planted conifers, was artificially created in the 1860s from several smaller tarns by the damming of a beck. Landscaped in the 'picturesque' style popular at the time, by the powerful Marshall family of Monk Coniston Hall. The Monk Coniston estate was bought by Mrs Heelis (Beatrix Potter) in 1930, with the half containing Tarn Hows sold on in the same year to the National Trust, and the rest bequeathed in her will of 1944. A level and very popular broad 1.5 mile footpath encircles the tarn where red squirrels may be spotted amid views over the water to the Coniston fells.

Taylorgill Force NT -2C 23. On Styhead Gill, the outflow of Styhead Tarn, a series of tumbling cascades leads to an impressive main drop of around 25 m (82 ft). 'The waterfall in Taylor's ravine', the name probably derives from that of a local family who resided here in the early 18th century. Two footpaths ascend from Seathwaite Farm. The path north-west of the gill, which begins by crossing the River Derwent on a wooden footbridge immediately west of the farm approaches closest after 1 mile, and provides the best view. Both paths join before Styhead Tarn.

Tilberthwaite Gill -1C 31. Impressive steep sided ravine with swift-flowing cascades on Yewdale Beck. There are high level paths on both sides, but a footpath links the two descending to a footbridge crossing the beck at a scenic location, wooded with larch and rowan, at the lower eastern end, just before the impressive narrow part of the gorge begins.

Wast Water NT -3B 22. The deepest lake in England at 76 m (249 ft), with its floor below sea-level. Waste Water is also famous for The Screes, a massive scree slope below Illgill Head and Whin Rigg, which drops dramatically around 540 m (1772 ft) to the lake surface below. To the north-east behind Sca Fell is Scafell Pike, England's highest mountain (see also Wast Water lake description).

Whitewater Dash -1D 15. Tumbling waterfall on Dash Beck, also known as Dash Falls, in an extensive series of cascades below Little Calva in a short valley between Skiddaw and Uldale Fells. The total drop is around 100 m (328 ft), being regarded by some as the best cascade set in Lakeland. The top of the falls, one of the highest situated waterfalls in the Lake District, are visible for a considerable distance from the north-west. They are reached by using the Cumbria Way from Skiddaw House (formerly a shooting lodge, one of the most remote buildings in England).

Nature Reserve / Bird Sanctuary

See also Forest Walk

Ash Landing Nature Reserve NT -2D 31. 2.6 hectare heather and rhododendron garden on west shore of Windermere. 3 ponds, stream and small wildlife garden displaying woodland, wetland and grassland habitats. Notable for dragonflies.

Bassenthwaite Lake National Nature Reserve -2C 15. 23 hectare national nature reserve comprising Bassenthwaite Lake and areas of adjoining wet woodland. Noted for its extremely rich aquatic flora and over-wintering birds, the reserve is permit only off public rights of way. Ospreys have recently been encouraged to nest on the west shore, and fish on the lake (see 'Dodd Wood Osprey Viewpoint' entry). The lake is home to the protected vendace, a fish limited to just two populations in the United Kingdom (here and Derwent Water).

Brown Robin Nature Reserve -see Grange-over-Sands plan -1D.

Burns Beck Moss Nature Reserve -1B 38. 15 hectare nature reserve featuring a rare combination on the same site of nutrient poor valley mire, or bog, and raised mire, together with a few isolated patches of willow carr and reed bed. Burns Beck bisects the reserve. Peat was dug here for compost and fuel, which has left an uneven surface. Roe deer, common lizard, tawny owl, curlew, reed bunting, sedge warbler and fritillaries can be seen. Many species of sphagnum moss, one of the main peat-forming plants, have been recorded here. A circular recommended footpath traverses part of the reserve.

Calder Woods Nature Reserve -3D 21. Broad-leaved woodland owned by the national park near to River Calder. The old names of the different sections of the woods-Chapelholme Wood, Brigholme Wood and the steeper ground of Crake Nest, suggest a long tradition of woodland management. There are areas of sessile oak, reminiscent of the sessile oak forest which used to cover the Lake District, as well as other native species such as alder, ash, birch, rowan, wild cherry and wych elm and the once common greater woodrush. Two overgrown quarries are thought to have been the source of stone for nearby Calder Abbey.

Cliburn Moss National Nature Reserve -2B 18. 26 hectare national nature reserve of basin mire colonised by Scots pine and birch. An unusual variety of fen, bog, grassland and heathland plants grow in an environment of former peat workings. Woodland birds include great spotted woodpecker, tawny owls, sparrowhawk and common buzzard.

Clints Quarry Nature Reserve -2C 21. 9.2 hectare disused limestone quarry noted for its industrial archaeology, geological interest and grassland with a rich flora. Plants include bee orchid and prolific ox-eye daisies and there are several ponds, with scrub woodland on the eastern edge. Last worked in the early 1930s, the quarry produced limestone for the Cumbrian steel industry and lime for agriculture (well preserved lime kilns are located at the south of the site). A steep footpath circles the quarry.

Cowraik Quarry Local Nature Reserve -1A 18. 4 hectare wildlife haven in former quarry noted for its geological importance. Key faces, which have been cleared of vegetation, reveal the geological structures of the Penrith Sandstone noted for its spectacular large scale sedimentary cross-bedding. Red squirrels can be seen.

Crosscanonby Carr Nature Reserve -1B 12. Small marsh in the Solway Coast Area of Outstanding Natural Beauty. The

reserve has a mosaic of wildlife habitats with meadows, carr woodland, beck and pond crossed by a boardwalk. It is home to damp-loving species such as meadowsweet and alder, reed-grasses and rushes. The Crosscanonby Carr Nature Trail explores the site.

Dorothy Farrer's Spring Wood Nature Reserve - 2B 32. Approximately 4 hectare reserve comprising 3 separate woodland enclosures-Dorothy Farrers Spring Wood and Beddards Wood in the south linked by a short permissive footpath over Grubbing Spring to High Wood in the north. These are fine examples of sessile oak woodland typical of the area. Wild daffodils, bluebells, wood anemone, and ramsons (wild garlic) provide colour in spring while foxgloves can be seen after coppicing. The reserve also supports many mosses, liverworts and fungi.

Drigg Dunes Local Nature Reserve -2B 28. 383 hectare reserve of sand dunes backed by marsh and saltings, home to Europe's largest colony of black headed gulls. Declared in 1954, the reserve is on the opposite side of the Esk estuary to Eskmeals Dunes Nature Reserve, accessed from a sea-front car park at the end of Shore Road, Drigg.

Dubbs Moss Nature Reserve -2A 14. 7.4 hectare reserve with habitats ranging from birch woodland, where the shade and wet ground allow mosses and ferns to thrive, through fen grassland, to hawthorn scrub on the drier ground. The reserve is a haven for small birds such as most common species of tit, together with warblers and butterflies. The fen vegetation is at its most colourful in July and August when yellow iris, common spotted orchid, meadowsweet and angelica are prevalent.

Dufton Ghyll Wood Nature Reserve -3D 19. Semi-natural ancient woodland (a mix of beech, oak and birch) in a narrow stream fed valley, situated just off the Pennine Way. 10.5 hectare Distant views, information board. Parking nearby.

Eskmeals Dunes Nature Reserve -2B 28. 67 hectare sand dune system with fossilised shingle ridges noted for its very rich flora. The spit was created by shingle deposited across the mouths of the Rivers Mite, Irt and Esk causing the later two to alter course, join and flow out to sea in one channel. The high dunes are dominated by marram grass, which binds the sand together, whilst the valleys between the dunes have the majority of plant growth at their most attractive in the summer. Birds on the estuary in winter include shelduck, redshank, curlew and widgeon. No access when yellow flags are flying on adjacent MOD Eskmeals Gun Range (gatehouse tel.- 01229 712200). Access via the minor road from Waberthwaite may be flooded at high tide.

Gait Barrows National Nature Reserve -3D 37. 69 hectare national nature reserve containing perhaps the most important single example of Carboniferous limestone pavement flora in Britain, hidden in the heart of a mixed woodland of coppiced hazel under oak, ash and sycamore. Limestone pavements are sensitive environments with many rare plants such as ferns, rare wildflowers and very rich fungi flora. The reserve also has notable high brown and pearl-bordered fritillary and around the fen and reedbed of Hawes Water are pastures grazed by Exmoor Ponies between November and March. There is no car park or other facilities. The sensitive nature of the reserve means it is strictly permit only off the permissive path (see 'Gait Barrows Nature Trail' entry).

Great Asby Scar National Nature Reserve -2D 27. 307 hectare national nature reserve containing some of the best examples of limestone pavement in Britain. The shaded humid conditions of the deeper grikes provide a micro-environment for many plants which, due to grazing pressure, very rarely grow above the surface of the clints. These plants include those more reminiscent of the woodland floor such as harts tongue fern, wood anemone and also the extremely uncommon limestone fern. The herb rich limestone grassland is dominated by blue moor-grass and abundant rock rose and wild thyme. The reserve is a remote upland site reached by footpaths from Great Ashy or Orton and is best

visited in the summer when the limestone pavement flora is at its best (see also 'Gait Barrows National Nature Reserve' and 'Hutton Roof Crags Nature Reserve' entries).

Hallsenna Moor National Nature Reserve -1B 28. 24 hectare national nature reserve of peatland with habitats such as heath, poor fen, basin mire and a small woodland. The reserve is permit only but is crossed by several public footpaths in different directions. On site visitor information signs give more details.

Harrington Local Nature Reserve -2B 12. 7 hectare reserve comprising a small former reservoir, with wooded valley, traversed by board walks and bridges. Fed by Eller Beck, the site is sometimes flooded.

Haweswater Bird Sanctuary -2D 25, Tel: 01931 713376. 9,395 hectare RSPB reserve comprising steep oak and birch woodland surrounded by fells, with streams and some heather moor, surrounding Haweswater Reservoir. Special plants include bird's-eye primrose. Limited parking is available in a car park at the southern end, while a public footpath on the west side, and permitted footpath on the east, encircle the reservoir on a 9 miles route. Haweswater is famous for its golden eagle pair which best nest in Riggindale at the southern end of the reservoir. A warden run observation post visitor centre is open daily from April to August between 11am and 4pm, reached by a 1.25 mile uneven path from the car park. There is free access to the fells, but not to the eagles' valley during

the breeding season.

High Leys National Nature Reserve -1D 21. 9 hectare national nature reserve comprising lowland grassland in 5 fields of unimproved grassland once part of nearby High Leys Farm. Managed as a hay meadow and grazed to encourage the growth of a large variety of wild flower species the site is best visited in the summer. The reserve is close to limestone quarries and the Whitehaven to Ennerdale Cyclepath.

Hodbarrow Bird Sanctuary -3B 34, Tel: 01697 351330. 105 hectare coastal RSPB reserve occupying the eastern half of a quiet slightly brackish coastal lagoon, bordered by limestone scrub and grassland. The lagoon, encircled by a level path, forms the largest coastal open water body in the north-west of England. There is a bird hide just off the sea wall on the south side overlooking a small island with the rare little tern, oystercatcher, redshank, great-crested and little grebe, ringed plover. Nesting waders can be seen during the summer. On the lagoon hundreds of wigeon, mallard, goldeneye, pochard, shoveler, red- breasted mergansers and coots over-winter. The grassland, alive with whitethroats and willow warblers in the summer months, has the largest colony of bee orchids in Cumbria.

Humphrey Head (The Joy Ketchen Memorial) Nature Reserve -3B 36. 23 hectare reserve leased from Holker Estates in 1992 and named after the Cumbria Wildlife Trust's first conservation officer. The main interest is the flora of the cliff tops on the west side of the reserve which displays plants such as common and hoary rockrose, bloody cranesbill, blue moor-grass, limestone bedstraw, green-winged orchid and wild thyme. (see also 'Humphrey Head' natural attraction entry).

Hutton Roof Crags Nature Reserve -3A 38. 99 hectare national nature reserve with some of the best areas of limestone pavement in Britain. Made up of the two 19th century enclosures of Lancelot Clark Storth and Burton Fell including Pickles Wood, an ancient woodland. The reserve has grassland, dominated by blue moor-grass, scrub and heath supporting colonies of fritillary butterflies, as well as birds such as tawny owl, green woodpecker and nuthatch. (see also 'Gait Barrows National Nature Reserve' and 'Great Asby Scar National Nature Reserve' entries).

Latterbarrow Nature Reserve -2C 37. 4 hectare reserve of mixed grassland, woodland and scrub with some limited limestone pavement and rock outcrops. There are over 200 species of flowering plants throughout the summer months such as cowslip, various orchids and columbine, and butterflies including brimstone, speckled wood and common blue. The woodland, predominantly of ash and yew, is also home to the rare Lancastrian whitebeam, recognised by its white flowers followed by red berries, which is entirely confined to the limestones around Morecambe Bay.

Leighton Moss Bird Sanctuary -3D 37, Tel: 01524 701601. 130 hectare RSPB reserve, and one of the RSPB's most popular, comprising a large reedbed in a part wooded limestone valley close to Morecambe Bay. Leighton Moss is the largest remaining reedbed in north-west England and the shallow meres and fringing sedge and woodland attract a wide range of wildlife. It is one of the few places in Britain, and the only regular site in northern England, where the rare bittern, a sort of stocky heron breeds. Other birds include a thriving colony of bearded tit, sedge and grasshopper warblers and the secretive water rail. Waders include redshank, lapwing and woodcock with large flocks of wintering wildfowl such as mallard, teal, pintail and shoveler. The marsh above the reedbed is a diverse mixture of species including unusual small marsh dandelion. 5 observation hides are linked by paths through the reeds. A small separated section of the reserve, comprising a steep wooded bank at Crag Foot, overlooks the RSPB Morecambe Bay Bird Sanctuary and Nature Trails.

Linskeldfield Tarn Nature Reserve -1B 14. Six acres of peat and wetland located on farmland home to 16,000 free-range laying hens. Wide variety of wildlife including birds, otters, frogspawn, red squirrels and carp. Twelve person birdwatching hide. Excellent range of birds include shelducks, oyster catchers, shovelers and pintail little grebes. Flat terrain, ideal for wheelchair access.

Longlands Lake Bird Sanctuary -2C 21. Large lake near the confluence of the rivers Ehen and Keekle on the site of the former Longlands iron-ore Mine. Remains of the mine buildings and railway embankments are covered by herb-rich grassland, gorse scrub and broad-leaved woodland. A large number of bird species and winter wildfowl include teal, goldeneye, mallard, warblers, swifts and great crested grebes. A circular footpath encircles the lake. The Longlands Mine was abandoned by 1924 due to economic factors (see Egremont description). Pillars, supporting the roof between the stalls where iron was worked, were subsequently 'robbed' causing subsidence which led to the flooding of the area now called Longlands Lake.

Millom Ironworks Local Nature Reserve -2B 34. Reserve on a former Millom Ironworks slag bank area adjacent a youth hostel. Pathways lead to a viewing platform overlooking the Duddon Estuary. The species-rich grassland supports yellow-wort, rare in Cumbria, and bee orchid. Skylarks breed here, as does the rare natterjack toad (see 'Sandscale Haws National Nature Reserve' entry).

Moor House-Upper Teesdale Nature Reserve (Moor House section) -1D 19. 3,894 hectare national nature reserve forming part of the combined massive 7,387 hectare Moor House-Upper Teesdale Nature Reserve, the Upper Teesdale section being to the east near Cow Green Reservoir (off map). Moor House is made up of the steep scarp slopes of the western flanks of the Pennines with grasslands, limestone outcrops and incised becks leading to huge areas of unburned blanket peat bog or mire, the most significant such area in the North Pennines. It is also the highest area of carboniferous limestone in the country, capped on the fells by thick layers of sandstone.

Next Ness Nature Reserve -see Ulverston plan -2D.

Park Wood National Nature Reserve -3B 38. 14.7 hectare ancient woodland, on a series of limestone terraces divided by areas of limestone pavement, with a small areas of blue moor-grass grassland. The woodland is predominantly ash with a hazel understorey and contains a large number of field maples, usually a southern species. The ground cover includes bluebells and ramsons (wild garlic) and there are many species of fritillary butterflies.

Roudsea Wood and Mosses National Nature Reserve -2A 36. 388 hectare national nature reserve at the head of Morecambe Bay comprising both acid and limestone ancient broad-leaved woodland with trees such as oak, birch, ash, lime and some impressive areas of yew. There are also areas of salt and freshwater marsh and raised bog habitats. The reserve requires a permit to explore.

St Bees Head Bird Sanctuary -2A 20. RSPB reserve featuring the largest cliff seabird colony on the west coast of England, along a 3 mile strip of sandstone cliffs. Best in spring and early summer, nesting colonies of guillemots, razorbills, kittiwakes, fulmars, auks, a few puffins and the only English colony of black guillemots can be seen. 4 viewpoint viewing stations (north of Fleswick Bay) overlook the colony. Plants such as rock samphire, bloody cranesbill and heath spotted orchid flower on the cliff-top, whilst on the shingle beach below, reachable by a footpath at Fleswick Bay, there are a variety of shellfish, crab, mussels and large 'coral' made of sand and shell fragments. Access is via a car park on St Bees beach (and a disabled car park at Tarnflatt Hall, east of St Bees Head Lighthouse on a private road from Sandwith) (see also 'St Bees Head' natural attraction entry).

Sandscale Haws National Nature Reserve NT -3B 34, Tel: 01229 462855. 263.5 hectare national nature reserve comprising one of England's largest and most important sand dune systems stretching for over 3 miles along the southern shore of the Duddon estuary. The huge open bay backed by grassland is home to a thriving and nationally important community of natterjack toads. The extensive dune system has marram grass, sea holly and sea spurge, whilst the mudflats are home to large numbers of wading birds including dunlin, knot and redshank. Nearby is evidence of the haematite iron mines of Roanhead and Park, which along with nearby sites such as Hodbarrow, were a key 19th century industry in Cumbria.

Siddick Pond Local Nature Reserve -1C 13. 21 hectare reserve comprising a large reed-fringed freshwater pond. An important wetland habitat for wildfowl which includes mallard, little grebe, reed bunting and migrating birds. A cycle-route on a former railway line crosses the site. Adjacent was the possibly 4th century Roman fort of Burrow Walls, a part of the 'Western Sea Defences' line of forts and watch towers along the north-western coastline of Cumbria.

Smardale Gill Nature Reserve -3D 27. 42.7 hectare national nature reserve containing some of the most important limestone grasslands in East Cumbria comprising a large area of ancient semi-natural woodland and rich limestone grassland dominated by blue moor-grass. This supports, along the entire length of the reserve, the scotch argus butterfly which flies between late July and early September. The reserve, which was designated a National Nature Reserve in 1997, follows a 3.3 mile section of the former South Durham and Lancashire Union Railway. The central feature, worth a visit in itself, is the impressive Scandal Beck viaduct restored in 1990.

Tarn Moss National Nature Reserve -2C 17. 16 hectare basin mire developed in a hollow where ground water collects. The resultant poor fen has sedges, bog mosses, heather and plants such as marsh marigold. This national nature reserve is of specialised interest and to avoid any damage is best viewed from the rather better drained former Cockermouth, Keswick and Penrith Railway alignment (closed 1972) running along the north of the reserve. This was the highest point or summit level of the railway at 271 m (889 ft).

Trowbarrow Quarry Local Nature Reserve -3D 37. 13.7 hectare former limestone quarry. Quarrying here dates back to around 1870 and ceased in 1959. In 1992, because of its geological and wildlife interest and its location in the Arnside and Silverdale area of outstanding natural beauty, Tarmac abandoned its rights to extract further minerals and in 1996 gifted the site to Lancaster City Council who declared it a protected 'local nature reserve' the following year. The site is a wildlife haven, with much interesting flora and fauna, and is also of national importance to climbers possessing shear cliffs over 30 m (98 ft) high. Waymarking and interpretation boards.

Whitbarrow (Hervey Memorial) Nature Reserve -1C 37. 100 hectare national nature reserve occupying a large enclosure on the highest part of Whitbarrow Scar, a carboniferous limestone escarpment rising to 215 m (705 ft) marked by a summit cairn at Lord's Seat, inscribed in memory of Canon G. A. K. Hervey who founded what is now the Cumbria Wildlife Trust in 1962. The reserve is generally open dry upland with juniper scrub and shelves of grassland between limestone

exposed as a series of parallel north-south ridges, thin and brittle limestone pavement and small cliffs. The grassland is dominated by blue moor-grass, with plants such as dropwort, bird's-foot trefoil, wood sage and common rockrose. The limestone pavement (see 'Gait Barrows National Nature Reserve' entry), the largest examples being on the south-eastern side of the reserve, has a specialist flora with rare species such as rigid buckler fern and Lancastrian whitebeam. Breeding birds include meadow pipit, green and great spotted woodpecker and redstart. Mid-summer is good for butterflies including high brown, pearl-bordered and dark green fritillaries. Information boards.

Whitbarrow (Howe Ridding Wood) Nature Reserve -1C 37. 29 hectare national nature reserve of broad-leaved woodland, mainly ash-hazel with some small-leaved lime, overlying Carboniferous limestone, rising in a series of small crags, terraces and scree slopes to the bottom of Whitbarrow Scar. The northern part of a large expanse of ancient semi-natural woodland, the rich ground flora includes green hellebore, wild daffodil in the spring and the rare dark red helleborine and rigid buckler fern. The lower scree slope immediately below the scar is colonised by yew and Lancastrian whitebeam (see 'Latterbarrow Nature Reserve' entry). In contrast, Calfclose Wood in the west of the reserve overlies impervious Silurian slate with springs leading to wet acidic conditions supporting oak, birch and alder. Birds include buzzard, tawny owl, woodcock and great spotted woodpecker, and roe and red deer can be seen. Butterflies include the rare high brown and pearl-bordered fritillaries.

Picnic Site

Astley's Plantation Picnic Site, Newby Bridge -1B 36.
Beech Hill Picnic Site, Storrs -3D 31.
Birks Bridge Picnic Site, Seathwaite -2A 30.
Bogle Crag Picnic Site, Satterthwaite -3C 31.
Brown Howe Picnic Site, Water Yeat -3B 30.
Cinderbarrow Picnic Site, Yealand Redmayne -3A 38.
Coniston Boating Centre Picnic Area
-see Coniston plan -3C.
Crosscanonby Salt Pans Picnic Site -1B 12.
Dodd Wood Picnic Site, Little Crosthwaite -2C 15.
Ennerdale Water Picnic Site, Ennerdale Bridge -2A 22.
Ennerdale Water Picnic Site, Ennerdale Bridge -1A 22.
Ennerdale Water Picnic Site, Ennerdale Bridge -2A 22.
Eskdale (Dalegarth) Station Picnic Site, Boot -1D 29.
Farra Grain Picnic Sites, Satterthwaite -3C 31.
Fell Foot Park Picnic Area, Newby Bridge NT *-1B 36.*

Force Beck Picnic Site, Force Mills -3C 31.
Grasmere Picnic Area -see Grasmere plan -2B.
Greenodd Picnic Site -2A 36.
Grizedale Beck (China Plantation) Picnic Site -2C 31.
Grizedale Picnic Site -3C 31.
High Bowkerstead Picnic Site, Force Mills -3C 31.
High Cross Picnic Site, Hawkshead Hill -2C 31.
Hursthole Point Picnic Site, Thornthwaite -2C 15.
Killington Reservoir Picnic Site, M6 (Southbound), Killington -3D 33.
Knott Coppice Picnic Site, Grizedale -3C 31.
Lakeland View Picnic Site, Braithwaite -3C 15.
Legburthwaite Picnic Site -1A 24.
Longlands Lake Picnic Site, Cleator -2C 21.
Low Dale Park Picnic Site, Force Mills -3C 31.
Machell's Coppice Picnic Site, Coniston -3C 31.
Machell's Coppice Picnic Site, Coniston -2C 31.
Moor Top Picnic Site, Roger Ground -2C 31.
Noble Knott Picnic Site, Braithwaite -3C 15.
Oldside Picnic Site, Workington -2B 12.
Park a Mor (Rigg Wood) Picnic Site, High Nibthwaite -3B 30.
Rayrigg Meadow Picnic Site, Windermere
-see Windermere plan -1B.
Revelin Moss Picnic Site, Braithwaite -3C 15.
Whinlatter Visitor Centre Picnic Site, Braithwaite -3C 15.

Place of interest (General)

Borrowdale Yews NT **-2C 23**. 3 ancient yew trees above the River Derwent. near Seathwaite Farm, west of the road south from Seatoller. There were once 4 trees (one was blown down in a storm of 1883). The biggest tree at 6 m (20 ft) girth is estimated at over 2,000 years old and is hollow enough to stand in. It is rare for great yews to survive on a bare hillside away from the shelter of a park or graveyard. They are also remarkable for growing on 'Borrowdale Volcanic' strata, when they prefer limestone, and in Borrowdale, the wettest inhabited place in England with an average 3,302 mm of rainfall a year. Such is their significance, they are also the only yew trees marked by the Ordnance Survey. Recognised by their dark green needle like leaves, red berries present in the autumn tell that these are all female trees. English yew is one of the longest-lived trees in the world, its orange-brown dense timber was the best for longbows; a tree with a girth of 3 m (10 ft) or more will be over 400 years old, but note that yew bark, leaves and seeds are all poisonous (see also 'Lorton Yew' and 'Martindale Yew' entries).

Coniston Brewery -see Coniston plan -1B.

Crookabeck Angoras / Herdwicks -1C 25, Tel: 017684 82742. Small flock of Herdwick sheep and angora goats on a 16 hectare farm situated beneath Place Fell, south of Ullswater. Herdwick and mohair fleeces are spun, dyed and made into rugs, throws, scarves, socks, knitting yarns etc. which are sold in the farmshop. By appointment only.

Crow's Nest -see Whitehaven plan -3B.

Dora's Field NT **-3B 24**. The sloping Dora's Field, formerly The Rashfield, next to the churchyard of Rydal St Mary's Church was bought by Wordsworth in 1826 to build a house for his daughter Dora. Grieved by her death in 1847 he planted, aided by his wife and sister, hundreds of daffodils as a memorial to her. Given to the National Trust in 1935 by his grandson, the field hosts a spectacular display in the spring.

Fairy Steps -3D 37. An intriguing narrow set of rough steps cutting up through the sheer limestone cliff face of Whin Scar. Until 1866, when the church at Arnside was completed, villagers had to walk the 2.5 miles to the church at Beetham, crossing Arnside Moss and using the steps on the way. Known as the Coffin Route, the footpath was also used to carry the dead for burial in the churchyard at Beetham; an iron ring in the cliffs north face is thought to have been used to haul coffins up the cliff as the steps were too narrow. On the Limestone Link long distance footpath.

(Giant's Grave, Penrith) -see Penrith plan -3D.

Gosforth Cross -1B 28. 10th century red sandstone Viking cross, in its original stepped stone base, dating from c.940 AD in the churchyard of St Mary's church, Gosforth. At over 4.3 m (14 ft) high, it is the tallest Viking cross in England, the survival of such a slender shaft covered with well preserved intricate carvings being exceptional. The carvings are a mixture of pagan Scandinavian (Norse) mythology and Christian symbolism and are important in representing the transition period between the two cultures. There was another ancient cross in the churchyard but this was converted into a sundial in 1789; the head is on display in the church.

High Head Sculpture Valley -2D 11. Tel: 016974 73552. Set on a working dairy farm, the life-size sculptures carved from wood, stone, iron and bronze are scattered throughout the landscape. The gallery displays changing exhibitions of traditional and contemporary sculptures, paintings, photography and ceramics and there is the opportunity to see the artists at work in the workshop. The River Ive runs through the Sculpture Valley and is home to an abundance of wildlife such as herons and kingfishers. Waymarked trails, play area, tearoom and Alice's Wonderland (an independent museum) complete this eclectic attraction.

Irton Cross -1B 28. 3 m (10 ft) high carved red sandstone cross dating from the early 9th century. One of 2 'Celtic' crosses in the churchyard of St Paul's church, one is ancient and the other a more modern copy, it is important as one of the oldest crosses in Cumbria. Dating from before the Norse invasion, unlike Gosforth Cross, it has no obvious Scandinavian design traits and no figures, but is decorated instead with Celtic spiral and fret patterns of Irish origin similar to those found in the famous Book of Kells of c.800 AD.

Jennings Brewery -see Cockermouth plan -2C.

Lakeland Maize Maze -1A 38, Tel: 015395 61760. Seasonal attraction designed by the world's leading maze designers, the maze is cut out of a nine acre field of maize with a specially designed farm quiz trail to attempt along the way. There are plenty of other activities to entertain young visitors; go karts, smaller themed mazes, pedal tractors and table top puzzles. Farm animals can be seen grazing in nearby fields. Open from July to September annually.

Lakeland Miniature Village -3B 36, Tel: 015395 58500. Cumbria's only miniature village with over 140 buildings expertly made from local Coniston slate. Cumbrian houses, farms and barns, including half timbered period houses, re-create the local architecture of the Lakeland landscape. Included are authentic models of Beatrix Potter's Hill Top and a replica of Slaters Packhorse Bridge in Little Langdale.

Lakeland Sheep and Wool Centre, The -2A 14, S, Tel: 01900 822673. A face-to-face meeting with up to 19 different breeds of sheep including herdwick, cotswold, shetland, soay and jacob, displayed together on stage during an indoor presentation (four times daily, except Friday and Saturday) in a special 300 seat indoor arena or theatre. Visitors can discover many different facts about each breed, witness a sheep shearer at work and the skills of highly trained sheep dogs. A surprisingly entertaining and educational experience, especially suitable for children.

Lakes Glass Centre, The -see Ulverston plan -2D.

(Lanternhouse (Centre for Celebratory Art), Ulverston) -see Ulverston plan -3B.

Lorton Yew -2B 14. Growing on the bank of Hope Beck, half hidden behind the wall of a derelict brewery, the original site in 1828 of Jennings Brewery now part used as the village hall, stands the forgotten Lorton Yew. Described by William Wordsworth over 200 years ago in his poem 'Yew Trees', this famous tree was recorded in the Domesday Book in 1085 AD. A storm in the early 19th century, after Wordsworth's visit, destroyed half the tree reducing its girth to 4 m (13 ft), however nothing can remove the tangible sense of history of this location (see also 'Borrrowdale Yews' and 'Martindale Yew' entries).

Lourdes Grotto -2C 21, Tel: 01946 810324. The 'Grotto of Our Lady of Lourdes' was built by the unemployed men of the parish during the depression of 1926 in response to the large number of Catholic immigrants that had been arriving in the town since the 1850s. Built in exchange for vouchers for footwear and clothing, money raised by the parish priest Father F. C. Clayton, and opened on 30th October 1927, it was restored in 1979 being rededicated by Cardinal Basil Hume in July 1980. Still a place of annual pilgrimage, open to all for prayer and quiet enjoyment, it is one of many replica 'Lourdes Grottos' around the world based on the original shrine in south-west France which was built to commemorate the 18 apparitions of the Virgin Mary to a 14 year old French girl, Bernadette Soubirous, which took place between 11th February and 16th July 1858 at the Grotto of Massabielle. The grotto stands in the grounds of St Mary's Roman Catholic church.

Low Sizergh Farm Trail -1A 38, Tel: 015395 60426. Organic dairy farm, leased from the National Trust, with award winning organic farm shop and craft gallery, keeping dairy cows and free range laying hens. 3 waymarked farm trails, following short (0.5 hour), intermediate, and long (1 hour) routes allow an organic farm to be seen in action, with conservation areas including a pond, 400 year old hedges, limestone walls, replanted orchard and Low Park Wood. The milking parlour (milking around 3.45pm) is viewable from a special window in the tea room.

Martindale Yew -1C 25. Ancient yew tree situated in the churchyard of Martindale St Martin's Church, sheltering the tomb of a former rector. This is a male yew thought to be some 1,300 years old and may have been planted when a church was first established here. Without a hollow centre usual in ancient trees, it is possible the prevailing climatic conditions may have slowed its growth (see also 'Borrrowdale Yews' and 'Lorton Yew' entries).

MeadowVole Maze -2C 29, Tel: 01229 717614. The MeadowVole Maze is a millennium project designed to make learning about conservation fun and a perfect accompaniment to Muncaster Castle gardens and the 'World Owl Centre'. The maze dramatises the perils faced by Muncaster's real meadow voles from predators such as badgers and owls. After viewing a short film young visitors are 'reduced' to just two and a half inches tall and led onto a pathway on a high summers day edged by what appears to be seven feet high meadow grass, before journeying with Max Meadowvole through the maze to the safety of his home by nightfall in an environment that mirrors the real wildflower meadow above it in a 'circle of life' story. The route ends in dusk, then darkness...when the owls come out.

(Puzzling Place, The, Keswick) -see Keswick plan -3C.

Rydal Stepping Stones -3B 24. Splendid line of tall rectangular cut stepping stones fording the River Rothay, opposite Stepping Stones house on Under Loughrigg (1.5 mile walk from Ambleside (via Miller Bridge) or a third of a mile walk south from the car park at Pelter Bridge). The stones would have been familiar to members of the Wordsworth family, as in 1881 William Wordsworth's youngest son William, purchased the house. The house remained in the family until 1935.

St Bees Lifeboat Station -2B 20. Operating an Atlantic 75 class inshore rescue boat, the fastest (32 knots) lifeboat design in the RNLI (Royal National Lifeboat Institution) fleet after the E class. Its hull of length 7.5 m (24 ft 6"), hence the name, is constructed of glass reinforced plastic, the class having being first introduced in early 1994. The first St Bees Inshore Lifeboat (a D class) was commissioned in 1985. The station is one of 231 (in 2003) in Great Britain and Ireland whose crews are estimated to have rescued over 127,000 people since the foundation of the RNLI in 1824. The station is open during lifeboat exercise.

West Coast Indoor Karting -1A 12, Tel: 01900 816472. One of the largest indoor go-karting tracks in the country. 520 m (569 yds) full racing circuit with 25 mph kids karts and 40 mph adult karts fitted with engines of between 160 and 200cc. Suitable for ages 8 years and above, protective overalls, helmets and gloves are provided.

Whitehaven Labyrinth, The -see Whitehaven plan -4B.
Whitehaven St Nicholas' Church Tower
-see Whitehaven plan -3B.
Whitehaven Quest -see Whitehaven plan -3A.
World of Beatrix Potter Attraction, The
-see Windermere plan -4B.

Prehistoric Monument

See also Hill Fort
Blakeley Raise (Kinniside) Stone Circle -2D 21. Remote circle, 16.5 m (54 ft) in diameter, of probably early Bronze Age or Neolithic origin, on Blakeley Moss beneath Blakeley Raise close by an unfenced road sometimes frequented by wild horses. Restored in 1925. A wide gap to the south between the two tallest stones may have been an entrance. The Great Stone of Blakeley, a third of a mile to the east, is thought to be a natural rock feature.

Castlerigg Stone Circle EH -3D 15. This is the finest, and most visited, of all the stone circles in Cumbria because of its easily accessible and unrivalled setting. On a low hill encircled

by a backdrop formed of a ring of distant mountains comprising Skiddaw, Lonscale Fell and Blencathra to the north, High Rigg and Helvellyn to the south-east, the Derwent Fells to the west and the north Pennines through a gap to the east. It is also one of Britain's earliest stone circles thought to date from the late Neolithic period around 3200 BC. 38 stones (33 standing) of variable size and shape are set in a 30 m (99 ft) flattened circle (at the widest point) with a rare rectangle, or sanctuary, of a further 10 stones, adjoining the circle in the south-east corner, within. It is thought there were once 41 stones making this a relatively well preserved monument. The main entrance is to the north flanked by two of the tallest stones. Owned by the National Trust, but under English Heritage guardianship, there is a display board at the main field entrance.

Cockpit Stone Circle, The -3D 17. Part of the Moor Divock Group or Complex of small mainly undistinguished stones, cairn circles, fragments of avenues, and shallow holes called shake holes. Thought to date from the early Bronze Age, The Cockpit is the biggest and most recognisable of the Moor Divock circles, set near a junction of footpaths on the course of

the High Street Roman Road, just before the land drops away to Ullswater. The circle is said to be a pair of concentric rings, or double ring stone circle, now mostly single, except on the north-west and south-west sides.

Elva Plain Stone Circle -1B 14. Of a comparatively early late Neolithic date, set on the south-eastern slope of Elva Hill, this circle has 15 fallen boulderous stones set in a large perfect circle of 35 m (115 ft) diameter. Of an estimated original count of 30, most of those remaining are on the southern arc, only a few are to the north. With an average height of about 0.3 m (1 ft) many are hardly visible above ground level, except for the tallest, about 1 m (3 ft) high, set on the western axis. In the middle of a field, accessed by a permitted footpath requiring a 0.25 mile walk from the road to the south, this site is not the most impressive you may encounter, however it is pleasantly sited with views east across the north end of Bassenthwaite Lake to Skiddaw and to the low Ling Fell and Sale Fell to the south.

Eskdale Moor (Burnmoor) Stone Circles NT -1D 29. A complex of 5 stone circles on Eskdale Moor set against a wide panorama of fells. A 1 mile steep uphill walk from Boot Packhorse Bridge, they are easy to miss from footpaths that pass on either side. Brat's Hill Stone Circle, the largest at 32 m (105 ft) in diameter at its widest, is barely visible on the heather covered moor but is important because of 5 small cairns with kerbstones contained within the ring. Of 42 stones, of average height of about 0.5 m, only 7 or 8 appear to be upright. Close by, to the north-west are the two 16 m (52 ft) diameter circles, with central cairns, of White Moss Stone Circle, visible well above the surrounding grass; these are the best of the group and the real reason for a visit to the complex.

Gamelands Stone Circle -3C 27. Around 34 stones, most fallen, in an oval 44 m (144 ft) across at its widest, with the majority in an arc on the northern side. Originally there were 42 stones. Situated in a quite natural landscape amphitheatre below Knott Hill the circle has much in common with Castlerigg Stone Circle and Swinside (Sunkenkirk) Stone Circle although in a less complete condition. Situated in a field 250 m (273 yds) down a byway off the Orton to Raisbeck road, it is visible over a tall wall. The landowners permission is required for closer inspection. Exterior view only.

Giant's Grave -2A 34. Two pointed upright stones, carved with ancient cup marks, situated on flat land in the shadow of Black Combe, between Lacra Stone Circles in the east and the sea. Adjacent to a public footpath, the stones are 2.5 m (8 ft) and 3 m (10 ft) high separated by around 4 m (13 ft), resembling a giant's grave, a not uncommon analogy.

Goggleby Stone -1B 26. 2 m (6.5 ft) high solitary standing stone of suggested late Neolithic date. Part of the denuded Shap Avenue of stones (which is thought to have run from the part destroyed Kemp Howe stone circle, south of Shap, towards Skellaw Hill barrow). Beside public footpath running from Shap to join minor road to Keld.

Grey Croft Stone Circle -1A 28. 10 stones, of a reported original 12, in an 27 m (88.5 ft) diameter circle dating from the late Neolithic period c.2500 BC, form a visual paradox in a setting immediately to the south of the huge BNFL (British Nuclear Fuels Ltd.) reprocessing plant. Restored in 1949, after being buried by a farmer to facilitate his ploughing in 1820, the stones are large irregular boulders with an average height of around 1.2 m (4 ft) each standing in a slight hollow, with a low outlier to the north. The site is best approached from the Seascale Banks on the coast footpath (the road to the plant has strict no parking restrictions). On private land the landowners permission is required to enter the field. Exterior view only.

King Arthur's Round Table EH -2A 18. Circular earthwork henge of possibly early Bronze Age period. 90 m (295 ft) in total diameter, and bounded by a ditch and irregular outer bank both of about 1.5 m (5 ft), there is a raised entrance at the south east corner. Until the 17th century there was another entrance with 2 standing stones outside on the north, but the site was heavily damaged in the 19th century by the building of the road to Pooley Bridge and use as a tea garden. A smaller 'table' was once located a short distance to the south (see also the older Mayburgh Henge nearby).

Lacra Stone Circles -2A 34. 4 Bronze Age stone circles formed of irregular boulders, and a ring cairn, notionally lettered from A to E, accessed by a footpath from Kirksanton. Lacra A, nearest a ruined farmhouse has 2 stones standing of only 6. Close by to the east is the indistinct, difficult to find Lacra D, in poor condition, it is best recognised by a stone slab in the middle, two stone rows supposedly run from it adding to the confusion. Also near here is Lacra E, a ring cairn. Around 320 m (350 yds) further south, Lacra B, the best of the group is clearly visible with 6 stones of maybe an original 11; with binoculars the Giant's Grave standing stones can be seen to the west from here. Lacra C close by to the east has only 3 fallen stones in an apparent arc, the most enigmatic, it is not certain whether they are part of the largest circle (21 m or 69 ft) or the remains of a stone row.

Mayburgh Henge EH -see Penrith plan -6D.

Oddendale Stone Circle -2B 26. An unusual concentric double stone circle on a flat site west of a bridleway south of Oddendale, with an outer 26.2 m (86 ft) diameter ring of 32 stones and an inner 7.5 m (25 ft) diameter ring with the stones almost touching; this is probably a ring cairn, the remains of a central burial mound which was flanked by kerb stones. No stone is larger than 1 m (3 ft) high with the largest boulders on the east side, being part hidden in the moorland grass.

Swinside (Sunkenkirk) Stone Circle -1B 34. Very well preserved Bronze Age stone circle in a tranquil setting on a moorland plateau beneath Swinside Fell, regarded as one of the finest in Western Europe. Unlike many circles, here 55 large stones (many more than Castlerigg but in a less spectacular setting) of an estimated original 60, around half of which are still standing, are closely spaced at around 1.5 m (5 ft) intervals in a compact circle approximately 28.5 m (93.5 ft) in diameter making the whole extremely impressive. There is a well defined entrance with double portal stones outside the circle perimeter to the south-east, with the tallest stone, a slender 2.3 m (7.5 ft) high pillar in the north. On private land, reached by a signposted 0.75 mile uphill walk along a bridleway from near Cragg Hall, the site is visible adjacent. Although there is a gate and stepped stile in the wall close by, the landowner's permission is required to enter the field. Exterior view only.

Railway (Heritage, Narrow Gauge, Miniature)

Cinderbarrow Miniature Railway -3A 38, S. 7.25" gauge miniature railway operated by the Lancaster and Morecambe Model Engineering Society, usually on Sundays in season located at Cinderbarrow picnic site in Cinderbarrow Quarry.

Curwen Park Miniature Railway, Workington
-see Workington plan -2E, S.

Lakeside and Haverthwaite Railway -2A 36 to 1B 36, S, Tel: 015395 31594. 3.5 mile long standard gauge railway operated by predominantly steam locomotives. Stations are at Haverthwaite (car park and picnic area), Newby Bridge and Lakeside. The line occupies the sole surviving part of the Furness Railway branch line from near Ulverston to Windermere Lakeside, opened in full in June 1869 to establish a tourist link with the Windermere United Yacht Company steamers on Windermere in which the railway held shares. The Lakeside branch was closed to passengers in September 1965, and reopened as a heritage line in May 1973. The railway connects at Lakeside with the Aquarium of the Lakes,

and with Windermere Lake Cruises who operate ferry services on the lake to Bowness (Windermere) and Waterhead (Ambleside), both popular destinations.

Port Haverigg Holiday Village Railway -3B 34, S, Tel: 01229 772880. 7.25" gauge, approximately 366 m (400 yds) long circular miniature railway opened in 1997. Running from Little Hoddy station in Port Haverigg Holiday Village. The railway is open to non-residents of the site.

Ravenglass and Eskdale Railway (La'al Ratty)
-2B 28 to 1D 29, Tel: 01229 717171. 6.75 mile long 15" gauge railway operated by narrow gauge predominantly steam locomotives. Stations are at Ravenglass, Muncaster Mill, Miteside, Murthwaite, Irton Road, The Green, Fisherground (Halt), Beckfoot and Dalegarth for Boot station. Known locally as 'La'al Ratty', the 3 ft gauge line opened in 1875, to transport iron ore to the Furness Railway at Ravenglass, conveying passengers the following year and later carrying granite from Eskdale quarry west of Beckfoot to a crushing plant at

Murthwaite. The line was closed in 1913, but was reopened using 15" gauge track in 1915-7 by Mr Wynne J. Bassett-Lowke, a model maker who became famous as a supplier of quality model railways during the period 1900-65. The granite quarries eventually closed in 1953 and, without the benefits of today's tourist industry, the railway was sold at auction in 1960, being saved from scrap by a group of railway enthusiasts. There is a children's playground at Ravenglass station. A delightful fairly level 4 mile walk from Dalegarth for Boot station, or the adjacent Picnic Site (and car park), taking in either side of the River Esk (crossing it at the Eskdale (Doctor) Bridge), the beautifully sited Eskdale St Catherine's Church, Gill Force, Stanley Force, and Eskdale Mill at Boot, is not to be missed.

Safari Railway -3C 35, S, Tel: 01229 466086. 7.25" gauge, approximately 183 m (200 yds) long out and back miniature railway opened in 1995. Running from the zoo shop of the South Lakes Wild Animal Park to a point overlooking the Indonesian otter enclosure, this short line is operated by a diesel engine.

Threlkeld Quarry Line -3A 16, S, Tel: 01768 779747 / 01228 561883. 2 ft gauge, 0.5 mile long demonstration line running from the locomotive shed at the Threlkeld Quarry and Mining Museum to the bottom level of the former Threlkeld Quarry. Passenger carrying using ex-industrial diesel (and eventually steam) locomotives and rolling stock is planned.

Roman Remains

Alauna Roman Fort (Maryport) -1A 12. Earthworks of a large Roman fort, built by legionaries probably during the reign of the emperor Hadrian (AD 117-138), together with an associated Roman town (the vicus) outside the gates. One of the biggest forts on Hadrian's frontier, built for around 1,000 soldiers, and linked by the Carlisle road to Derventio Roman Fort at Papcastle and Old Carlisle Roman Fort near Wigton. It is thought to have been the command headquarters for the

'Western Sea Defences' chain of fortlets and watch towers along the Solway Coast, an extension of Hadrian's Wall. Alauna imported supplies for the wall and the city of Carlisle and handled a large export trade. In use for some 280-300 years it was abandoned in the 5th century. Some of the Roman town could still be seen in the 1700s but the stone was used to build 'Mary-Port'. Exterior view only.

Alauna Roman Fort (Natland) -see Kendal plan -7B.

Brocavum Roman Fort -2A 18. Low earthworks of a 1.5 hectare Roman fort built at the confluence of the rivers Eamont and Lowther, and at an important strategic crossroads of a north-south Roman road with the route east to York. From here a road (High Street) ran south-westwards over the mountains above Ullswater to Galava Roman Fort, Waterhead, and then over the high passes of Wrynose and Hardknott (see Hardknott Roman Fort entry) to the port of Ravenglass. Later the fort was used as the bailey for Brougham Castle, and had to be crossed to reach the original entrance to the castle. Carved stones from the fort are on display in the castle.

Derventio Roman Fort -1A 14. Barely visible earthworks of a late 4th century Roman fort at Papcastle, north of the River Derwent. One of the larger forts in northern England (at 2.8 ha, bigger than the famous Housesteads fort (2 ha) on Hadrian's Wall) it was built in a significant cereal growing area, its role being a re-supply base and support to forts on the wall to the north. The Roman presence here is considered the foundation for the town of Cockermouth nearby. Like many other forts Derventio was robbed of stone after the Romans had left, much being used in the walls of Cockermouth Castle. On private land, the only possible views are from the A595 which runs along the north-west of the site. A footpath north-west off the minor road over this road follows the Roman road route towards Maryport and the A595 itself to the north-east has a long straight section typical of Roman road alignments. Exterior view only.

Galava Roman Fort EH -see Ambleside plan -5A.

Hardknott (Mediobogdum) Roman Fort EH -1A 30. Excavated and partially restored remains of a Roman fort of the 2nd century built between 120 and 138 AD to control the road over the Hardknott and Wrynose Passes, from the port of Ravenglass to Galava Roman Fort at Waterhead. Regarded as one of the most dramatic Roman sites in Britain, spectacularly sited on a spur of land projecting from the western side of the Hardknott Pass overlooked by the crags of Border End, there are stunning views down the Esk Valley to the coast at Ravenglass and to some of the highest fells in Lakeland. The substantial remains include the square plan outer walls up to 1.7 m (5.5 ft) thick and about as high, with 4 gateways, and the foundations of the inner buildings including the headquarters, commandant's house and granaries. Outside the fort to the south-east is a bath house with 3 rooms and a large artificially flattened parade ground to the north-east. There are interpretative panels at various points.

Low Borrowbridge Roman Fort -1D 33. Well defined rectangular earthwork of a 1.1 hectare Roman fort, once with stone walls, occupied until the 4th century. Roads ran north to Brocavum Roman Fort and south to Calacum Roman Fort at Nether Burrow, near Kirkby Lonsdale. Coins, found during the construction of the Lancaster to Carlisle Railway (opened December 1846) adjacent, are in the Penrith Museum. On private land but visible from adjacent minor road. Exterior view only.

Old Carlisle Roman Fort -1B 10. Very well preserved fort ditches and mound covering the stone walls (not visible) and earth rampart of a rectangular plan Roman fort of around 1.8 hectares, together with ridges and humps between the fort and the A595 to the south thought to be of a civilian settlement. The fort was linked by road to Alauna Roman Fort, Maryport to the south-west. On private land, the only possible distant views

are from the main road or adjacent minor road to the east. Exterior view only.

Ravenglass Roman Bath House (Walls Castle) EH -2B 28. Remains of about half of the Roman bath house of Glannoventa Roman Fort. The bath house (known as 'Walls Castle'), 12 m (39 ft) by 27 m (89 ft) with intact partly plastered walls 3.5 m (11.5 ft) high, higher than any other Roman building in the north of England, has remains of the hot and cold rooms, some of which had hypocausts (under-floor heating). There is an interpretative panel. The wide estuary, sheltered by sandbars with a navigable channel, made Ravenglass a natural safe harbour for Roman galleys, becoming an important naval port which it remained until the 17th century, by which time the channel had silted up. From here a difficult and steeply graded road ran over the Hardknott Pass to the spectacular Hardknott (Mediobogdum) Roman Fort and then on via the Wrynose Pass to Galava Roman Fort at Waterhead. The fort, the subject of many fanciful legends over the years, can be reached by a third of a mile walk along the Cumbria Coastal Way from the southern end of Main Street in Ravenglass.

Roman Milefortlet 21 -1B 12. Fully excavated Roman milefortlet with interpretation panels, and reconstructed Roman palisade viewing platform, overlooking the Solway coast on a low, red-sandstone cliff just over the brow of Swarthy Hill. The milefortlet formed part of the 'Western Sea Defences', a series of fortlets, interspersed with small towers, which linked with Hadrian's Wall, built to defend against the possibility of invaders from Galloway circumventing the wall end. Its placement just off the brow of the hill is thought to be keep it exactly one Roman mile (just over nine tenths of a normal statute mile) from the next milefortlet. This is the only element of Hadrian's coastal defences of the Roman Empire's north-west frontier to have been wholly excavated (in 1990-1). It is thought the fortlet was only occupied for a short period during the reign of Hadrian, at the time of the initial planning and construction of the wall (around 122 AD), being decommissioned after a very short period of time.

Spot Height

Blencathra (Saddleback) 868 m (2,848 ft) -2A 16. Blencathra ('blaen' is the Celtic word for summit) is one of the great mountains of Lakeland. Although lower than its neighbour Skiddaw, across the Glenderaterra Beck to the west, it is an awe inspiring sight from the main A66 road to the south, 4 gouged valleys on its precipitous south face adding to its ominous dominance. By contrast the northern slopes are gentle, but all main ascents are from the south.

Cross Fell 893 m (2,930 ft) -1D 19. The highest summit in the Pennine chain set in a high expanse of moorland. Prolonged slopes lead to the flat top with extensive views. The source of the River Tees, which flows to Middlesbrough, is just below in the bleak moorland to the east. A 'golf-ball' air traffic control radar station can be seen to the south-east atop the neighbouring Great Dun Fell.

Fairfield 873 m (2,864 ft) NT -2B 24. Fairfield, the Lake District's 13th highest mountain, is most popularly reached by the classic 'Fairfield Horseshoe' walk (see Ambleside description). Fairfield, a domed grassy plateau has northern slopes comprising deep corries and impressive crags giving views north to St Sunday Crag (841 m or 2,759 ft), and north-east into Deepdale, however the top of Fairfield can be confusing in low cloud and mist and a compass is essential.

Great Gable 899 m (2,949 ft) NT -2C 23. The Lake District's seventh highest mountain and regarded as one of the finest and most popular mountains in the national park, the classic pyramid or cone shape of Great Gable (as seen from Wasdale) forms the basis of the Lake District National Park's logo.

The fell was originally known from Viking times as Great Gavel, referring to the 'gable end of a house'. The mountain is approachable from every direction, the most direct is north-east from Wasdale over Gavel Neese (Gable Nose). A bronze topographical relief with inscription (of 8th June 1924) on the summit of Great Gable is a permanent memorial to the 20 members of the Fell and Rock Climbing Club who died in the war. In October 1923, as part of the memorial, the title deeds of 1,214 hectares of high mountain fells acquired by their fellow-members, were gifted to the National Trust to preserve this archetypal Lakeland landscape for future generations.

Helvellyn 950 m (3,117 ft) -1A 24. The third highest mountain in England, Helvellyn lies between Thirlmere and Ullswater halfway along, and at the most elevated point of one of the longest mountain ranges in the Lake District. It is claimed that it is climbed by more people than any other British mountain. The west side of Helvellyn presents an uninteresting smooth face over Dunmail Raise, but to the east are fine buttresses and wild hanging valleys. A small tablet just south of the large cross-shaped summit shelter celebrates the first successful landing of an aeroplane on a British mountain top in 1926. Helvellyn is most popularly climbed from the east by the famous route along Striding Edge above Red Tarn.

High Street 828 m (2,717 ft) -2C 25. High Street is the highest of the group of fells east of the Kirkstone Pass. The wide flat-topped elongated plateau forming the summit has a trig pillar and gives views in all directions including east to the Pennine chain. It was once used as a racecourse. A well known landmark to the south-west is a tall pillar of stones on Thornthwaite Crag. There are long ridges, with deep corries in between, on the eastern side (one holding Blea Water) and it is one of these, Rough Crag and Riggindale Crag, that form the most direct and easiest followed 3.5 mile route to the summit. Parking at the car park at the southern end of Haweswater Reservoir. High Street famously refers to the Roman Road which followed the ridge top for most of the way between Galava Roman Fort, near Ambleside and Brocavum Roman Fort, near Penrith.

Langdale Pikes 736 m (2,415 ft) NT -3D 23. The Langdale Pikes are a classic icon of the Lake District. The distinctive twin silhouettes of the sugar-loaf shape of Pike of (o') Stickle (709 m or 2,326 ft) and the highest point of Harrison Stickle (736 m or 2,415 ft), although not of exceptional height, are considered one of the Lake District's finest and most recognisable group of summits, being visible from most of Lakeland's south-east approaches. The pikes are climbed by a very popular and relatively easy 4 mile circular walk from car parks at the New Dungeon Ghyll Hotel. Just east of Pike of Stickle, at the top of a badly eroded scree slope, is the famous Great Langdale Neolithic axe factory. It produced the raw material for green-stone polished axes of the period found all over Britain (finds are in the Kendal Museum).

The Langdales are considered two of the Lake District's most beautiful valleys. A circular drive from Skelwith Bridge along the narrow Little Langdale, climbs up past Blea Tarn before spectacular views enfold as the route drops down into Great Langdale. Located here is the Old Dungeon Ghyll Hotel (now owned by the National Trust) famous for its Climber's Bar visited by many of the early climbers of Everest and other Himalayan expeditions.

Old Man of Coniston, The (Coniston Old Man) 803 m (2,635 ft) -2B 30. Sometimes known as Coniston Old Man, this is the most southerly of the great Lakeland peaks, popular, and relatively easily climbed from Coniston. From the substantial summit cairn there are panoramic views to the Scafell range, the highest fell in England, and a seascape of the Furness Peninsula and the Isle of Man. Closer by, the entire length of Coniston Water is visible to the east, and immediately to the west the forbidding shear rock wall of Dow Crag (778 m or

2,552 ft), above Goat's Water, one of the best rock climbing faces in the Lake District.

Pillar 892 m (2,927 ft) NT -2B 22. Pillar occupies a fine situation at the head of the Mosedale and Ennerdale valleys and is named after, and famous for, the great buttress of Pillar Rock (780 m or 2,559 ft) on the north-east flank which overlooks Ennerdale, 566 m (1,857 ft) directly below. A direct

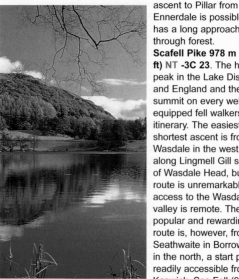

ascent to Pillar from Ennerdale is possible but has a long approach walk through forest.

Scafell Pike 978 m (3,209 ft) NT -3C 23. The highest peak in the Lake District and England and the summit on every well equipped fell walkers itinerary. The easiest and shortest ascent is from Wasdale in the west, along Lingmell Gill south of Wasdale Head, but this route is unremarkable and access to the Wasdale valley is remote. The most popular and rewarding route is, however, from Seathwaite in Borrowdale in the north, a start point readily accessible from Keswick. Sca Fell (964 m or 3,163 ft), the second highest peak in England is only 0.75 miles to the south-west of Scafell Pike.

Skiddaw 931 m (3,054 ft) -2D 15. Skiddaw, England's fourth highest mountain (one of only 4 in the Lake District over 3,000 ft), with its distinctive triangular slate bulk soaring high above Keswick, is the oldest mountain in the Lake District, famous for its unsurpassed views to Derwent Water and, at the summit, as far as the Isle of Man and the Pennines. Not for those seeking solitude, it is one of the most popular fells for walking in the Lake District, readily accessible with well worn paths and easy terrain.

Viewpoint (180 degree)

See also Viewpoint (360)
Arnside Knott Viewpoint NT -3D 37.
(Ashness Bridge Viewpoint, Watendlath -1D 23.)
Birker Fell Viewpoint, Ulpha -2D 29.
Biskey Howe Viewpoint, Bowness-on-Windermere -see Windermere plan -5C.
Castlehead Wood Viewpoint, Keswick NT -see Keswick plan -4C.
Castle Howe Viewpoint, Kendal -see Kendal plan -4B.
Dodd Wood Osprey Viewpoint -2C 15, S. Low level outdoor viewing platform in Dodd Wood, reached by a short uphill walk from the Forestry Commission's Dodd Wood car park (see 'Dodd Wood Forest Walks' entry). Here there are views to a specially constructed osprey nest site about 1 mile away on the opposite south side of Bassenthwaite Lake, built in 1998. Free telescopes are available to use from project staff and a live video camera link of the nest site operates from April to early September at the Whinlatter Visitor Centre (see also 'Bassenthwaite Lake National Nature Reserve' entry).
(Dunmallard Viewpoint, Pooley Bridge -3D 17.)
Friar's Crag Viewpoint, Keswick NT -see Keswick plan -5B.
Hammarbank Viewpoint, Windermere -2A 32.
Hause Bridge Viewpoint, Low Borrowbridge -1D 33.
High Bowkerstead Viewpoint, Force Mills -3C 31.
Jenkin Crag Viewpoint, Waterhead NT -1D 31.

Loughrigg Fell Viewpoint, Clappersgate NT *-1D 31.*
Loughrigg Terrace Viewpoint, Rydal NT *-3A 24.*
Noble Knott Viewpoint, Braithwaite -3C 15.
Orrest Head Viewpoint, Windermere -2A 32.
Post Knott Viewpoint, Bowness-on-Windermere NT *-see*
Windermere plan -6C.
Queen Adelaide's Hill Viewpoint, Windermere NT *-see*
Windermer plan -1B.
Seat How Viewpoint, Braithwaite -2C 15.
Strutta Wood Viewpoint, Watendlath NT *-1D 23.*
Surprise View, Watendlath NT *-1D 23.*
White Moss Common Viewpoint, Rydal NT *-3A 24.*
Yewbarrow Viewpoint, Grange-over-Sands
-see Grange-over-Sands plan -1B.
Yew Crag Viewpoint, Dockray NT *-3C 17.*

Viewpoint (360 degree)

See also Viewpoint (180)
Beacon Hill Viewpoint, Penrith -see Penrith plan -1E.
Bowness Knott Viewpoint, Ennerdale Bridge -1A 22.
Carron Crag Viewpoint, Grizedale -3C 31.
Castlebarrow Head Viewpoint, Silverdale NT *-3D 37.*
Dodd Summit Viewpoint, Little Crosthwaite -2C 15.
Gummer's How Viewpoint, Newby Bridge -1B 36.
Hallin Fell Viewpoint, Martindale -1C 25.
Hampsfell Viewpoint, Grange-over-Sands -3B 36.
Hoad Hill Viewpoint, Ulverston -see Ulverston plan -1C.
Kendal Castle Viewpoint -see Kendal plan -4D.
Latrigg Viewpoint, Keswick -3D 15.
Latterbarrow Viewpoint, Colthouse NT *-2D 31.*
Scout Scar Viewpoint, Underbarrow -3B 32.
Skiddaw Viewpoint, Applethwaite -2D 15.

Visitor Centre / Information Centre

Bowness Bay Information Centre, Bowness-on-
  Windermere NP *-see Windermere plan -5B.*
Bridge House Information Centre, Ambleside NT
-see Ambleside plan -2B.
Grizedale Visitor Centre -3C 31, Tel: 01229 860010. The
visitor centre is the starting point for eight waymarked walking
trails, three cycle trails and a mountain bike trail. Mountain
bikes are available for hire. It is also the base for Go Ape!, an
aerial assault course through the tree- tops. The centre has an
exhibition area and a shop with a guide available to the trails
and the sculptures in the forest. The forest café serves hot
meals, drinks and snacks. Nearby is a large purpose built play
area.
Hawkshead Information Centre NT
-see Hawkshead plan-2B.
(Keswick Information Centre NP) *-see Keswick plan -3C.*
Keswick Information Centre NT *-see Keswick plan -4B, S.*
Lake District Visitor Centre at Brockhole, The NP *-1D 31,*
S, Tel: 015394 46601. (Home to England's first national park
visitor centre opened in 1969. There is also a national park
information desk and a wide variety of special events
throughout the season - see also 'Brockhole Gardens' entry).
Leighton Moss Bird Sanctuary Visitor Centre, Silverdale
-3D 37, Tel: 01524 701601. Information and interpretative
displays at Myers Farm on Leighton Moss Bird Sanctuary.
Lilliput Lane Visitor Centre -see Penrith plan -6B.
Rheged - The Village in the Hill -2D 17, Tel: 01768 868000.
Named after Cumbria's ancient Celtic kingdom in the Dark
Ages (c.590 AD), Rheged is housed in Europe's largest grass-
covered building. Built in a former limestone quarry, the
building, designed to look like a Lakeland Hill, has 5 levels and
two adjacent lakes. 3 films are shown daily on a Mega
systems large format cinema screen as big as 6 double decker
buses. Also to be seen are waterfalls, limestone crags, an

indoor brook in the Mountain Hall, artist's exhibitions, pottery
demonstrations and a paper mill shop. Home to The Helly
Hansen National Mountaineering Exhibition and an indoor
children's play area (see 'Rheged Indoor Play Centre' entry).
Sellafield Visitors Centre -3C 21, Tel: 019467 27027. First
opened in 1986 and totally redesigned in 2002, the visitors
centre adjacent to the Sellafield nuclear site provides an
exciting free family day out for budding scientists of all ages.
Interactive exhibits allow the visitor to experiment with gravity
and static electricity, recreate the chimes of Big Ben, turn off
29 power stations and discover the Top Secret Science Labs.
Visit the Immersion Cinema, the only exhibit of its kind in
Europe, where you can help a country in danger of energy
shortages. The Visitors Centre is a great way to discover how
you can save electricity and join in the energy debate.
Ullswater Information Centre, Glenridding NP *-1B 24.*
Whinlatter Visitor Centre -3C 15, Tel: 017687 78469.
Exhibition with information and audio-visual about the
Whinlatter Forest Park, and the work of the Lakes Forest
District. Visitors can meet the giant badger in his sett. A live
video camera link to the Lake District Osprey Project's osprey
nest site near Bassenthwaite Lake near Dodd Wood (see
'Dodd Wood Osprey Viewpoint' entry) operates from April to
early September. During autumn and winter a red squirrel live
video camera link brings images from a red squirrel feeding
station in the forest. The visitor centre is the start point for
waymarked forest walks (see 'Comb Forest Trails' entry), cycle
routes and a permanent orienteering course. There are 2
children's trails- the Rabbit Run (0.5 mile, marked by rabbit
footprints), about different animals and their homes, and for
slightly older children the Fox Trot (or Foxtrot Foodweb) (0.75
mile, marked by fox footprints), about forest food webs. There
is also a picnic site, nearby outdoor adventure playground with
unique forwarder climbing frame, zip wire and obstacle course,
and Mountain Forest Tearoom with panoramic views.

Wildlife Park

See also Animal Collection, Farm Park, Zoo
Trotters World of Animals -1C 15, Tel: 017687 76239.
Hundreds of wild animals, and traditional domestic farm
animals, including endangered species, birds of prey and
reptiles on a 10 hectare farm with many under cover areas.
Many of the animals can be hand fed or held including guinea
pigs, giant rabbits and mice in special participation events held
throughout the day including bottle feeding goats and handling
snakes, lizards and a giant python. Flying displays of birds of
prey are held here by the British Birds of Prey Centre. There
are also tractor trailer rides, pony rides and a playground (see
also 'Clown About' entry).

Zoo / Safari Park

See also Animal Collection, Farm Park, Wildlife Park
South Lakes Wild Animal Park -3C 35, Tel: 01229 466086.
Small zoo covering 7 hectares but exhibiting a wide diversity of
over 100 species from Africa, South America, Australia,
Madagascar, Asia and Indonesia housed in unusual
combinations and enclosures, such as the African paddock
which white rhino, giraffe and baboons share, and the
'Australian Experience' where visitors can enter a large
enclosure through which black swan, kangaroos, emu and
lemurs roam freely. The park is home to the largest and most
varied kangaroo collection in Europe. Special feature of the
park are the animal feeding and conservation talks (April-
October) including rhino, spectacled bears, lemurs, lion, and
tiger (both Sumatran, and the Amur, the smallest and largest of
the 5 remaining sub-species of tiger, which are encouraged to
climb 6 m (20 ft) poles to obtain their food).

INDEX TO PLACES OF INTEREST

The Places of Interest entries throughout this publication have written descriptions to assist you in your choice of destination.
This Index for the places of interest will enable you to look them up alphabetically with reference to where the descriptions can be found in this publication.

Entries with town name references in BLUE, will be found in the 'Town Plan section' (pages 40 to 84).
e.g. 'Abbot Hall Art Gallery - Whitehaven **77**' will be found in Whitehaven Town Plan text that starts on page 77.

Entries with references in RED, will be found in the 'Guide to Places of Interest section' (pages 85 to 110).
e.g. 'Aira Force - Natural Attraction **97**' will be found under the heading for 'Natural Attractions' that starts on page 97.

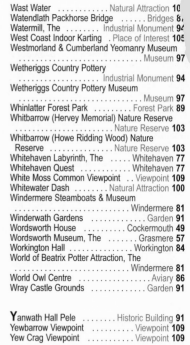

Every possible care has been taken to ensure that, to the best of our knowledge, the information contained in this atlas is accurate at the date of publication. However, we cannot warrant that our work is entirely error free and whilst we would be grateful to learn of any inaccuracies, we do not accept any responsibility for loss or damage resulting from reliance on information contained within this publication.

The representation on the maps of a road, track or footpath is no evidence of the existence of a right of way.

The Grid on this map is the National Grid taken from Ordnance Survey ® mapping with the permission of the Controller of Her Majesty's Stationery Office.

Photo Credits : All photo's Copyright J.Salmon Ltd., Sevenoaks, England © ; except 2, 6(left), 89, 91, 106 & back cover © Digital Vision; 7, 71, 94 © Photodisc; 6(right), 53, 81, 102 © Geographers' A-Z Map Co. Ltd.